Lords of the Mountain

Social Banditry and Peasant Protest in Cuba, 1878–1918

Louis A. Pérez, Jr.

University of Pittsburgh Press

Published by the University of Pittsburgh Press,
Pittsburgh, Pa. 15260
Copyright © 1989, University of Pittsburgh Press
All rights reserved
Feffer and Simons, Inc., London
Manufactured in the United States of America

Library of Congress Cataloging in Publication Data

Pérez, Louis A., 1943–
  Lords of the mountain: social banditry and peasant protest in Cuba,
1878–1918 / Louis A. Pérez.
    p.   cm. — (Pitt Latin American series)
  Bibliography; p.
  Includes index.
  ISBN 0–8229–3601–1
  1. Peasant uprisings—Cuba—History—19th century.   2. Peasant
uprisings—Cuba—History—20th century.   3. Land tenure—Cuba—
History.   4. Cuba—Rural conditions.   5. Outlaws—Cuba—History.
6. Sugarcane industry—Cuba—History.   I. Title.   II. Series.
HD1531.C9P47   1989
322.4'4'097291—dc19   88–19815
                                                                  CIP

For my brother

We are sad, it is true, but that is because we have always been persecuted. The gentry use the pen, we the gun; they are lords of the land, we of the mountain.—An old brigand from Roccamandolfi, quoted in F. Molfese, *Storia del brigantaggio dopo l'Unità*

Todo es según el color del cristal con que se mira. —Félix Hernández ("Según el color")

Contents

Tables

Acknowledgments

In the years during which this book was in preparation, I have incurred a large number of debts—some are professional, some are personal, and all serve to remind me, again, how much an undertaking of this type is necessarily a collaborative venture.

I am especially grateful to the Cuban Academy of Sciences for its hospitality, attention, and most of all, for providing me with the opportunity to use Cuban research facilities. I owe a particularly large debt to the professional staff and personnel at the Archivo Nacional de Cuba. I received a warm welcome during the full length of my stay in Cuba. It is impossible to name all who were so generous with their time and assistance, but particular acknowledgements must be made to Amalia Angulo, Nieves Arencibia, Mercedes Maza, and Julio Vargas. They provided professional assistance and personal attention. Their support was always given generously and graciously.

The opportunity to conduct research in Cuba also provided the occasion to confer with colleagues engaged in similar pursuits. I benefited much from their interest and insight into the subject of my investigation. My time with José Luciano Franco will remain always valued moments. His erudition was surpassed only by his generosity. I am grateful also to Fe Iglesias for her attention and assistance. She provided thoughtful rejoinders to arguments and constructs with which she did not always agree. Her knowledge of and facility with the Archivo Nacional saved me from hours of fruitless searches. I benefited greatly both through her published works and her personal assistance. My debt extends also to Olga Cabrera, whose insight into the Cuban past were consistently thoughtful and thought-provoking. Our discussions suggested new approaches and fresh perspectives, and for this I am very much in her debt. I am grateful also to John Dumoulin and Jorge Ibarra, both of whom provided useful advice and helpful suggestions in the course of my research in Cuba.

Greatest of all is my debt to Marel García. This book would not have been possible without her kindness. She shared generously with me her friendship as well as her friends and extended to me a hospitality that went well beyond professional courtesy. The success of this research is in no small part due to her efforts in my behalf.

Colleagues in the United States also gave unstintingly of their time and wisdom. I have relied much on the counsel and criticism of others. They all came to my assistance from different perspectives, with different questions, from the rigor of different methodologies, and advocates of different points of emphasis: from stylists and statisticians, specialists and generalists, from social scientists and humanists. Some read early drafts of the full manuscript, others read portions of the completed manuscript. It is impossible to repay their generosity. I can only offer them my heartfelt appreciation for their efforts in my behalf. Raymond H. Wheeler read key sections of the manuscript and saved me from any number of egregious errors. He also offered thoughtful counsel and constructive criticism as I made these initial forays into the world of demography and population studies. Linda M. Whiteford read the completed manuscript. She provided helpful advice and assistance with the formulation and organization of much of the demographic data. I am indebted also to Nancy A. Hewitt for reading the completed manuscript. Her criticism ranged wide and far, and was always thoughtful. Her extensive marginal comments on various aspects of this study reminded me again of her versatility and devotion to the larger purpose of what we do. Robert P. Ingalls subjected the manuscript to an especially rigorous review. His careful reading and attention to detail was especially gratifying and is most appreciated. Susan J. Fernández reviewed the completed manuscript and provided helpful suggestions. Thomas P. Dilkes also read the final version and made useful comments.

There were, lastly, those friends who gave me their time and patience: they provided company and companionship in the course of the travels and travails of research and writing, all along the way. They commiserated and counseled, but most of all they listened over the years as new ideas and insights began to take initial form. A particular thanks is owed to Etta Bender Breit, José Keselman, and G. Kelly and Brenda M. Tipps. A particular debt is owed to Steven F. Lawson: we have been doing this for a long time. We have ridden the waves together through many ups and downs. We will have much to talk about on the porch. The aforementioned individuals provided gratifying response to and stimulation for much of the material that follows. I look back upon with some nostalgia and a great deal of appreciation for the many hours of discussion, with a great number of people, during which the ideas herein expressed were first advanced and tested, reformulated and advanced again. They gave me their time as well as the benefit of their insight.

I also received vital courteous assistance from librarians and archivists at every step of my work. I am grateful to the staffs at the National Archives and Library of Congress in Washington, D.C., the Sterling Memorial Library at Yale University, and the Public Record Office in London, England. I owe a special acknowledgement to the staff at University of Florida Library, and especially to Carl Van Ness in the Archives Department. The staff at the University of South Florida Library came through, as always, splendidly. My research taxed the resources—and often the patience! —of the personnel in the Inter-Library Loan office, and they rarely failed. To Mary Kay Hartung, Cheryl D. Ruppert, and James F. Wood in the "front office," my deepest appreciation.

I benefited from generous financial assistance during the course of this research, without which this work could not have been completed. I acknowledge with gratitude the support provided by the National Endowment for the Humanities in the form of a summer research stipend. I am grateful also for a generous grant from the Joint Committee on Latin American Studies of the Social Science Research

Council and the American Council of Learned Societies with funds provided by the National Endowment for the Humanities, the Mellon Foundation, and the Ford Foundation. Other support for this research was provided by the University of Florida in the form of a State University System Faculty Development Grant and a Library Travel Grant. Research support was provided also by the University of South Florida by way of a President's Council Grant, for which I am especially grateful to Carl D. Riggs.

I cannot adequately express my appreciation to Cecile L. Pulin for her part in the completion of this book. She presided over the preparation of drafts too many to count, from beginning to end. I am sensible of my enormous debt to her. She has been a wonderful collaborator. Sylvia Wood provided ongoing and day-to-day support and always was ready to assist in every way possible. In this regard, my debt to Peggy Cornett continues to deepen. It is impossible to repay her generosity. I am grateful also, and again, for the effort made by Jane Flanders on my behalf. Her expert editing skills have improved the final draft in ways I would not have thought of.

My daughters, lastly, continue to play an essential part of all this. They are becoming young women. Along the way, I lose some things, I gain some things. What remains constant, however, is their place at the center of my world. And from the permanence of that position, Maya and Amara provide the vantage point from which that world is measured.

Introduction

"This is an outrage!" protested the Havana daily *Diario de la Marina* on March 12, 1886. Another planter had been kidnapped, the nineteenth abduction in almost as many months. There was no mistaking the portents: the persons and property of the planter class were under siege. The countryside had become a hostile place for *hacendados*, and neither their family nor their farms were safe from attack. "It is inconceivable," *Diario de la Marina* chided colonial authorities, "that the well-being of the most respected citizens of the Island cannot be assured by the government. When can we expect relief? Where will it all end?"

Official responses to these questions were not readily forthcoming, and for good reason. The authorities knew in fact what the citizenry only could suspect, and the citizens' worst suspicions were correct: banditry was approaching unmanageable proportions. It was widespread, and spreading. Bandits roamed the countryside, in untold numbers, in unchecked movement. Brigandage was only part of the problem, however. In fact, during the 1880s, rural Cuba was in the throes of economic disruption and social disarray, and all Cuba was in depression. These were years of transition, as Cuban planters sought to adjust at once to uncertain market conditions, changing labor systems, advancing technologies, and new production modes. Economic recovery required economic reorganization, and nowhere were the effects of the emerging order experienced as immediately and with such disruptive consequences as in rural communities of western Cuba. Sugar production expanded and land concentration increased, both at the same time and both at the expense of farmers and peasants. The sugar latifundia was everywhere on the increase, absorbing diverse land units, eliminating divergent agricultural activity, and expelling the small cultivators. In the process, a class of small-scale landholders was transformed into a new class of rural wage-earners. The rural economy was in transition, in flux between two competing—and conflicting —forms of economic organization: production for use and production for exchange. What was happening in the western agricultural zones during these years was nothing less than the destruction of traditional rural society. Old land tenure forms collapsed in the wake of encroaching market forces, and a way of life was coming to an end. Some accepted their fate, others migrated—to the cities in search of new livelihood, others into the interior in search for new land. Still others turned to outlawry as a means of subsistence, but also the release of frustration and the redress of grievances. They struck back against the planters, kidnapping them for ransom, burning their fields, derailing their trains, destroying their mills. In the interior zones of the western provinces, Cubans were more or less in a state of revolt, primitive rebellion in anticipation of a general uprising. It was improvised resistance by the prepolitical rural poor, spontaneous protest against the encroachment of rural capitalism. When revolution erupted in the name of *Cubre Libre* in 1895, socioeconomic discontent combined with political dissent, and together formed an irresistible force of national liberation.

The war of independence (1895–1898) summoned Cubans to dramatic action but failed to produce dramatic change. When it was over, Cuba was not independent. The United States intervention (1898) and the subsequent military occupation (1899–1902) subjected the island to foreign rule, again. Of greater significance, the arrival of the North Americans introduced into Cuba new competitors for the resources of the island. With the inauguration of the republic in 1902, Cubans faced a new round of displacement and dispossession. The source was again the reorganization of the sugar system and its expansion, this time into the eastern provinces. But the east was also the place of last resort for generations of Cubans. By the tens of thousands they had migrated eastward, in search of open land and the opportunity for work. They had not been disappointed.

But change was overtaking them, too, and it occurred suddenly during the 1910s. The war in Europe resulted in an increase in the world price of sugar, and producers in Cuba responded with expanded production. Once more, rural communities faced disruption, dislocation, and, ultimately, displacement. And, once more, peasants resisted, in the form of banditry and spontaneous armed protest in 1912 and again in 1917.

In the course of these years, peasants were displaced as free and independent cultivators. They searched for available land, and many ultimately found sanctuary in the foothills and folds of the sprawling mountain ranges of Oriente, regions largely unsuitable for commercial agriculture but of use for subsistence farming. There they lived as outcasts, at the margins of the body social and outside the body politic. They lived by their wiles, by stealing and as squatters, never reconciled to the conditions of indigence to which they had descended. They continued in this state of more or less rebellion until the 1950s, when they became part of a revolution.

**Lords
of the
Mountain**

.

1 The Passing of the Old

Under the present value of sugar, in its exchange for all imported merchandise, it is plain that the Cuban population languishes and dies. It is therefore necessary to arrange affairs in a way that its production may duly remunerate both planter and laborer, and stimulate their efforts to further production.

—*El País*, May 20, 1886

To say that almost every business and perhaps with one, or possibly two exceptions, every sugar estate is either bankrupt, or on the perilous edge of bankruptcy, would be within the most captious bounds of a correct statement of the condition of every business enterprise in the Island.

—Vice-Consul David Vickers, July 1884

Labor is becoming dearer and sugar cheaper. . . . Brigandage is on the increase, as poverty and want of legitimate employment prevail.

—Maturin M. Ballou, *Due South,*
or Cuba Past and Present, 1885

The alarm caused by the attacks upon individual security has so spread throughout the Island that it has now become a necessary duty to exhaust all means for the reestablishment of confidence and the banishment of all fear of danger from the rural districts and towns.

—Governor-General Manuel Salamanca, March 1889

I War brought in its wake economic disarray. Peace was followed by depression. The Ten Years War (1868–1878) spanned an era of transition. Property relations and production modes were in transition. Social formations were in flux. Commercial ties were changing. So were political loyalties. Even the nature of change changed. The Peace of Zanjón (1878) marked more than the end of the war—it announced the passing of an age. For the million

3

and a half inhabitants of the island of Cuba, life soon returned to normal, but it would never be the same.

The war had profoundly disrupted the colonial economy. Planters who operated before the war on marginal profits, who lacked either the finances or the foresight to modernize their mills, were among the earliest casualties. Of forty-one mills in operation around Sancti-Spíritus in Las Villas province in 1861, only three remained after the war. In Trinidad only sixteen out of forty-nine, in Santa Clara only thirty-nine of eighty-six, in Cienfuegos seventy-seven out of one hundred seven. In Güines, almost two-thirds of the eighty-seven mills operating before the war had disappeared by 1877. In some districts of the eastern provinces, the collapse of sugar production was all but complete. In Puerto Príncipe, only one out of one hundred survived the war.[1] None of the twenty-four mills in Bayamo and the eighteen mills in Manzanillo survived. The sixty-four mills of Holguín were reduced to four. Of the hundred *ingenios* operating in the district of Santiago de Cuba in 1868, only thirty-nine resumed production after Zanjón.

These developments announced at once a climax and a portent. Sugar production declined markedly during the Ten Years War. In 1868, Cubans had produced a record crop of 749,000 tons. Production decreased to 547,000 tons in 1871 and to 520,000 tons during the last full year of war. Producers enjoyed a brief recovery in 1879 with a crop of 670,000 tons, but suffered successive setbacks in 1880 (530,000 tons) and 1881 (493,000 tons).[2]

Nor did the end of the war end the crisis. Planters faced new problems. Capital was scarce and credit dear. High rates of interest precluded any likelihood that local credit transactions would stimulate economic recovery in post-Zanjón Cuba.[3] Prevailing high rates, often as much as 30 percent, all but guaranteed that foreign capital would serve as the principal source of credit for the heavy and long-term investments necessary to revive sugar production.

The war and the attending disruption of local sugar production set the stage for the next series of misfortunes to descend upon Cuban producers. The decline of Cuban sugar exports had stimulated the expansion of sugar production

on a worldwide basis. After Zanjón, Cuban planters faced a
new adversity in the form of expanded competition from
new producers and expanded production from old competitors. Not since the end of the eighteenth century, when
revolution in St. Domingue ended French supremacy over The
sugar production, did rival international producers have as Passing of
great an opportunity to extend their share of the world the Old
market. They did not hesitate. In the United States, new
varieties of cane were introduced in the South, while beet
sugar production expanded in the West and Southwest. Beginning in 1876, cane sugar from Hawaii entered the United
States duty free. Sugar production also expanded in Latin
America, most notably in Argentina, Peru, and Mexico.
Many displaced Cuban planters resettled in Santo Domingo
and contributed to the expansion of Dominican sugar. Between 1875 and 1882, thirty new sugar haciendas were established in the Dominican Republic.[4]

But it was in Europe that production recorded its most
significant advances, principally in the form of beet sugar.
By the mid-1880s, France, Austria, and Germany had become the largest suppliers of sugar for the world market.
Beet sugar, accounting in 1853 for only some 14 percent of
the total world production in sugar, had by 1884 come to
represent 53 percent of the international supply. By the early
1880s, beet sugar had displaced Cuban cane sugar from the
European markets; by the 1890s, Europe had been transformed from a net importer of sugar to an exporter.[5]

And the worse was yet to come. Even as Cuban planters
prepared to resume production after Zanjón, they discovered that they faced more than new sources of competition
and the loss of old markets. They confronted, too, a sharp
increase in local taxes and a precipitous decline in the value
of their principal product. A rise in public spending during
the 1870s to finance the cost of the war in Cuba and an
increase in the circulation of paper money in the 1880s
brought on the first in a series of devastating inflationary
spirals. After the Pact of Zanjón, Madrid transferred the war
debt directly to Cuban producers and consumers. At about
the same time, the value of sugar collapsed. In 1884, the
price of sugar plummeted to a new low, dropping from

eleven cents a pound to eight. The decline of sugar prices and the imposition of a new series of crushing taxes occurred at just the time planters were adjusting to the transition from slave labor to wage labor.[6] All at once, the Cuban planter class encountered mounting debts, shrinking markets, declining prices, increasing taxes, and a dwindling labor supply. "Out of the twelve or thirteen hundred planters on the island," the U.S. consul in Havana reported early in 1884, "not a dozen are said to be solvent."[7] Vice-Consul David Vickers reported similar conditions in Matanzas province. Heavy taxes assessed against agriculture and livestock, municipal taxes on land, sales taxes, transportation taxes, duties on imported equipment and food— "everything that the people eat comes from abroad"— threatened the planter class with extinction. Vickers continued:

> Through want of frugality and foresight and with enormous taxation, added to the competition of other sugar countries, the planter, to meet all demands, has discounted his crops at such ruinous rates of interest, piling mortgage upon mortgage, that to-day he finds himself irrevocably involved in debts equal to at least one year's excellent crop and in some instances much more. In the event of a poor crop, he would not have enough money either to pay current expenses or even to commence grinding his cane when the harvest begins and no one to loan it to him.[8]

Many planters resumed postwar production perched on the brink of disaster, heavily in debt, without capital to modernize, and lacking the resources to renovate their mills. In the past, Cubans had worried about producing large harvests as a hedge against disaster. During the 1880s, they produced good crops, but their markets had dwindled and prices had declined, and disaster struck. The combination of rising taxes, increased operating costs, and declining sugar prices forced many planters into bankruptcy. Property changed hands at accelerating speed as planters struggled desperately to stave off insolvency. Over a span of ten years, the U.S. vice-consul in Cienfuegos reported in 1883, "almost every sugar estate [in] the jurisdiction of Cienfuegos has either changed ownership by reason of debt or is now encumbered with debts to an amount approximating the value of the estate."⁹

Nor was the crisis confined to rural property; planters were also ruined in the cities. The value of urban real estate suffered. Many were forced to liquidate their urban property as a way to stave off total bankruptcy, often at great losses. Some of the most sumptuous homes in the Havana suburb of Cerro sold at a fraction of their value. Houses appraised at $220,000 in 1875 were sold for $30,000 a decade later.¹⁰

Crisis in sugar announced calamity for Cuba. By the mid-1880s, all of Cuba was in the throes of depression. Business houses closed and banks collapsed. Seven of the island's largest trading companies failed. Credit dear after Zanjón was almost nonexistent a decade later. In October 1883 the Bank of Santa Catalina closed. In March 1884, one of the most important savings institutions in Havana, the Caja de Ahorros, suspended payments, ostensibly in response to the suicide of the bank's president. The U.S. consul in Havana speculated tersely, "It is more probable that the Director committed suicide because the bank was unable to meet its engagements."¹¹ Two weeks later the Caja de Ahorros went into liquidation, and in the same month, panic runs on the Banco Industrial and the Banco de Comercio forced both institutions to close. Two months later, the Banco Industrial went into liquidation. The Bank of Santa Catalina was closely linked to agricultural interests, and its failure affected principally *hacendados*. The Caja de Ahorros, on the other hand, served a much broader clientele, including professionals, merchants, shopowners, civil servants, and workers, and when it failed small depositors of all kinds faced catastrophe.¹² In the first three months of 1884, business failures totaled some $7 million. "The entire population is reduced . . . to blank despondency and universal ruin," the U.S. consul reported in 1884.¹³

Similar conditions prevailed in the provinces. In March 1884 the prestigious house of Rodríguez in Sagua la Grande, together with its affiliate in Havana, Mijares and Company, failed. In Cienfuegos, the value of rural and urban property declined by half.[14] The once opulent city of Trinidad was in an advanced state of decay. Depopulation threatened the very existence of the city. Business houses closed and retail shops were abandoned. The vital rail link to Casilda, the port of Trinidad, ceased operation due to the disrepair of the track.[15] A similar account came in the form of a brief news cable from Santiago de Cuba: "Failures, extra-judicial arrangements, and the liquidation of commercial houses follow each other in rapid succession."[16] In Matanzas, economic collapse was almost total. The surplus of unsold sugar mounted as prices dropped and markets declined. In 1885, the cost of local sugar production was exceeding the world price. "Our planters," the *Diario de Matanzas* complained editorially, "are becoming alarmed at the low prices for sugar, which do not even cover the cost of production."[17] Hundreds of estates faced imminent ruin. "Firms are going into bankruptcy every day," Vice-Consul Vickers reported in July 1884; "planters are discharging their laborers and threaten—to save themselves further disaster—to abandon their estates; gold fluctuates two and three and sometimes ten points a day; all credits are denied even to the most substantial and men are wondering how and where they will obtain the means to live; and in many cases relatives are doubling up apartment style to save expenses."[18] A month later, conditions had deteriorated further. "Unless some happy change comes before the grinding season," Vickers predicted soberly,

> enormous numbers of plantations will be abandoned for want of funds to commence the harvest with. It is estimated that three hundred estates will be abandoned. Every day the situation is becoming more and more serious and the condition of the people more and more sad. All credits are being suspended. . . . House owners are receiving little or no rent. In a word the condition of all classes, rich and poor alike, is most lamentable; and what is worse, there is no hope in the future.[19]

Foreign travelers confirmed this generally bleak picture of late nineteenth-century Cuba. Maturin M. Ballou, traveling east to west, encountered distress and despair everywhere he visited. In Santiago de Cuba, Ballou reported the local gas monopoly "on the verge of bankruptcy, like nearly every-thing else of a business character in Cuba." In Cienfuegos, he found sugar in crisis. One planter was preparing to use his molasses as fertilizer on canefields, he informed Ballou, rather "than send it to a distant market and receive only what it cost." The planter vowed to permit "thousands of acres of sugar cane to rot in the fields this season as it would cost more to cut, grind, pack, and send it to market than could be realized for the manufactured articles." "Mercan-tile credit may be said to be dead," Ballou noted upon his arrival to Havana, "and business is nearly at a standstill." And as he prepared to leave Cuba: "Financial ruin stares all in the face."[20] Wrote Tesifonte García Gallego in 1890:

> Guanabacoa, the old summer residence..., more sparkling than silver, until recently proud of itself, today weeps for the misery of the solitude.... Matan-zas, a graceful and gay city, formerly wealthy and magnificent—there it is, melancholic and mourning its enormous decadence.... Remedios was a wealthy and prosperous city: today it is ruined.... We see Trinidad decadent, to such an extreme that its resi-dents threaten the city's existence with abandon-ment.[21]

"Money is no longer to be made," reported A. C. Crowe, the British consul-general in Havana; "those who had any mostly lost it."[22]

These conditions affected too, the colonial treasury. Gov-ernment revenues diminished. In one year alone, from 1883 to 1884, customs revenues fell by almost $500,000—from $1,433,741 to $945,386.[23] Inevitably, public service declined. Sanitation services decreased; public works programs were suspended. The city of Havana faced a staggering utility bill of $400,000—and a threat from an impatient Spanish-American Light and Power Company in New York to sus-pend gas service for city street lights unless the debt was speedily and satisfactorily settled.[24]

Indeed, public administration itself was in crisis. Across

the island the salaries of thousands of public officials fell hopelessly in arrears, with no relief in sight. "Employees of the government and municipalities have received no pay for months," wrote Vice-Consul Vickers from Matanzas in 1884. "As a sample, this city is in arrears to the Gas Company over $95,000—to the schools about eighteen months, the police nine months. Even the public hospital—which collects a tax of $2—has been obliged to beg bread from the *bodegas,* and from door step to door step."[25] In Havana, the capital press reported the plight of public officials obliged to pawn their furniture in one last desperate effort to stave off destitution.[26] Wrote Maturin M. Ballou of Havana:

> The streets, even about the *paseos,* are so impregnated with filth, here and there, as to be sickening to the senses of the passer-by. Once in 3 or 4 weeks somebody is awakened to the exigency of the situation, and a gang of men is put to work to cleanse the principal thoroughfares. . . . We were told that the reason for this neglect was that no one was regularly paid for work; even the police had not received any pay for seven months; and many refused to serve longer. The soldiery had not been paid their small stipend for nearly a year.[27]

II During the 1880s, unemployment reached desperate proportions. Jobs were few and competition fierce. And whether in public office or private occupations, prospects for Cubans were everywhere dismal, and getting worse. Spaniards continued to monopolize public office as the normal perquisite of empire. These were hard times in Spain, too, and of political necessity, public administration in Cuba served as a source of relief for economic distress in the metropolis. These were also years of remarkable population growth in Spain; the number of Spaniards doubled from 9.3 million in 1768 to 18.6 million in 1900.[28]

Cuba late in the nineteenth century remained very much what it had been early in the sixteenth century: a place for the destitute of Spain to start over. Public office and political appointments in Cuba were themselves little more than the overseas extensions of the Spanish patronage system. The rise of one government ministry announced the arrival of countless thousands of new office seekers and the departure of countless thousands of others, a vast turnover of person- nel from which Cubans were by and large excluded. "There is no permanence in the Civil Service," British Consul- General Crowe reported in 1889. "Each Spanish mail brings a new list of arbitrary removals and new appointments, and a stream of ex-officials and their substitutes is constantly travelling to and fro at great expense and detriment to the colony."[29]

Peninsulares also dominated private property. Spaniards controlled trade and commerce, banking and finance, in- dustry and manufacturing. Spaniards owned the factories and the farms, managed the plants and plantations; they were the retail shopkeepers and wholesale merchants as well as the moneylenders and land brokers. Spaniards were artisans and apprentices, clerks in offices and day laborers in the fields. They dominated the economy, and most of all they controlled the jobs. Spaniards preferred to hire Spaniards, a private practice that coincided with public policy. Spain actively encouraged immigration to Cuba as a convenient and cost-effective method through which to reduce the size of a socially unstable population and in- crease the number of loyalists in Cuba.

Beginning in 1886, Madrid formally adopted a policy of subsidizing the cost of travel for all Spaniards seeking em- ployment in Cuba. And they arrived in shipload after ship- load. In the decades after Zanjón, a quarter-million Spaniards emigrated to the island.[30] And these were differ- ent Spaniards. The new immigrants were from the north, mostly from Galicia and Asturias, Spaniards destitute, and often desperate, but strong-willed and determined to make it. They worked hard and long, often for little and always for less. It was a labor market in which Cubans could not compete.

These were hard times in Cuba. In Havana alone, some 20,000 workers were without jobs. In 1885, the once thriving Havana naval yard closed, dismissing hundreds of workers.

The decline of cigar exports in the late 1880s and early 1890s caused havoc in one of the major labor-intensive economic sectors: cigar production had provided employment for over 100,000 people in all phases of agriculture and manufacturing, the vast majority of whom resided in the western provinces of Pinar del Río and Havana. The cigar factories alone provided employment for some 50,000 workers. As cigar exports decreased, cigar factories closed. By the early 1890s, some 35,000 cigar makers were totally without work, with the balance of workers reduced to part-time employment.[31] Against this generally bleak economic landscape, the abolition of slavery was completed. Tens of thousands of former slaves joined Cuban society as free wage earners in a depressed economy.

Times in post-Zanjón Cuba were difficult, for everyone certainly, but for Cubans especially. There seemed to be no place for Cubans in Cuba. For many members of the planter class and peasantry, as well as members of the professions and the proletariat, Spanish administration was incapable of discharging the central clause of the colonial social contract: providing the opportunity for livelihood. Cubans seemed in danger of becoming a superfluous population, outcasts in the society they claimed as their own. They faced both exclusion and expatriation. Indeed, emigration gave dramatic expression to the crisis. Thousands of working-class families left for Key West, Tampa, Ocala, and Jacksonville. Some 10,000 cigar workers found employment in the expanding cigar industries of Florida during the 1880s and early 1890s, creating in exile a flourishing community in which Cuban emigres of all occupations could find employment.[32] In sum, during the last third of the nineteenth century, a total of some 100,000 Cubans in all occupations and professions, of all ages, from all classes and races, emigrated to Europe, to the United States, to Latin America.[33]

III Dislocation in the cities was itself symptomatic of disruption in the countryside. A new stage of capitalist organization was about to transform sugar production, and with it all of Cuba. The demise of the sugar mills continued well after the war ended, and announced new property relations and a new system of production. The solvency of Cuban sugar production, planters recognized, required such changes. Not since the first third of the nineteenth century had Cuban sugar producers expanded so aggressively and with such speed as they did in the decade after Zanjón.

The incentive for greater concentration of land originated with the Ten Years War. Property destroyed in war, or vacated by the forced relocation of rural families and the death of owners killed in the war, enabled ambitious land-owners to expand their holdings. Abandoned or destroyed farms were simply seized by larger estates. Municipal records were also destroyed and titles lost, and inevitably land claims became confused and contested. Then, too, the property of many Cubans who had enrolled in the separatist cause was expropriated and subsequently auctioned off to finance the war.

During the war years, expansions were haphazard and scattered, more in response to opportunity than the result of organization. This changed during the 1880s. Mobilized into action in response to international developments, Cuban producers undertook far-reaching and systematic changes that foreshadowed the transformation of production and property. Greater efficiency was needed to market sugar profitably, given the intense international competition and prevailing world prices. Until the Ten Years War, sugar production had expanded horizontally—that is, by the construction of additional mills to expand output.[34] After 1878, production strategies shifted from increasing the number of mills to increasing the production capacities of those already in operation. New credit, fresh capital, and new ownership, originating principally in the United States, provided larger enterprises with the necessary resources. Sugar production had always been an agro-industrial venture requiring high capital stakes. After the 1880s, the ante increased markedly. Improved varieties of cane, innovation in manufacturing techniques, and other advances became generally available to planters by the late 1880s and enabled Cuban producers to respond aggressively to new conditions.

New machinery to extract maximum sugar from cane and efficiently grind the increased volume of harvested cane was introduced. New vacuum pans, boilers, and centrifugal equipment were installed to distill and crystallize more sugar from improved strains of cane.[35]

Transportation advances added another impetus to the expansion of sugar cultivation. In the late 1870s the Bessemer steel process reduced substantially the cost of railway construction, bringing the cost of steel rails down from $106 per ton in 1870 to $44 in 1878. Producers acquired cheap and rapid access to added sugar distribution centers and areas of cultivation. They acquired, too, an efficient means with which to transport the newest machines and latest technology into the interior. The expansion of rail facilities relieved the bottleneck problem created when production overloaded the transportation system. The two-wheeled wooden carts drawn sluggishly by a yoke of oxen *(carreta)* over dirt roads, many in wretched condition, could not accommodate the growing needs of expanded sugar production.[36] The new rail system promised to increase efficiency and reduce costs just when Cuban planters were in dire need of economy of production. It also served to widen the export market by linking hitherto isolated sugar regions with the principal ports. It encouraged, lastly, the expansion of sugar cultivation, and brought new land into production as remote regions formerly beyond the efficient reach of existing mills were linked by rail.

The expansion of the railroad gave producers access to new lands on a scale previously unattainable, for it solved a longstanding obstacle to expansion. Sugar cane once cut began immediately to ferment, with an attending loss of sucrose content. The longer the time between the harvesting and grinding, the lower the extract. This predicament of time was in reality a problem of space. Planters were restricted in the expansion of their fields by the efficiency with which they could transport cane to the factory. The use of the *carreta* had created objective limits to the radius of cane cultivation, but with the expansion of rail facilities, producers acquired rapid and reliable access to new lands, and this expansion came at the expense of smaller farms, sugar and nonsugar alike.[37]

The shift in production strategies led immediately to a sharper division between field and factory. These developments made growth and specialization not only attractive but also imperative. Planters unable to meet the growing capital requirements of sugar manufacturing abandoned the industrial end of production altogether and devoted themselves exclusively to the expansion of cane cultivation. The prevailing system whereby the grower milled his own cane gave way to a new specialization of operations and, increasingly, separation of ownership in which the mill owner concentrated on manufacture and the farmer *(colono)* tended to cultivation.

The modernization of the mills, further, led to new and greatly enhanced production capabilities of Cuban *centrales.* In 1891, Spain and the United States negotiated a reciprocity treaty giving Cuban sugar privileged access to North American markets. The effects were immediate. Planters expanded, and sugar production increased. They more than doubled their output in the decade between 1883 (460,000 tons) and 1892 (976,000). Two years later, Cuban producers reached the historic 1 million–ton harvest.

These advances placed additional pressures on supporting production sectors, including transportation and storage. Railroad facilities expanded. So did wharf and pier construction. Warehouse facilities increased. But most of all, and especially, land—and more land—was essential to derive optimum advantage from the new technology.[38] If the newly renovated mills were to operate at optimum efficiency and a maximum level of production, they would require much greater quantities of cane, which was possible only by expanding the zones of sugar cultivation. The more efficient mills of 1860 ground an average cane from 1,000 to 1,265 acres of land. By 1890, the average *central* was capable of handling cane from 4,000 acres, and mills with the capacity to grind the cane from as many as 6,500 acres were not at all uncommon.[39] The first requisite for sugar producers, hence, turned on the acquisition of more land. The second was the acquisition of cheap labor. The abolition of slavery in the 1880s required producers to locate alternative sources of workers. And as the scope of sugar production increased, so too did the planters' need for a reliable supply of labor: in the *centrales,* along the railroad lines, but most of all on the expanding fields of sugar cane.

Sugar producers attempted to secure both new land and cheap labor at one and the same time. To produce sugar for commodity sale as the overriding consideration of agriculture required planters both to eliminate rival agricultural activity and competing land tenure systems and appropriate units incompatible with the new purpose of the land. This meant immediately converting land devoted to tobacco, coffee, fruit and vegetables, and grazing to sugar production and attaching it to the sugar latifundia. It also required the abolition of diverse forms of landownership. These conditions invited the powerful to move against the powerless, and circumstances in the decade after Zanjón made these opportunities irresistible. The communal farm *(haciendas comuneras),* the small commercial estates *(sitios),* and livestock pastures *(hatos* and *corrales)* were doomed. Unincorporated land was attached and public property was absorbed.

Small cultivators were facing displacement at every turn. They plunged deeper into debt to stave off insolvency. They were obliged periodically to sell small parcels of land to creditors. Rates of interest were increasing, returns on investments were decreasing. Farmers sold parts to save the whole, but it was only a matter of time, for many, before nothing remained.[40]

The capitalization of agriculture required also the elimination of the peasant as an independent farmer. Traditional land tenure forms and marginal agricultural production obstructed both the monopolization of land and the consolidation of the latifundia. As long as the peasant held on to the land and engaged in subsistence agriculture, the sugar estate could not expand. But exclusive command over the ownership of land through concentration of land was itself a means of coercion to obtain social control over the workers of land. Farmers and peasants able to provide for their own subsistence were not inclined to offer their labor for depressed wages. Monopolization of land offered a method calculated to end the self-sufficiency of farmers and create a labor force disposed to work at low wages. Possession of the land—as much land as possible—was as much to use it as it was to withdraw its use, to transform the self-sufficient farmer into a subsistence wage worker. The unreliability of the local labor supply was just as important a motivation for the territorial expansion of the sugar latifundia, which often appropriated land it could not and did not intend to cultivate. The estates compressed peasants onto land incapable of producing enough to support its possessors, who were then obliged to sell their labor to the sugar latifundia.

The expansion of sugar production thus had two interrelated objectives: first, the expropriation of peasant lands to increase the output of sugar production and, second, the appropriation of peasant labor to decrease the cost of sugar production. Planters were successful on both counts. Land and labor served production, and the increased need of the latter was a function of the increment of the former.[41]

The capitalization of agriculture and the proletarianization of peasants transformed the character of Cuba's rural political economy. The boundaries of the estates expanded. Communal lands, commercial farms, and ranches passed under the control of the new sugar plantations.

These developments affected all regions of Cuba in varying degrees, but the effects were most pronounced in the sugar zones of the west. The traditional livestock farms in Havana province all but disappeared. Coffee and tobacco farms declined.[42] In the municipio of Santa Ana in Matanzas province, the area of sugar cultivation expanded from 5,733 acres in 1881 to 11,266 acres in 1885.[43] In the region around Remedios grazing land and forests disappeared under sugar cane. The number of sugar estates declined—from forty in 1878, to thirty-two in 1888, twenty-five in 1890, and seventeen in 1894—while the concentration of land increased. So did production, which almost doubled: from 251,528 sacks of sugar to 501,343.[44] Through the late 1880s and early 1890s, tens of thousands of Cubans, white and black, appeared in the census records as landless agriculturists, working on the sugar estates in Havana, Matanzas, and Santa Clara.[45]

IV The crisis in rural Cuba began with the Ten Years War. The separatist conflict caused havoc in the countryside, obliging thousands of rural families to migrate to the cities in search of sanctuary. Spanish military policy exacerbated conditions. The forced removal of the rural population into urban reconcentration centers meant dislocation in the countryside and congestion in the cities. Rural refugees were transformed immediately into urban indigents. Families displaced by war were deprived of a livelihood in the peace. Pauperization followed.

The end of the war did not end the crisis in the countryside. The modernization of the mills and the expansion of fields created new pressures. The concentration of land into the sugar latifundia uprooted the farmer, destroyed the rural landowning and farming class, and impoverished the rural population.[46] Small planters, commercial farmers, and peasants maintaining a precarious existence through subsistence farming and ranching lost permanent control over production and in the process experienced immediately a decline in their material well-being. Independent peasants were transformed into wage laborers. To the swollen ranks of those who had no reason to leave the cities after the war were added those who had no reason to remain in the countryside after the peace. Some migrated to the cities, where conditions were materially worse than those from which they sought to escape. At a time of severe economic depression, large numbers of unemployed workers, displaced farmers, and emancipated slaves competed in the cities with just as many Spanish immigrants for decreasing numbers of jobs.

Cuba in the 1880s was a society in transition: from slave labor to wage labor, from peasant to proletariat, from family farming to corporate agriculture. Spaniards were immigrating to Cuba, farmers were migrating to the cities, and Cubans were emigrating to the United States. By the end of the decade, a difficult situation became an impossible one. Problems associated with vagrancy and mendicancy reached unmanageable proportions. For many, the only alternative to destitution was begging. For some, the threshold between marginality and criminality was easy to cross. Cuba neared Malthusian conditions, in which the basic fact of life was an inexorable struggle against death. Entire sectors of the urban population became permanent indigents. Illness and disease pursued the destitute into Havana. Mortality rates suggest a grim and unremitting life-and-death struggle in the capital throughout the latter part of the nineteenth century. Epidemics struck again and again: yellow fever, cholera, smallpox, typhoid fever, dysentery, and malaria. Asiatic cholera struck in 1868, raising the annual death rate of the capital to a staggering 51.75 per 100,000 inhabitants. Yellow fever struck in 1873–1879 and 1895. Smallpox epidemics occurred in 1871–1872, 1874–1875, 1878–1881, 1887–1888, 1891, and 1894. Pulmonary tuberculosis claimed some 1,200 lives in 1886. Between 1881 and 1890, the Havana death rate averaged 34.18 per 100,000 inhabitants.[47]

The rural dispossessed became the urban destitute. Most drifted aimlessly from job to job: the women from domestic service to peddling to prostitution, the men from casual day labor to unemployment or crime. They lived by their wits, through petty pilfering, begging, and stealing.

Vagrancy increased through the 1880s, and beggars soon became a permanent feature of the urban landscape. Prostitution increased. In 1885 there were more than two hundred registered brothels in Havana. Crime increased, too. "Sexual immorality keeps up with criminality," reported Consul-General A. C. Crowe in 1888, and two years later: "Prostitution is prohibited but there are hundreds of houses with showrooms to the street dedicated to this traffic."[48] Robberies, assaults, and petty theft of all kinds spread across the island.[49] By 1890, the average number of criminal cases before the High Court of Havana averaged between 10,000 and 12,000 annually.[50]

"Personal security in Cuba is a myth!" one Spanish traveler complained in 1887. "No one who leaves his house there knows if he will be able to return alive and well. Robbery occurs as much on the most central streets of Havana, at any time of day or night, as in unpopulated areas."[51] A Cuban wrote in the same year:

> In the cities we have the rapacious land sharks, the pickpockets, the snatchers of watch chains—the terrifying cry of "your money or your life," assailing the ear of the defenseless passer-by at every obscure corner; the stabbings, the shootings, the cries, the incessant alarms, the rushing to and fro—everywhere a bloody picture of shameful and abominable barbarities.[52]

"Havana has more police to the square foot than any other city on earth," exclaimed a North American correspondent. "People are often waylaid and robbed in the streets, and there is much wailing in Havana . . . because with all this great protection the thieving cannot be stopped."[53] Reported Consul Crowe:

> Life in the country has long been attended with personal risk, and the towns are apparently becoming equally unsafe. Prudent people no longer wear trinkets in the streets, and only those who have a staff of servants care to keep valuable portable property in their homes, notwithstanding that all available ingress to them is protected by iron bars.[54]

Few who traveled to Cuba during these years could fail to notice conditions in the cities, especially the beggars. Visiting Cienfuegos in the mid-1880s, Marturin M. Ballou wrote:

> It was very pitiful to behold the army of beggars in so small a city, but begging is synonymous with the Spanish name. Here the maimed, halt, and blind meet one at every turn. Saturday is the harvest day for beggars in the Cuban cities, on which occasion they go about by scores from door to door, carrying a large canvas bag. Each family and shop is supplied with a quantity of small rolls of bread, specially baked for the purpose, and one of which is nearly always given to the

applicant on that day, so the mendicant's bag becomes full of rolls. These, mixed with vegetables, bits of fish, and sometimes meat and bones when they can be procured, are boiled into a soup, thus keeping soul and body together in the poor creatures during the week.[55]

"Numerous mendicants," wrote one North American journalist, "are daily seen in nearly all the principal streets, clothed in filthy rags, and soliciting alms with much impunity."[56] The U.S. consul in Havana wrote often of the "numerous vagrants infesting this city," attributing the "scarcity of employment for its people" to the widespread "vagrancy and kindred social evils."[57] English historian John Anthony Froude, visiting Havana during the mid-1880s, described legions of beggars crowding the capital's narrow streets. Squalor and destitution were everywhere manifest.[58] Some years later, North American tourist Richard Davey struck a similar tone:

> Never . . . have I seen such terrible beggars as those of Cuba. They haunt you everywhere, gathering round the church doors, whining for alms, insulting you if you refuse them, and pestering you as you go home at night, never leaving you till you either bestow money on them or escape within your own or some friendly door.[59]

V Not all these problems were new. Vagrancy had caused authorities concern during the Ten Years War when the relocation of rural families had caused overcrowding in the cities. The expectation that the end of the war would relieve the urban congestion and destitution, however, proved short-lived. Within a year after Zanjón, Spanish authorities undertook a thorough policy review of the relationship between vagrancy and rising lawlessness. It was a connection readily established, but at first officials were preoccupied with finding a remedy to the causes of vagrancy as a means of reducing its effects. Attributing vagrancy to unemployment, colonial authorities proposed three courses of action, each designed to meet problems associated with a specific age group. First, vagrant youths under twenty were to be assigned to local factories and farms as a way to promote a work habit and a trade. In the second program, the government established a workhouse for beggars and vagrants on the Isle of Pines. In the *protectorado del trabajo*, as the Isle of Pines project became known, vagrants between the ages of twenty and fifty were to be sentenced to work rehabilitation programs with minimum compensation. Lastly, vagrants over fifty were to be assigned to local municipal *ayuntamientos* as day laborers in public works and government service with compensation adequate for their upkeep.[60]

In the best of times, these would have been imposing programs. In post-Zanjón Cuba, they were impossible. The *protectorado del trabajo* was hardly launched when revenue deficits forced its suspension. By the early 1880s it was no longer feasible to condemn the idle to work when workers were condemned to idleness. Nor could municipal authorities bear the rising cost of subsidizing antivagrancy programs at a time when declining revenues and deepening indebtedness were edging local government ever closer to bankruptcy. Public payrolls were already hopelessly in arrears, and all but totally foreclosed new municipal expenditures.

Through the 1880s, authorities resorted to a variety of measures to end vagrancy, all of which failed. As early as 1881, the civil governor of Santa Clara organized the Junta de Represión de la Vagancia designed to halt the rising crime rate through the summary arrest of all vagrants.[61] In 1888, deteriorating conditions in Havana led to the promulgation of severe repressive measures. "The disagreeable spectacle offered by the great number of individuals of all classes who are continually found asleep or given over to idleness, in the promenades and other public places, when not to worse acts," the civil governor of Havana, Carlos Rodríguez Batista, proclaimed,

> must not and cannot be tolerated any longer. The measures adopted by this Civil Government on differ-

ent occasions for the disappearance of such scenes were intended also to guarantee individual security, particularly at night, when people on foot are easily surprised and attacked by criminals under the disguise of peaceable persons, thus originating the commission of crimes that were it not for those circumstances would be easy for the police to prevent.

Rodríguez Batista decreed the arrest of "every person without occupation or known address found in the parks, streets and other public places of the city." Vagrants were sentenced to mandatory employment in public works projects in Havana, without compensation.[62] At the same time, the colonial government sought to revive the *protectorado del trabajo*, this time imposing a tax levy on each province to subsidize the program.[63]

These measures had little immediate effect. Within months, a new governor complained of rising crime and continuing vagrancy. In 1889, Governor Manuel Salamanca pledged his administration to create new jobs as an antidote to vagrancy, "the single largest cause of crime."[64]

But Spanish authorities knew, too, that colonial revenues were not adequate either to promote public works projects or to create new jobs. Nor could officials expect relief from private quarters, for the Cuban economy continued to languish. By the end of the decade, the colonial authorities devised still another solution to the problem: to expel vagrants and criminals. In the late 1880s and early 1890s, Spanish authorities offered moral encouragement and material incentives to "undesirable" Cubans to emigrate to Florida. Convicts received the choice of prison on the Isle of Pines or passage to Key West. Fugitives at large were offered pardons if they surrendered to authorities before emigrating. A new population of Cubans thus joined the growing expatriate communities in Florida, and although the number of Cubans emigrating to Florida under these circumstances is impossible to determine, it was apparently large enough to prompt the mayor of Key West in 1888 to protest Spanish policy to the State Department.[65]

Not all farmers migrated to the cities or acquiesced in
VI their impoverishment and the new order of things.

Rural Cubans had developed a tolerance for the vagaries of subsistence agriculture. They accepted the relentless providence to which they were subject. Bad times alternated with good times—the cycle was not an unfamiliar
one. But all such cycles had an element of predictability, a
rhythm that itself served as a source of stability and continuity: a beginning, an end. By the 1880s, this predictability
had vanished: now bad times were followed by worse times,
with no end in sight. Peasants were prepared to endure
grinding poverty, but not the rupture and collapse of the
world as they knew it. The reaction was not long in coming.
Within a decade of Zanjón, banditry reached epidemic proportions in the countryside—palpable expression of crisis
and tension in rural Cuba. In many western regions, communities were disintegrating. A way of life was being destroyed as a new oppression overtook the old communities.
Many displaced farmers and dispossessed peasants refused
to submit to the regimen of the plantation, choosing independence and life outside the law. But banditry was more
than individual rebellion and personal revolt. It was also an
expression of collective resistance by communities threatened with ultimate extinction.

Lawlessness in the countryside increased during the
1880s, in good part the result of the Ten Years War. For
veterans and *pacíficos* alike, the requirements of peace were
often more exacting than the rigors of war. The prospects of
peace provided many Cubans little material incentive to
abandon their arms. Jobs were few and agriculture was in
ruins. Even when farms could be reclaimed, the destruction
of crops, the dispersal of livestock, and the disrepair of
equipment was so complete that all but the most determined were discouraged from returning to the land. For
some, it was preferable to seek survival as unrepentant
fugitives than scratch out a subsistence as indigent farmers.[66]

But to propose that the Ten Years War caused the increased lawlessness of the 1880s is not sufficient. For the
better part of ten years, the war had been contained largely

in the east. It was the eastern population that had suffered the primary effects of the military campaigns, and it was in the eastern provinces that the war had released its most destructive force with the most disruptive effects. But the east experienced nothing comparable to the lawlessness that occurred in the west. Certainly postwar banditry was not unknown in Camagüey and Oriente. Incidents of banditry were fewer, however, and the extent of lawlessness was less. Even as banditry assumed epidemic proportions in the west, peace and order still prevailed in the east. Between May 1885 and November 1887, the governor of Camagüey reported no instance of banditry. It was not until June 1888 that authorities in Camagüey recorded the first act of banditry. In Oriente, lawlessness was confined to scattered cases of arson and sporadic assaults.[67]

Hence, the disruption produced by the separatist war does not in itself explain the increase of lawlessness in the west. A more direct and relevant correlation can be found in the different patterns of land tenure and tenancy between the two regions. Vast expanses of eastern Cuba remained uninhabited and unchartered. More land was available to more people in Oriente than in the west. Even as the Ten Years War was in progress, official maps described vast areas of Oriente province as "waste and uninhabited mountains" and "uncultivated and unexplored regions."[68] It was this availability of land that served to mitigate effects of postwar disarray and destitution. Certainly the war had caused profound dislocation in the east, but access to land provided individuals with subsistence and communities with sustenance, easing the transition from war to peace.

It was not war that disrupted community organization and property relations in the west. It was peace. The concentration of land into larger units and the consolidation of property under fewer owners signaled displacement and dispossession on a vast scale. Long after communities of small farmers had declined in the west, communal tenure and individual tenancy continued to flourish in the east. The western provinces reorganized around sugar latifundia, to the detriment of divergent agricultural purposes and diversified land tenure, while mixed small farms continued to dominate the east. Even as late as 1899, Oriente contained the largest number of independent farms with the smallest average acreage. Only .5 percent of the farms in Oriente were over 330 acres, and they comprised only 26.9 percent of the total area under cultivation. The average size of the 21,550 farms in 1899 was approximately 82 acres. Oriente claimed not only the highest number of individual landowners, but also the highest number of renters, a total of 43,721. The contrast with the western sugar regions in 1899 was striking. Matanzas had the fewest number of farms (4,083) with the largest average acreage (247), followed by Havana with 6,159 farms averaging 135 acres, and Santa Clara with 16,129 farms of an average of 115 acres in size.[69]

In the west, the capitalization of agriculture created a rural proletariat for which there existed neither permanent employment nor guaranteed work. Employment was seasonal, and the length of employment was variable, subject always to the vagaries of the market economy. During the *zafra* (harvest), typically between late autumn and early spring, work was available, and often plentiful. The *tiempo muerto*, the aptly named dead season, followed the *zafra*. It arrived with the tropical summer and brought idleness. The completion of the harvest created instantly unemployment and indigence. The sugar system minimized full-year work and maximized seasonal fluctuation of labor demand. Underemployment was constant, except at the height of the *zafra*. For all the vaunted labor requirements of sugar production, plantations were in the end incapable of providing full-time employment to all workers all year long. A rural labor surplus population was formed, creating in its wake destitution among workers where once there had existed self-sufficiency.

Farmers earlier tied to the land, preoccupied year round with planting, cultivating, and harvesting, once transformed into wage laborers, acquired a new mobility. In the absence of work, the unemployed ex-farmer could take—and was often required to take—temporary leave of field and family in pursuit of alternative sources of income. Outlawry offered a way out of privation, a livelihood during periods of personal destitution. "Laborers on the plantations," the U.S vice-consul in Matanzas reported during the *tiempo muerto* of 1884, "have turned into highwaymen."[70] During the long months of summer idleness unemployed workers found in banditry an adequate if hazardous means of subsistence.

By the late 1880s, entire districts of the west were in the throes of social unrest. Discontent gave way to open rebellion, ambiguous and amorphous, to be sure, disorganized and desultory, too, but rebellion nevertheless, more in response to local injustice than to colonial inequities, more parochial than national. It flourished through communal collaboration. At its source and in its scope, banditry gave expression to a popular refusal to conform to the new order of things. It was an assault against property, property owners, and inevitably the authorities charged with their defense.

Brigandage had existed intermittently throughout western Cuba from the beginning of the nineteenth century. Indeed, fugitives had operated outside the law almost as far back as the century of conquest.[71] But the banditry of the late nineteenth century was different. Banditry after Zanjón was a localized phenomenon and did not affect all regions equally. In those districts where banditry flourished, it was ubiquitous, persistent, and proliferating. It gathered recruits from among those expelled from the land or seeking escape from poverty. It was different, too, in that bandits operated in comparatively large and close-knit groups. The size of the approximately fifteen distinct bands operating in post-Zanjón Cuba averaged between fifteen and thirty permanent members, bound together by shared values in common activities against shared sources of oppression.[72]

VII Developments in western Cuba after Zanjón conform generally to those conditions that Eric J. Hobsbawm has suggested engender a specific form of rural protest identified as social banditry: peasants transformed into outlaws who enjoy the support of local residents. Social bandits operate with the acquiescence, often with the approval, of peasant communities and always within the bounds of the moral order of rural society. They are perceived as heroes and noble robbers who plunder from the prosperous to provide for the poor. They are avengers, redressing grievances and righting wrongs. Banditry as an expression of premodern protest, Hobsbawm suggested, reaches epidemic proportions during times of pauperization and economic crisis. More specifically, banditry "may reflect the disruption of an entire society, the rise of new classes and social structures, the resistance of entire communities or peoples against the destruction of its way of life."[73] Peasants become bandits, Hobsbawm wrote elsewhere, to protest oppression and impoverishment, as an outcry against the advent of agrarian capitalism that comes to them from the outside, "insidiously by the operation of economic forces which they do not understand and over which they have no control."[74] Hobsbawm writes:

> [Social banditry] consists essentially of relatively small groups of men living on the margins of peasant society, and whose activities are considered criminal by the prevailing official power-structure and value-system, but not (or not without strong qualifications) by the peasantry. It is this special relation between peasant and bandit which makes banditry "social": the social bandit is a hero, a champion, a man whose enemies are the same as the peasants', whose activities correct injustice, control oppression and exploitation, and perhaps even maintain alive the ideal of emancipation and independence.[75]

Along similar lines, Aníbal Quijano Obregón writes: "In a primitive way [social banditry] is often the beginning of the secularization of social action. Since social banditry in Latin America has always been directed against the domination and the abuse of landlords, it reflects an incipient process of identification of the most important social enemy of the peasants."[76]

Bandits operated across western Cuba throughout the 1880s and 1890s, directly involving at the height of rural unrest an estimated 800 men.[77] Outlaw groups consisted of a mixture of former soldiers and former slaves, but mostly displaced farmers and destitute laborers. Bandits ranged in age between twenty-five and thirty-five years; some were younger but few older.[78] Bands under Juan Vento, José Inocencio Sosa ("Gallo" Sosa), and most famously Manuel García ("El Rey de los Campos") operated in Havana province. Victoriano and Luis Machín dominated the Vuelta Bajo region in Pinar del Río. José Plasencia, José ("Matagás") Alvarez Arteaga, Nicanor Duarte, Regino Alfonso, Desiderio and Nicasio Matos, and Aurelio Sanabria ranged across the interior districts of Matanzas province. Bandits operating in Santa Clara included Florentino Rodríguez and Bruno Gutiérrez, Matías Rodríguez, Diego Comezanas Valdivia, Nicasio Mirabal, and Sacarino Ruiz.

These were clever country people. They had the aptitude to plan mischief and the audacity to execute it. They employed disguises of every type: sometimes dressed as the Guardia Civil, sometimes mail carriers, often bearing false messages. They did whatever was required to penetrate the defenses of the embattled planter class. They succeeded.

VIII Unrest in rural western Cuba during the late 1880s and early 1890s assumed fully the proportions of a social upheaval. This was not quite an organized peasant rebellion against landlords. Rather, it was an improvised assault against the dominant social class, and no planter or plantation was safe. Resentment was directed at the propertied, the privileged, and the powerful. Attacks against planters expressed first the social content and later the political context of peasant grievances. Planters were subjected with increasing frequency to kidnapping and ransom demands. During the 1880s, the abduction of individual planters, as well as family members, assumed epidemic proportions. In 1885, authorities reported fifteen kidnappings: seven in Matanzas, seven in Santa Clara, and one in Havana. Another ten were reported the following year.[79] Between 1883 and 1888, government authorities in Matanzas province recorded nineteen abductions involving total ransom payments in excess of 70,000 pesos in gold.[80] Similar conditions were reported in Havana province[81] and Santa Clara.[82] Between November 1886 and May 1887, the kidnapping of planters in the provinces of Pinar del Río, Havana, and Matanzas occurred at the rate of one per month.[83] The patriarchs of some of the most prestigious planter families, including Nicolás Pérez Artiles, Genaro Roque, Antonio Galíndez de Aldama, Eulogio Nodal López, and Pedro Sardiña, fell captive to kidnappers and were released only after the delivery of ransom payments.[84]

Attacks against property also increased. Bandits attacked plantations, destroyed buildings, sacked stores, and confiscated livestock.[85] But most often, they torched the canefields—again, again, and again. Because the vastness of open and unprotected fields made arson all but impossible to defend against, arson was easily the most common expression of peasant discontent. During the *zafra* of 1891, lasting some 150 days, Spanish authorities reported a total of 461 canefield fires.[86]

Because of the vulnerability of their fields, planters were subject to another type of harassment in the form of extortion. Bandits routinely exacted annual tributes from planters in exchange for guarantees of the security of their property. Manuel García enjoyed considerable success in imposing an annual levy on landowners for permitting them to plant and harvest.[87] Indeed, many planters settled directly with bandits, rather than risk damage to property or interruption of the *zafra*. North American planter Edwin F. Atkins recalled that many landowners in the Cienfuegos region paid tribute to García, although Atkins preferred "to incur the expense of maintaining a strong field guard to paying tribute."[88]

Beginning in the 1890s, García expanded his operations to include the Ferrocarriles Unidos de La Habana, the major railroad service in Havana province and the principal means of transport for sugar and plantation equipment. The railroad shared one fateful similarity with the plantations: miles of unprotected tracks and isolated stations. When, in 1891, railway officials ignored a demand for 10,000 pesos in annual tribute, García attacked the Ferrocarriles Unidos, derailing trains, destroying rail stations, and assaulting railroad crews.[89]

IX Banditry transformed the Cuban countryside into something of a war zone. Travel in rural Cuba soon became a hazardous undertaking, and few travelers of means ventured very far into the interior without adequate security precautions. "There are many lawless people— banditti, in fact," commented Marturin M. Ballou in the course of his travels through Cuba, "who make war for plunder both upon native and foreign travelers, even resorting in some cases to holding prisoners for ransoms. . . . It is, therefore, necessary to carry arms for self-defense upon the roads in some parts of the island, and even the countrymen wear swords when bringing produce to market. Residents having occasion to go any distance inland take a well-armed guard with them, to prevent being molested by the desperate refugees who lurk in the hill country."[90] The new English consul-general completed a tour around the island in 1893, and could scarcely contain his disbelief: "The banditti, who, much to my astonishment, infest many parts of the Island . . . are apparently able to carry on their lawless life and commit their depredations on society with an impunity almost inconceivable."[91] "The results of all this," Vice-Consul David Vickers reported from Matanzas, "has been an alarming increase of brigandage all over the Island. In a year it has been unsafe to go into the country unless armed like a pirate, and even then one is constantly in danger of assassination. Owners of estates cannot visit their plantations without running the risk of kidnapping and the cities are becoming as dangerous as the country."[92]

The issues involved more than the safety of travel in rural Cuba, however. Deepening social tensions in the west threatened the most productive agricultural regions of the island with ruin. Planters lived in constant fear for their personal safety and the security of their family and property. Trade and commerce suffered. Transportation was disrupted. Uncertainty increased, and incidents of banditry grew in frequency and audacity. By the 1890s, sugar estates once immune from bandit depredations by their nearness to the capital were subject to increasing attacks. "Brigandage is still rife," A. C. Crowe wrote from Havana in 1890, "and life and property are not secure even within a few miles of the towns. Sequestrations, murders, and incendiarism are frequently reported from the country and at the present moment there is a band of 20 to 30 of these miscreants at large in the Province of Havana."[93] In January 1893, Ignacio Herrera, a prominent planter and the son of the count of Barreto, was kidnapped within the Havana city limits and held for 10,000 pesos in ransom. In 1894, Manuel García kidnapped Antonio Fernández de Castro, a member of one of the most prominent sugar families and brother of the leader of the Autonomist party. A year later, the sugar mill "Portugalete," located almost within view of Havana, was attacked and destroyed by Manuel García.[94] The U.S. consul in Havana described local conditions with a growing sense of urgency. "Small bands of marauders have often existed in Cuba," wrote Ramon O. Williams as early as 1887, "but heretofore the Government has always succeeded in speedily capturing or dispersing them. Never before, however, have they been so bold and defiant as now."[95] On the occasion of the abduction of Fernández de Castro, La Lucha wrote:

> The impression caused by the kidnapping of Antonio Fernández de Castro has been sobering. . . . Never have we been at such an extreme, in such a grave situation. For what is surprising is not that bandits abduct, and above all besiege the wealthy and comfortable people, but that they can do this with nearly the absolute impunity that they have been doing. Against the legal authority, against public administration, they have established a clandestine administration and power that appears more formidable, better organized, more clever . . . than the former. That is what is scandalous.[96]

The metaphors the press employed to characterize banditry reveal as much about the popular state of mind as the actual state of brigandage: "pestilence," "infestation," and "scourge" were among the most common. The Havana daily Diario de la Marina denounced the "lamentable plague" of banditry. The increasing incidents of planter kidnappings in particular aroused editorial ire and prompted the newspaper to demand immediate official action: "The evil is a very grave one, and it is necessary to stop it, for the personal tranquility of many families and of thousands of persons in the country is involved, all of whom ask for support and protection against these thieves and murderers. . . . Special energy is required for the extinction of this plague."[97]

X   But it was not for want of government efforts that banditry persisted and flourished. Indeed, it may very well have increased as a result of those efforts. Few other issues between 1878 and 1895 so fully preoccupied colonial authorities, for social unrest in the countryside had grave political and economic implications. The assault against the planter bourgeoisie struck at the linchpin of the colonial system, threatening the vital interests of the very class upon whose continued collaboration Spain depended for successful rule. The inability to defend the planter class bode ill to authorities, already on the defensive against growing political dissent and deepening economic dislocation. The mere existence of bandits, and particularly in the numbers that flourished in post-Zanjón Cuba, weakened the moral authority and prestige of colonial government. The authorities, beleaguered planters protested, could not provide even minimum guarantees of security to the producing classes.[98] This became the stuff of separatist propaganda, too, allegations that Spain could not provide stability or protect citizens.[99] Rural disorders in the rich agricultural zones of western Cuba, moreover, threatened to thwart Cuban efforts to recover its former primacy in sugar. Under prevailing conditions, the prospect of revival remained tentative, if not bleak—a prospect that threatened the planter class with ruin and ultimately extinction.[100]

These conditions had far-reaching political implications. Most immediately they served to encourage annexationist sentiment among planters, as increasingly the belief took hold that in union with the United States landowners would obtain greater security. The stirrings of discontent were everywhere on the increase. Local elites in growing numbers were experiencing a crisis of confidence, and more than a few publicly questioned the efficacy of continued colonial relationships. Growing impatience over the deteriorating state of affairs, the British consul in Havana reported in 1888, was "for the first time echoed by the Conservative papers, which shows that even the Government supporters have abandoned their reserve, and think the time has come to adopt drastic measures if Cuba is to continue inhabitable for the white races."[101]

These were portentous developments, and no one misconstrued their meaning. "Many are already talking of resistance and annexation to the United States," reported Vickers from Matanzas as early as 1884, "not that they love Spain less, but their interests more."[102] The Havana daily *El Popular* predicted confidently in 1887, "Annexation to the United States would make Cuba a rich, enlightened, and tranquil country."[103] "The very gloomy and depressed state of affairs now affecting Cuba," editorialized *La Razón* of Pinar del Río, "makes some of those persons extend their eyes toward the United States for measures of salvation."[104] Wrote the U.S. consul in Havana: "A great many persons here, who years ago hooted the idea of annexation to the United States now advocate it, as the only remedy for the preservation of public order and the attainment of future commercial prosperity in the island."[105]

XI Spanish authorities were not slow to respond to rural lawlessness. Across the western interior, the government military presence increased. As early as 1884, in an attempt to provide better protection to planters in Matanzas during the harvest, colonial authorities augmented the number of Guardia Civil detachments.[106] In 1889, Spain established a Rural Guard Corps, organizing a network of permanent rural outposts throughout the sugar zones.[107] In the same year, Governor General Manuel Salamanca ordered all Guardia Civil posts on the island linked together by telephone to coordinate operations against outlaws. Salamanca subsequently authorized the establishment of telegraph lines between the larger sugar estates and provincial headquarters of the Guardia Civil.[108]

Government efforts also included increased rural surveillance. In late 1887, the civil governor of Santa Clara formalized surveillance procedures by ordering sugar mills to sound their steam whistles upon the first sighting of an outlaw. Each estate was to repeat the warning until the sound of the successive whistles reached the local Guardia Civil station, whereupon chase would be given.[109] In addition, new emphasis fell on the collection and analysis of intelligence. In 1890, the government established a special intelligence unit to deal exclusively with banditry. At the same time, the authorities continued to alternate offers of amnesty with the posting of generous rewards for information leading to the capture of known fugitives.[110]

The most ambitious government undertakings were full-scale military operations in disaffected zones. The first one, in 1888, in direct response to a sudden increase of planter kidnappings and, as a consequence, rising public impatience, resulted in the most formidable Spanish military offensive since the end of the Ten Years War. Governor Sabas Marín proclaimed a state of war in the four western provinces of Pinar del Río, Havana, Matanzas, and Santa Clara, placing the administration of justice entirely under military authorities.[111] The state of siege and military operations continued through 1889 without much effect and were subsequently suspended during the brief administration of Governor Manuel Salamanca. With the appointment of Camilo G. Polavieja as governor-general in 1890, however, military operations resumed. Polavieja mounted a second and even more formidable military offensive against bandits within weeks of his arrival in Havana. Some 10,000 troops were amassed in major—but in the end, again, futile—military operations.[112]

Certainly not all government efforts were ineffective. Many bandits were captured by the police and killed in military operations.[113] Indeed, between 1889 and 1891, some of the most prominent bandit leaders, including Sixto Valera, Andrés Santana, and Domingo Montolongo, were captured by the authorities. Officials claimed to have captured a total of 164 bandits. Public executions were revived, ending a longstanding moratorium on capital punishment. They were calculated to give maximum publicity to the meager progress made by the government—a public demonstration to calm public disquiet. Between 1889 and 1891, hangings proceeded at the rate of one a month.[114]

But success against individual bandits in the field and convictions in the courts failed to establish order in the countryside. Outlaw bands had been neither defeated nor dispersed. After almost ten years and nearly as many different colonial administrations, the mightiest of Spanish efforts had failed to end what was officially referred to as "the plague." Banditry would not go away. As colonial officials knew only too well, military authorities faced more than the task of suppressing bands of hundreds of outlaws operating in the interior. They were engaged in a low-level war, and not only against the bandits. They confronted the daunting task of controlling communities of thousands of peasants and rural workers who served as the natural allies and loyal accomplices of fugitive bands. Either by passive acquiescence or active participation, local residents formed a complex support network, involving men, women, and children. They provided outlaws with aid and alibis, protection and provisions, sanctuary and support. In the remote villages and hamlets of rural Cuba a difficult problem became impossible. Bandits were themselves local men whose familiarity with the often inaccessible terrain in which they operated accounted in part for the ease with which they eluded the authorities.

More important, however, were the ties of kinship and friendship that served to bind outlaws to the body social of rural Cuba. Bandit groups represented a cross section of their communities. They shared common experiences and traditions, but most of all shared similar grievances against common sources. They gave form to local resistance to the new socioeconomic order and inspired rebellion against the old politico-military system. Attacks were directed principally against sources of local oppression, and each deed was possessed of palpable symbolic content. "The peasants continue protecting Manuel García," an exasperated Governor General Camilo G. Polavieja reported in 1891, "for they see in him, not the bandit, but the partisan up in arms against Spain."[115]

Bandits were supported especially by those peasants who were themselves caught midway between the peasantry and the proletariat, moving inexorably toward rural wage labor, but still clinging to claims on the land.[116] The abduction of planters, the attacks against the plantations, and the assaults against the railroads were actions readily understood by rural communities. On occasion, bandits passed the spoils of war on to the rural population. Manuel García frequently used ransom money to distribute foodstuffs, supplies, and equipment among peasants and rural workers.[117] This gesture may have been motivated as much by practical considerations as political conviction, for it served to foster goodwill among the people upon whose support bandits depended for their survival.[118] And the villagers responded in kind. Runaway slave Esteban Montejo later recalled: "[Manuel García] was a friend of the *guajiro*, a real friend. If they ever saw the police getting close to a place where Manuel was, they used to take their trousers off and hang them on a rope waist down. This was the signal for Manuel to get moving, and that must be why he lived so long as an outlaw."[119]

Colonial authorities were not unaware of the magnitude of this collaboration and the meaning of its implications. Indeed, Spanish intelligence reports themselves provide the most comprehensive and detailed accounts of the character of the collaboration between fugitives and farmers. One military intelligence report from the *municipio* of Madruga in eastern Havana province compiled a lengthy list of local residents known to assist bandit leaders. These included: Rafael Almeida who sheltered the bandit Asunción Muerte; Victoriano Jacomino who provided bandit José Plasencia with changes of clothing; Miguel Mesa, who supplied Manuel García with food and horses; Joaquín Chávez, who regularly gave bandits shelter, supplies, and fresh horses; Manuel Hernández, whose home was a meeting site for several bandit groups; José Mario Brito, who acted as a purchasing agent for supplies; Severino Méndez, a nephew of José Plasencia, and Matias Domínguez Fundora, a cousin of bandit José Fundora, who served as intermediaries during kidnapping negotiations and ransom transactions; Juan Luis Bello, who acted as messenger among various bandit groups; Tomás Hernández, who sheltered Manuel García, José Plasencia, Vicente García, and Gallo Sosa and served as a collector of ransom funds for Antonio Santana.[120]

All had some role in the rural drama. Some provided intelligence information concerning the strength of local army units; others reported the movement of government forces; some prepared and delivered food, provisions, and daily newspapers to fugitives on the run, and all steadfastly professed ignorance of any knowledge concerning the activities or whereabouts of the outlaws. "He is protected absolutely by the country people," Governor Polavieja wrote of Manuel García.[121]

Nor was such collaboration restricted to passive support. Occasionally they served as auxiliary members of an outlaw band, participating in special operations that required augmented forces. "Every group of bandits," Polavieja later wrote, "counted upon a certain number of peasants who joined them armed for important actions, and who subsequently returned to their homes as peaceful citizens and ignorant of everything."[122] This practice was especially prevalent during the *tiempo muerto,* when the unemployed sought relief from idleness and indigence through banditry.

Spain's problems, hence, were not primarily, or perhaps even principally, with outlaw bands themselves. They were with the communities that sheltered them and the villagers who provided fugitives with supplies, sanctuary, and support. And increasingly, and inevitably, the full weight of government frustration fell upon the country people suspected of collaboration. The imposition of martial law in 1888 and 1890 and subsequent military operations were directed as much against the local rural population suspected of supporting bandits as the bandits themselves, who, in any case, routinely eluded even the most elaborate government military efforts. During periods of martial law peasants and rural workers were indiscriminately arrested and tried by courts martial. Peasants detained for questioning often disappeared. Some were beaten to death; others were subjected to the *ley de fuga:* "shot while trying to escape." They were killed in hot pursuit and in cold blood. Survivors recounted tales of murder and massacre, terror and torture. The Guardia Civil became a source of rural repression, deepening the estrangement between the country people and colonial authorities.[123] Each military campaign announced the disruption of local life, and communities dispersed in anticipation of new and sustained periods of government operations. Village marketplaces were destroyed and local trade and agriculture declined. The homes of suspected peasant collaborators were burned and razed. "The government has had at times as many as six thousand troops," one Cuban wrote, "besides the rural police *(Orden Público)* and volunteers, in pursuit of these brigands, and yet for every bandit captured or killed, the newspapers are filled with complaints from poor farmers who are beaten and insulted as harborers of criminals. All this show of force has been another source of squandering and tension as a result of the summary executions in unpopulated regions, on the pretext that suspects resisted arrest or tried to escape."[124]

Many countryside communities were in an advanced state of disarray. Villagers abandoned their homes and fled deeper into the remote interior in search of sanctuary. Some sought temporary safety with outlaw bands. Indeed, in 1889, Manuel García announced that government military operations had contributed to augmenting his band of nineteen to a battalion of 400.[125]

XII The failure of colonial authorities to defeat bandits led to greater emphasis on dominating the peasants who supported them. Responsibility and punishment for the actions of bandits were transferred to the country people, without whom, authorities insisted, fugitives could not long sustain their depradations. And, increasingly, it was against the rural communities that military authorities directed their actions. Many country people, the governor of Havana province, Luis Alonso Martín, warned in November 1877, "either through culpable complicity, or from lack of energy and courage, contribute to making more difficult, when not completely defeating, the action of the authorities, by maliciously concealing the passage of bandits through the fields, or reporting it too late, and in many cases withholding information of important matters." Martín proclaimed that all persons were under the "imperative duty" to report the presence or passage of all fugitives in local communities. Delay in communicating appropriate information, moreover, "if it exceeds the time deemed necessary in the judgment of the authorities," would be construed as "shielding the malefactors," and appropriate action would be taken.[126] In April 1888, only days after the kidnapping of planter Antonio Galíndez de Aldama, the Havana newspaper *Voz de Cuba* exhorted the government to prosecute all participants in the crime, particularly those who sheltered the outlaws: "Let the penalty for kidnapping be executed not only upon the bandits, but upon their harborers and accomplices, and upon all engaged in this detestable plot to ruin our agricultural wealth."[127] In proclaiming martial law in 1888, Governor Sabas Marín pledged to proceed with an equally "strong hand against the leaders, accomplices, and harborers of these crimes." Enjoining his field commanders to move against communities suspected of providing aid and comfort to bandits, Sabas Marín vowed: "I am resolved to exact of them the responsibility they incur, if they neglect to lend their moral and material support to the government which their duty as citizens imposes upon them." Indeed, it was precisely the growing collaboration between bandits and villagers, Sabas Marín explained, that required the government to impose martial law: "The aid given . . . in a part of the island by a few deluded persons . . . converting themselves into aiders and abettors, compel the adoption of extraordinary measures to put an end to disorders."[128]

Governor Manuel Salamanca demanded increased legal action in the courts and enjoined government attorneys *(fiscales)* to prosecute vigorously all suspects charged with aiding bandits. "Without doubt," he predicted in 1889, "the active and well directed efforts of the military forces against the bandits that infest the rural districts will have little effect if the attorneys entrusted with their prosecution do not display all the zeal and intelligence necessary not only for the discovery of crimes, but also for the bringing of accomplices, aiders, and abettors to trial regardless of their social rank or motive of relationships with those subject to the action of the court, and whom they help escape punishment and thereby directly or indirectly impede the administration of justice." Salamanca concluded:

> It is of great importance that these functionaries should take into consideration that one of the most efficient means for the destruction of banditry and preventing bandits from having their own way is the punishment of all persons who lend them help, and the exaction of due responsibility of those who sympathize with them, for it is an undeniable fact that if the bandit who respects neither life nor property finds no assistance in the districts where he exercises his criminal profession, nor finds even shelter afforded by the sentiment of indifference towards his acts, he would feel the dangers of his isolation and in a short time would be obliged to abandon the fields of his habitual incursion.[129]

Not all peasants and workers collaborated with bandits willingly. Some did so under duress: a request for food and supplies by armed bandits on the run could hardly be spurned by an isolated peasant family. But a transaction under these circumstances was often sufficient grounds for Spanish authorities to arrest the farmer. U.S. Vice-Consul Henry A. Ehringer wrote from Cienfuegos:

> Parties of these bandits numbering from 5 to 10 go about the country relying on the sympathy or toleration of the inhabitants of whom they exact food and horses, extorted in many cases by threats of personal violence or destruction of their property. A party visits the house of a countryman and demands food, money or horses. The person called upon dares not refuse them. Afterwards there arrives a party of troops or

police in pursuit of these outlaws, and hearing that they have been there, they arrest the already suffering countryman on the charge of having given aid and shelter to the bandits. In many cases taking into their own hands the punishment of those persons who acted from self-preservation.[130]

Certainly it is plausible that any peasant discovered by the authorities to have fed and sheltered bandits would have been wise to claim to have done so under duress. But it is also possible that some did indeed render assistance under coercion. These distinctions were often lost on the authorities. Peasants were placed in a terrible dilemma. They could neither collaborate with the bandits nor cooperate with the authorities without grave risks. Peasants known to have assisted the government were frequently the victims of murder.[131] These were powerful object lessons for country people. The authorities who could not protect the powerful planters could hardly be expected to protect the powerless peasant.

Hence the crisis of confidence that gripped the propertied also affected the propertyless. The colonial regime revealed itself incapable of discharging even the minimum guarantees for persons and property.

2 The Promise of the New

Exclusive wealth is unjust. Let this wealth belong to many
people. . . . A nation is indeed wealthy if it possesses many
small-property owners. A wealthy nation is not one in which
there are a few rich men but rather one in which every citizen
has a small share of that wealth. Both in political economy and
in solid government, by distributing these things we make the
people happy.

—José Martí, 1887

The centers of our sugar production contain great evils, partici-
pate in criminal negotiations, and contribute to the degradation
of our people. Work . . . there is the humiliation and exploitation of the weak. The redemptive Revolution . . . will show the
weak how the people express their protest.

—Colonel Fermín Valdés Domínguez, 1897

I have not been able to understand the fundamental cause of
such an unjust disproportion between the farmer and the
central-owner. . . . I felt indignant and profundly predisposed
against the upper classes of the country, and in an instant of
rage, at the sight of such a sad and painful disparity, I
exclaimed: "Blessed be the torch."

—General Máximo Gómez, 1897

Hard times after Zanjón affected all Cubans, certainly not all at once or in the same way. But ultimately, hard times aroused to action vast numbers of
Cubans for whom the promise of an uncertain future, even
though created at the cost of untold suffering, was deemed
preferable to the prospects of an unacceptable present and a
continuation of the status quo.

War came once more to Cuba in February 1895, once more
in the name of Cuba Libre. But the separatist effort of 1895
was dissimilar in character and composition from what had   **43**

gone before. Cuba had changed much between the Grito de Yara in 1868 and the Grito de Baire in 1895. No longer did the sources of Cuban grievances derive exclusively from the colonial rule of the distant European metropolis. By the late nineteenth century, Spain was neither the principal beneficiary nor the primary benefactor of colonialism. Inequity in 1895 had a peculiarly home-grown quality. That the sources of oppression in Cuba were more internal than external, and, further, that the forms of oppression were more social than political, served as the central premises around which the separatist movement assumed definitive shape during the 1880s and 1890s. Armed separatism in 1895 was committed to more than Cuba Libre. It had also a social imperative. What was different in 1895 was the recognition that injustice was principally caused not by Spanish political rule, for which independence was the obvious remedy, but by the Cuban social system, for which the transformation of Cuban society was the only remedy. Cubans continued to speak of war as a way to independence, of course, but they now also spoke of armed struggle as a method of economic reorganization and social redemption. Political separatism had expanded into revolutionary populism, committed as much to ending colonial relationships within the colony as to ending colonial rule. To the historic purpose of national liberation was added national revolution, and instantly a movement dedicated to the establishment of a new country became a force devoted to shaping a new society.

Different, too, were the social origins of separatist leadership. A new constituency joined the ranks of Cuba Libre: the dispossessed and destitute—Cubans for whom armed struggle offered the means through which to redress historic grievances against the social system. Large numbers were Cubans of color. Indeed, an estimated 40 percent of the senior commissioned ranks of the Liberation Army was made up of Afro-Cubans.[1] Armed separatism in 1895 offered oppressed groups the possibility of social justice and economic freedom. A decade of proletarianization and pauperization had more than predisposed tens of thousands of Cubans to embrace the promise of national liberation; for them the old regime was as much a social anathema as it was a political anachronism. They had committed themselves to a movement that promised to give them a new place in society, a new government they would control, and a new nation to belong to.

No small source of the change in the character of armed separatism was the result of changes in the Cuban countryside. Economic dislocation and social distress after Zanjón plunged colonial society into disarray. By the mid-1890s, the deepening socioeconomic crisis increasingly found expression in political discontent, and nowhere more dramatically than in the disaffected rural districts of the west. The disruption of life in rural Cuba more than adequately prepared the countryside for revolution. Banditry was at once cause and effect of crisis. It was not so much a form of peasant movement as it was symptomatic of peasant unrest. The pursuit of bandits and the persecution of their supporters had the net effect of transforming regions of the west into zones of intermittent and irregular warfare. Periodic government operations wrought havoc in rural communities and became a recurring source of insecurity. Discontent with socioeconomic conditions spurred resistance to the colonial political system.

During the early 1890s, bandit activities acquired distinctive separatist overtones. Individual bandit chieftains found the passage from social protest to political rebellion easy if not inevitable. Manuel García developed into an ardent supporter of Cuba Libre. He had been one of those fugitives who had earlier accepted the Spanish offer of safe-conduct passage to Florida. In the course of his three years as a cigar worker in Key West and Tampa, García made the conversion to the separatist faith. He returned to Cuba in 1888 and resumed his attacks against property and property owners, now as an agent of the Revolutionary Club of Key West and with the military rank of *comandante*.[2]

During the 1890s, too, funds obtained in the form of ransom payments found their way into separatist coffers. A portion of the ransom money collected by García during these years served to support the activities of various revolutionary clubs in Key West and Tampa. The payment obtained for the release of planter Antonio Fernández de Castro in 1894 was donated to the Cuban Revolutionary party in Havana and Matanzas. Another estimated 75,000 pesos were donated to revolutionary organizations in the United States. Money was also used to obtain arms, ammunition, and supplies, which served to place entire districts of rural Cuba on a war footing. Manuel García and José "Matagás" Alvarez Arteaga alone managed to distribute some 500 weapons.[3]

The promise of independence also gave fugitives hope for a new life. A change of government, particularly one to which individual bandit leaders contributed, offered many the opportunity to end their outlaw status. Only a month before the outbreak of the war in 1895, Manuel García acknowledged that his support of the separatist cause was in part motivated by the hope of obtaining from the new republic a pardon that would allow him to return to peaceful pursuits.[4]

III In the end, they were more avengers than redeemers, more the protectors of old ways than the prophets of new ones. By themselves, bandits failed to develop the organizational structures and the ideological systems necessary to transform parochial rebellion to national revolution. Nor was their protest well organized. Their objectives were modest: the restoration of traditional social relationships. They did not reject the exercise of privilege as much as the excesses of privilege. They protested the abuse of inequality, but did not propose the abolition of inequality. They resented and resisted the disintegration of the old order. They had not enjoyed equality in the old order, but they had at least some rights. That was their minimum objective: at least some rights. In refusing to submit to oppression, bandits set by example a standard of resistance that uplifted the downtrodden.

In their own time they passed into legend, the subject of songs and stories, of poems and parables. They responded to injustice with armed protest, rejecting the passive role of the submissive peasant and engaging on its own terms the coercive authority of the state. Their mere existence offered the possibility of remedy to oppression and redress of grievances. In this capacity bandits demonstrated that injustice was not irreversible and that the powerless were not helpless.

More than predisposing peasants to resist, they stirred peasants to rebel. On February 24, 1895, bandits passed from outlawry to insurrection, and in the process were overtaken by history and passed from the realm of criminality to the world of nationality. Many of the principal outlaw chieftains immediately proclaimed armed support for the cause of Cuba Libre. Manuel García and José Inocencio Sosa in Havana, José "Matagás" Alvarez Arteaga and Regino Alfonso in Matanzas, Desiderio ("El Tuerto") Matos in Santa Clara, and Lino Mirabal and José Muñoz in Camagüey passed directly into the insurgent army of liberation.[5] García reached the rank of colonel. In the first year of the war, Matagás and Alfonso reached the rank of lieutenant colonel. "El Tuerto" Matos held the grade of major. Other members of their bands attained officer rank, including Eutaquio Morejón, Ignacio Fundora, and Miguel Parra. By the end of 1896, the military unit under the joint command of "Matagás" and Matos included 300 men. They operated out of the Zapata Swamp in the area of the Bay of Pigs. The "Matagás"-Matos band was among the best-equipped units in the Liberation Army, possessing an assortment of Winchesters, Mausers, revolvers, and a plentiful supply of ammunition.[6]

Few bandit leaders survived the war. Manuel García was killed in the early days of the uprising in 1895. "Matagás" perished in 1896, Matos a year later. Their units were absorbed into the provincial regiment of the Liberation Army commanded by General Francisco Pérez. In the end, their contribution to creating a climate of rebellion was greater than their participation in the rebellion.

IV The war spread quickly across the island. By the end of 1895, the main columns of the Liberation Army had marched into the western provinces. First Santa Clara, then Matanzas, and finally Havana and Pinar del Río, and suddenly, everywhere, Cubans were on the march, making war in regions never before subject to the sustained assault of Cuba Libre. In the space of ten months, Cubans had secured what they had failed to achieve in all of the Ten Years War: the incorporation of the western provinces into the war for independence.[7]

The effects of the Cuban presence in the west were both immediate and far-reaching. Regional rebellion fused with national revolution, and they acted upon each other. Developments in the preceding decade more than adequately prepared Cubans in the west for a greater role in a widespread rebellion. They were ready to make common cause with a movement that promised to end injustice by ending colonialism. The regions in which outlawry had flourished provided ideal districts in which to expand the insurrection. The stunning sweep westward of late 1895 and early 1896— "the invasion," as it became known, viewed as the outstanding military achievement of the war—was in fact a succession of flashpoints precipitated by the arrival of advanced units of the Liberation Army. The appearance of insurgent columns in the west heralded redemption, and peasants enrolled in the insurgent army by the thousands. In Cartagena, Cuban General José Miró Argenter wrote in his campaign diary of the "great increment of the Revolution in western Las Villas," and added: "the peasant abandoned his farming, the tobacco farmer his planting, the artisan his tools, and the laborer his work: all the patriots took to the hills."[8] Antonio Maceo estimated that some 10,000 new recruits had enrolled in the army in the course of the westward march.[9] After the invasion, the total number of insurgent army regiments increased from thirty to eighty-six.[10]

The separatist cause also obtained the support of countless tens of thousands of civilians, the *pacíficos* who served the liberation effort as noncombatants in a variety of roles. They provided food and supplies, cared for the wounded and tended the horses, served as messengers and couriers, but most of all, they passed back and forth across enemy lines, collecting intelligence and gathering information on the movement and maneuvers of the Spanish army everywhere in Cuba.[11]

By the time the invasion was complete, in early 1896, vast

numbers of peasants had enrolled in the movement for national liberation. They looked forward to the future, to a new Cuba. But they looked backward, too, hopeful that in the new Cuba they would recover some of the old ways, and most of all, recover their place on the land. They wanted a future that lived up to their past. And they had reason to be optimistic. In 1896, in a sweeping agrarian reform decree, the insurgent army command pledged the future republic to the redistribution of land:

> All lands acquired by the Cuban Republic either by conquest or confiscation, except what is employed for governmental purposes, shall be divided among the defenders of the Cuban Republic against Spain, and each shall receive a portion corresponding to the services rendered. . . . All lands, money, or property in any and all forms, previously belonging to Spain, to its allies, abettors or sympathizers, or to any person or corporation acting in the interest of Spain or in any manner disloyal to the Cuban Republic are hereby confiscated, for the benefits of the Cuban Army and of all the defenders of the Cuban Republic.[12]

V The invasion had another effect: in moving the center of the armed conflict from the remote eastern districts to the west, it immediately announced a new phase of the war. After 1895, Cubans found themselves in the position of toppling the colonial system, fully and irrevocably, including both its politico-military structures and its socioeconomic substance. With the completion of the invasion, it was no longer necessary, or even practical —given the weakness of insurgent logistical support—for Cubans to engage the Spanish army in battle.[13] Instead, the war was now against the dominant social class, the local collaborators of colonialism: a war waged against the beneficiaries of colonialism by its victims. Bandit attacks against property as an expression of provincial protest had expanded fully into the separatist means for national liberation. In this new design for war, the Spanish army hardly figured at all. The war was directed more against the creole bourgeoisie than the colonial bureaucracy, and the material destruction of the former was an adequate substitute for the military defeat of the latter.

This was the new purpose of Cuban arms after 1895. The sugar fields became the battlefields, the enemy became the planter class, and the war against Spain became a siege within Cuba. The insurrection was now "an economic war," Colonel Fermín Valdés Domínguez recorded in his diary, "against capital and production."[14] As early as July 1895, General Máximo Gómez proclaimed a moratorium on all economic activity—commerce, manufacturing, agriculture, ranching, but most of all, sugar production: no planting, no harvesting, no grinding, no marketing. Any estate found in violation of the ban, Gómez vowed, would be destroyed and its owner tried for treason. "All sugar plantations will be destroyed, the standing cane set fire and the factory buildings and railroads destroyed," the decree warned. "Any worker assisting in the operation of the sugar factories will be considered an enemy of his country . . . and will be executed."[15] Five months later, as the Cuban army advanced westward, Gómez ordered his chiefs of operation to enforce the July decree. "The war did not begin on February 24," he proclaimed portentously on the occasion of the invasion, "the war is about to begin now."[16] In another decree in July 1896 the army command ordered insurgent chieftains to "burn and destroy all forms of property as rapidly as possible everywhere in Cuba."[17] In July 1896, the revolutionary provisional government enacted military field orders into statute:

> Property is the true enemy of the Revolution, for on it rests the power of the Spanish government, and on its defense rests all [Spain's] effort. . . . While Cuba is not independent, it is necessary to paralyze the social, political, and economic life of the country; our attacks should be directed principally against property that comforts and supports the Spanish—the essential means of securing that paralysis. Once this is obtained, Spain, its army notwithstanding, will de facto

no longer exercise its sovereignty over Cuban territory and will have no recourse but to end a futile war and abandon the island.[18]

At the end of July, the provisional government proclaimed a moratorium on the 1896–1897 *zafra* and ordered the destruction of all estates participating in the harvest.[19]

The most devastating weapon in the insurrectionary arsenal became *la tea*—the torch. Across the island, fire announced the Cuban purpose. Máximo Gómez made his point by analogy: "It is necessary to burn the hive in order to disperse the swarm."[20] The point was not lost on the Cuban insurgent command. "The invasion of the western end of the island," Antonio Maceo exulted in February 1896, "has produced the desired result: everything has changed and the Revolution is strong; the revolutionary fire has been lit even in the most remote corners of Vuelta Abajo."[21] And two months later, Maceo again wrote with satisfaction: "With great success . . . everything that could serve as a source of revenue and an object of support for our enemies has been ordered destroyed."[22]

The Cuban moratorium against sugar production threatened the planter class with ruin—which was exactly what it was supposed to do. To ignore the insurgent ban was to risk the destruction of property, and with Cuban army units operating fully across the breadth of the island, it was not a risk to be taken lightly. Some tried, unsuccessfully, and across Cuba fields and factories went up in smoke. Larger planters managed to defy the ban, but only after first organizing private squadrons of armed guards to protect their property.[23] Most producers, however, were obliged to observe the moratorium. "If any one had told us four months ago," wrote one planter in early 1896, "that [Gómez] would be able to stop the crushing of cane in the Province of Havana, or even in Matanzas, we would have laughed in his face. Today not a planter disobeys his orders."[24]

But the suspension of production by no means guaranteed either salvation or solvency. Indeed, the economic hardship caused by compliance with the ban was potentially no less calamitous, and often far more certain, than the military reprisal Cubans threatened for the defiance of the ban. Planters had traditionally borrowed against future crops at prevailing world prices, and years of accumulated indebtedness found the planter class operating with little margin for mishap. In those circumstances where planters tottered at the brink of bankruptcy from harvest to harvest, the loss of a single year's crop promised catastrophe.

VI The completion of the westward surge sent shock waves across the island and across the Atlantic. Cuban successes stunned Spanish authorities. Few could believe that the rebellion had spread westward with such speed. General José Lachambre, the Spanish military commander in the eastern provinces, later remembered:

> Though every precaution possible . . . was taken, . . . the Government was, in fact, taken by surprise and was quite unprepared to meet such a formidable revolution, and this condition was very seriously increased and intensified by the fact that almost the entire population, especially the rural population, including that of the small villages and towns, was with the insurrectionists; . . . this enabled them to conceal their movements and at the same time to keep themselves fully and constantly informed [about] the movement of the Government and measures to meet and repress them.[25]

Everything was different after 1895. No longer could the insurrection be dismissed as one more disorder in the long series of desultory provincial disturbances that had characterized separatist stirrings for thirty years. It was now national in scope and revolutionary in intent, and Spain could not be anything less than unequivocal in its response. The invasion challenged directly the basis of the colonial consensus, the unstated but understood sources of Spanish sovereignty in Cuba. Spain's support—indeed, its very claim on the allegiance of the planter class—had rested on its ability to protect property and privilege. This was the tacit understanding between officials in the metropolis and property owners in the colony, an understanding with origins early in the nineteenth century and upon which the loyalty of the Ever Faithful Island had since depended.

The expansion of the insurrection into the western provinces was no less a threat to the solvency of the colonial administration than to the social system over which it presided. What Cubans proposed to do, simply, was to make Spain irrelevant to the Cuban social reality, and to make the continued Spanish presence in Cuba itself the single largest liability to property. There would be no peace, no production, no protection of property as long as Spain exercised political power over Cuba.

Spanish authorities understood well the Cuban purpose. "The means of war by the Cubans," Spanish infantry Captain Ramón Sánchez Varona realized, "was to employ or use . . . all of the means of destruction, and which showed the inefficiency of Spanish Government in Cuba. . . . [This] policy did not arise due to a vandalic desire for destruction, but for the necessity of using those means which were the proper means of the weak against the strong."[26] Spanish authorities understood, too, the gravity of the crisis and recognized the urgency to end it quickly. The Cubans did not have to defeat the Spanish, they had only to avoid losing. Time was on the side of the Cubans, and if Spain failed to lift the insurgent siege in the west soon, all would be lost everywhere in Cuba.

Spain first reorganized the army command in Cuba and soon thereafter enlarged its army in Cuba to 200,000 officers and men. Appointed to oversee the new Spanish war effort was General Valeriano Weyler, a tough campaigner and a veteran of the Ten Years War. Weyler arrived in Cuba in early 1896, bringing with him some 50,000 new troops. He also brought an understanding of the task at hand. Any campaign that did not first deprive the insurgents of their support in the countryside, he understood, was doomed to failure. So long as the rural population remained at liberty to move between the cities and the countryside, free to transport medicine and supplies, and at large to relay intelligence and information across government lines, so long as peasants remained free to cultivate their crops and tend to their livestock, Spain would be facing insuperable odds.

After 1895 the focus of the Spanish war effort also shifted, and once again the peasantry became the object of government repression. That autumn Weyler issued the first in a series of decrees ordering the rural population to evacuate the countryside and move to designated fortified towns. Spanish field commanders were ordered to enforce the reconcentration decree and escort the rural population to the cities. Major Florentino Yriondo de la Vara, a member of Weyler's staff, later recalled the purpose of Spanish policy:

> to carry into effect the reconcentration under the conviction that it was impossible to terminate the war as long as the country people lived in the homes, because these country people gave news and provisions to the Cuban forces, and, besides, their continual visits to the town enabled them to take out all kinds of provisions and medicines and also information and at the same time the livestock which they had, the pigs as well as the cattle were given by them to the insurrection.[27]

In 1896 military operations were now directed against the rural population, its resources, its possessions. Subsistence agriculture and trade between the cities and the countryside were banned. Livestock owners were ordered to drive their herds into the cities.[28]

But the worst was to come. Not only was war directed against the peasant, it was declared against the land and its resources, the tools of its cultivation, and the bounty of its yield—against everything, in short, capable of sustaining life in regions beyond Spanish control. Weyler campaigned with determination, and ruthlessly. Laureano Llorente, a member of the Sancti Spíritus city council, later recalled his meeting with the general:

> Weyler told us that he had come resolved to put an end to the war, and that if it was necessary for that object to destroy everything that Máximo Gómez had not destroyed, he would do so. His exact words were the

following: "I shall leave the Island as bare as the palm of my hand."[29]

The Spanish, like the Cubans, found fire an efficient and cost-effective method of waging war. Spanish military forces scoured the countryside in search of all signs of human activity. Villages and planted fields were burned; food reserves were set ablaze, homes were razed, and livestock was seized. Animals that could not be driven to Spanish-held zones were slaughtered. In this way, thousands of head of cattle, horses, pigs, and mules were destroyed. To this was added the systematic plunder of anything of value and the destruction of the meager possessions owned by peasants. Peasants were herded into the reconcentration camps, and what they could not take with them was destroyed with their villages. After 1896 the human presence in the countryside was proscribed, and any human being found there was presumed to be a subversive. By the end of 1896, a stillness had settled over vast expanses of the Cuban countryside. The farms were untended, the fields unworked, the villages uninhabited. Entire communities disappeared. Vast stretches of rural Cuba were reduced purposefully to a wasteland. Wrote one traveler to Cuba a year after the reconcentration decree:

> I travelled by rail from Havana to Matanzas. The country outside the military posts was practically depopulated. Every house had been burned, banana trees cut down, cane fields swept with fire, and everything in the shape of food destroyed. It was as fair a landscape as mortal eye ever looked upon; but I did not see a house, man, woman or child, a horse, mule, or cow, nor even a dog. I did not see a sign of life, except an occasional vulture or buzzard sailing through the air. The country was wrapped in the stillness of death and the silence of desolation.[30]

For countless numbers of Cubans, life in the interior turned into an incomprehensible nightmare. An estimated 300,000 Cubans, young and old, all noncombatants, were crowded into hastily assembled and poorly constructed resettlement camps.[31] The camps filled the cities with sounds of women wailing, children shrieking, and men praying for deliverance, or swearing vengeance on their tormentors. An ill-conceived policy became inevitably an ill-implemented program. Municipal authorities were not prepared to assume the responsibility of caring for the *reconcentrados*. The Spanish government refused to assume responsibility. With only scant attention to living quarters, less to diet, and none to health, the overcrowded reconcentration centers became breeding grounds for disease and death.[32] Recalled an officer on Weyler's staff:

> I remember that the Mayor of Güines presented himself before General Weyler telling him that he had more than 6,000 women and children dying of hunger in his town, and . . . he begged him for resources with which to support them. Weyler answered him that he had effected the reconcentration precisely with the object that all might die, and the Mayor went back to Güines and there in the streets of Güines I saw women and children die of hunger.[33]

The reconcentration policy, the method Spain chose to defeat the Cubans, was not an entirely random affair. Spanish authorities waged war on the families of combatants. The grandparents and parents, the wives and children of Cuban soldiers were arrested and interned, and it was known by all at the moment of their internment: they were doomed.[34]

VII The belligerents divided the island between them. The Cubans controlled the countryside, and the Spanish occupied the cities. Peasants had the choice of fighting or not, but after 1895 not of choosing sides. Weyler's reconcentration program forced the issue. Countless thousands of *pacíficos* sought sanctuary behind insurgent lines, certain that their prospects of surviving were better as combatants in the countryside than as noncombatants in the cities. Cuban field commanders reported a new development in the war: a sudden and significant increase in recruits. "The sending here of ferocious Weyler,"

General José María Rodríguez wrote from Oriente, "has been a counterproductive measure for Spain: great numbers of Cubans who had remained pacific, in the countryside as well as in the towns, are found today swelling our ranks."[35] Antonio Maceo reported similar developments in the west: "The Revolution does not have a better ally than Weyler himself."[36] In central Cuba, Colonel Fermín Valdés Domínguez recorded his thoughts in his campaign diary: "The time for the definitive division has arrived. Those who are with the Spanish will go to the cities and our supporters will be with us in the countryside. Weyler works for us. The *good* result of his method of directing military operations will soon be seen."[37] The U.S. consul in Havana arrived at a similar conclusion. Weyler's policies, Fitzhugh Lee wrote, "has had the effect of filling [insurgent] ranks and binding them together in stronger union, as well as increasing the spirit of their resistance."[38]

The war took a curious turn after 1895. Spanish troops concentrated in the cities and fortified positions, and they were almost impregnable; Cuban troops overran the countryside, and they were virtually unconquerable. A good part of war passed in this way: the Spanish in the forts, the Cubans in the fields, each beyond the other's reach. So they both found surrogates to attack, those social groups allied by persuasion or proximity, or both, to an enemy that neither could get at, those social groups who were, above all, vulnerable and whose elimination promised an adequate alternative to the unobtainable military victory. The Spanish assaulted the peasants, the Cubans assailed the planters. They both attacked property, but the two sides were not fighting quite the same war. The Cubans waged an economic war for political objectives, the Spanish conducted a social war for military ends. Meanwhile, the destruction of the island continued unabated. The Cubans were determined to destroy the island in order to win, the Spanish were determined to destroy the island in order not to lose. By the third year of the war, the depopulation of the countryside was all but complete. So was the despoliation of the country.

3 Aftermath of War

The soldiers belonging to the rank and file of the Cuban army own or control no property on the island, and . . . they are discussing among themselves the question 'What have we gained by this war?'
> —Bureau of Detectives, "Confidential Report," 1899

They are absolutely destitute and have no property of any kind except a rifle or machete or both, and no means of substituting while waiting for a crop to mature. Nor have they any means for procuring the work cattle and farming implements needed in cultivating tobacco.
> —General George W. Davis, January 1899

We have no cash. We can not secure credit. We do not receive assistance, and can not obtain needed seeds, implements, and work animals. How will we survive?
> —Farmer, Santa Clara Province, 1901

The increase in the number of small farms is so small that one is inclined to think that the instinct and taste for farming has never existed in the Cuban, or if it has that it has been lost. If left to Cuban intelligence and industry, the Province of Santiago will never be thoroughly developed; it will have to be done by foreigners.
> —Matthew Hanna, U.S. Military Attaché, 1903

I The war ended in 1898, and no part of Cuba had escaped its ravages. It had been a brutal war, a war of excesses, at every turn disruptive and destructive, a war in which the opposing armies seemed determined more to punish the land than pursue the enemy. For almost four years, contending forces had laid siege to the largesse of the land, preying upon the bounty of its resources, and practicing pillage of every kind as the normal method of warfare.

And when it was over, in 1898, the price of independence was incalculable. The war may have brought deliverance, but it also brought ruin. Travelers to the island that first autumn of peace were uniformly appalled by the extent of destruction. "I saw neither a house, nor a cow, calf, sheep or goat, and only two chickens," one journalist reported from Camagüey.[1] "The country is wilderness," a "desert," another correspondent wrote from Las Villas.[2] General James H. Wilson wrote of Matanzas and Las Villas provinces:

> The desolation is scarcely conceivable. It has been shown that substantially every small farmhouse in the two provinces, as well as a large number of the sugar mills, were burned; that the growing crops were destroyed, the agricultural implements broken up, the poultry nearly all killed, and the farming population driven into the fortified towns and villages to starve. From the foregoing it will be perceived that nearly all the instruments of production in the hands of the poorer people have been swept away, and that production, outside of that carried on by the larger and richer sugar "ingenios," had entirely ceased. The people were rapidly dying of starvation and disease.[3]

General Fitzhugh Lee described conditions in Pinar del Río in similar terms:

> Business of all sorts was suspended. Agricultural operations had ceased; large sugar estates with their enormous and expensive machinery were destroyed; houses burned; stock driven off for consumption by the Spanish troops or killed. There was scarcely an ox to pull a plow, had there been a plow left. Not a pig had been left in the pen, or a hen to lay an egg for the poor destitute people who still held on to life, most of them sick, weary, and weak. Miles and miles of country uninhabited by either the human race or domestic animals were visible to the eye on every side. The great fertile island of Cuba in some place resembled an ash pile, in others the dreary desert.[4]

The people had dispersed, and hundreds of thousands had perished, and only a fortunate few could comprehend that they had survived a population disaster of frightful proportions. A population of nearly 1.8 million had declined to less than a million and a half, a net loss of almost 17 percent.[5] In 1899, Cuba had the highest proportion of widowed to married persons in the Western Hemisphere: 34.6 per hundred. There was one widow or widower for every three married persons. The proportion of widowed women was higher: 51.2 per hundred, or one widow for every two wives.[6]

It was not only that hundreds of thousands died; tens of thousands were never born. Births between 1890 and 1893 had increased steadily, averaging 32,000 births per year. The annual number of births through the war years 1895–1898 declined, falling to just over 17,000. If the prewar birth rate had not been interrupted, an estimated 60,000 more children would have been born during the quadrennium 1895–1898.[7] The combined effects of the high child mortality rate and low fertility produced an appalling reduction in the population structure of postwar Cuba: children under five made up only 8.3 percent of the total population. No country in the world for which data was available in 1899 had so small a proportion of children under five. The total loss of children dead and unborn was estimated conservatively at 100,000.[8]

The toll of the war was everywhere visible. Houses everywhere in the interior were roofless and in ruins. Roads, bridges, and railroads had fallen into disrepair. Mines had closed. Commerce was at a standstill and manufacturing suspended. Where towns and villages once stood, there remained only scattered piles of rubblestone and charred wood. What were previously lush farming zones were now scenes of scorched earth and singed brush. Livestock had been scattered, or slain. Of nearly 3 million head of cattle grazing on Cuban pastures in 1895, less than 200,000 remained in 1898.[9] In some districts the loss of breeding stock and work cattle was almost complete. Horned cattle in Matanzas declined from approximately 300,000 to 9,000 and in Las Villas from 967,000 to 66,000. The 50,000 yoke of cattle in Matanzas and the 150,000 in Las Villas were reduced to 5,500 and 15,000, respectively.[10]

Agriculture was in desperate crisis in an economy predominantly agricultural. Of the total 1.4 million acres under cultivation in 1895, only 900,000 acres returned to production after the war. The rich sugar provinces of Havana and Matanzas were each cultivating fully less than one-half the area in 1899 than in the year before the war.[11] Over 100,000 small farms, 3,000 livestock ranches, 800 tobacco *vegas*, and 700 coffee *fincas* had perished during the conflict.

Sugar mills were in an advance state of disrepair. In fact, most had disappeared. Of the 70 sugar mills in Pinar del Río, only 7 survived the war. Of the 166 *centrales* operating in Havana province in 1894, only 20 participated in the 1899 harvest. Of the 434 sugar mills located in Matanzas, only 62 survived. The 332 *centrales* in Las Villas were reduced to 73. In sum, of the 1,100 sugar mills registered in Cuba in 1894, only 207 survived the war, and not all these mills contributed either to the 1899–1900 harvest or the 1900–1901 crop.[12]

Tobacco *vegas*, coffee *fincas*, and sugar estates not destroyed or abandoned were paralyzed by the dispersal of labor. Because of the depopulation of the countryside, producers lost ready access to workers and the country folk lost crops, livestock, tools, and homes. When the war ended, no one was quite certain how, or where, to begin again. The total value of rural property *(fincas rústicas)* was set at some $185 million on which rested a mortgage indebtedness of $107 million.[13]

II The transition to peace was difficult. The U.S. military intervention in 1898 hastened the end of the war, ending too the conditions of siege that had so thoroughly disrupted life in Cuba. For tens of thousands of *reconcentrados*, relief was immediate. The distribution of supplies of food, clothing, and medicine eased some of the most desperate conditions in the cities. Sanitary conditions improved, and the cycle of disease and epidemic was broken. The ill and the indigent received care in hospitals and the parentless and homeless found refuge in public shelters. "The streets were cleaned," the U.S. military commander of Havana reported in September 1899, "refuse removed, sanitary and hygienic laws and regulations enforced, the hospitals and charitable institutions equipped and put in operation, the ailing and homeless provided for."[14]

But the impact of peace was not everywhere similar nor salutary. Behind the far-flung battle lines of Cuba Libre, a disaster of calamitous proportions was in the making. The formal armistice protocol of August 1898 divided control of the cities between Spain and the United States, isolating the 50,000 officers and men of the Cuban army in a countryside devastated by nearly four years of war. Throughout the conflict, Cubans had depended principally upon supplies exacted locally and under duress, forced to do so by the exigencies of war. They appropriated what they needed, whenever required, wherever found. They attacked the estates, plundered the ranches, and ambushed the railroads, all in the name of free Cuba.

Peace changed everything, and its effect in the armed camps of Cuba Libre was immediate and devastating. The sanction to forage lapsed, depriving the Cuban army of its principal means of subsistence. Idle veterans passed the autumn months in ill health, in constant want, without food, medicine, and clothing.[15] Soldiers who had survived the war succumbed to peace. "Our soldiers are dying at the gates of the city for lack of food," one Cuban officer wrote from an army camp outside Havana.[16] In Havana province, one correspondent reported a dozen Cuban soldiers dying daily.[17] "Before the war ended," another army commander wrote, "we lived better, as the enemy's provisions were at our mercy. The orders are now to discontinue foraging. . . . Last week the death in town was twenty to thirty daily."[18] "Hunger causes in our ranks more casualties than enemy bullets caused," another officer despaired. "If we do not receive more food within a month, more than a third of the Cuban Army and rural population will cease to exist. In another month, it will be too late to avoid the death of thousands by starvation. I am horrified by the scenes I am witnessing."[19]

III But the Cuban army was unwilling to disband, even if it possessed the means—which it did not. And it was this unwillingness to disband, together with the destitution among the Cubans, that caused concern with U.S. policy circles. Indeed, nothing so preoccupied North American authorities as the continuing presence of armed Cubans.

The Cuban army also represented a potential source of social disorder. The continued presence of 50,000 Cuban officers and soldiers, under arms, with lines stretched out across the interior countryside, in various states of destitution, had chilling implications.

The problem was twofold. On one hand, it was necessary to move with dispatch to disarm and disband the Cuban army, and thereby eliminate the only force capable of resisting U.S. rule. On this point all North American authorities agreed.[20] What was not clear was how to accomplish this. To disband the Cuban army without giving Cuban soldiers some means of support promised simply to transform a political problem into a social one, with similar consequences.

The U.S. military government attempted to deal with both problems at the same time. Efforts centered first on disarming and disbanding Cuban troops, a task facilitated by skillful exploitation of the Cubans' distress. North Americans transacted a straightforward exchange: they bartered rations for retirement. The orders were simple and clear from the U.S. army headquarters in Havana: "The issue of rations to Cuban soldiers still held together as an organization cannot be authorized; on the contrary, you should use all your influence to bring about the disbandment of such organization in your Department."[21]

While the distribution of rations did not everywhere lead to the disbandment of the Cuban army, it did lead in many places to disarming it. The final dissolution of Cuban army units responded to other incentives. In early 1899, the United States allocated a total of $3 million in the form of an outright cash allotment of $75 to each soldier. Used as mustering-out pay, the stipend served to complete the full demobilization of the Cuban army, and with it the elimination of rival armed claims to sovereignty.[22]

IV The disbanding of the Cuban army created immediately the problem of providing livelihood for the former soldiers. Specifically, by what means would nearly 50,000 former Cuban soldiers reenter a war-shattered, depressed economy? Everywhere in Cuba North American military commanders proceeded with demobilization both with relief and a presentiment of disaster. Concern over these developments began at the highest North American policy levels. It was not so much that demobilization would deepen distress and destitution, but rather bring discontent and disorder. In Washington, John Addison Porter, secretary to President William McKinley, warned the War Department:

> Even though without arms it would be extremely dangerous to cast thousands of men on the mercy of the community absolutely penniless and without resources. They would have to continue to live on the country in large numbers, and some might be driven by the extremity of their wants to take food and clothing by stealth and force. With such men wandering aimlessly about, the planters would not dare buy the cattle necessary to begin the operation of their plantations, and even those disposed to work would thus not find the opportunity of doing so. Unless this element of danger is entirely removed, a large American military force will be necessary to guarantee peace, involving a great expenditure of money.[23]

It was clear that $75 would not go very far. It was clear, too, that economic conditions would not improve quickly enough to absorb large numbers of Cubans into productive activities. The prospects for disorder loomed large. "Unless

employed in some manner," warned Major John Logan from
Santa Clara early in 1899,

> many of the Cuban troops themselves will soon be
> turned loose to find existence as best they can. That
> there is not sufficient employment this year in the
> agricultural districts or in the cities for even fifty per-
> cent of them, is evident. How they are to exist is a
> problem we have to solve. If allowed to wander aim-
> lessly about many of them will soon take to lawless-
> ness and brigandage.[24]

A similar warning came from the United States commander
in Pinar del Rio. The disbandment of the Cuban army,
General George W. Davis predicted, would turn "loose upon
the community some thousands of armed men who would
in many cases resort to highway robbery and pillage as a
means of support."[25]

If political considerations required the elimination of the
Cuban army, social conditions demanded the employment
of Cuban soldiers. Warned Major Logan:

> It seems to me that it is preferable to give these men an
> opportunity to earn an honest and respectable living
> for themselves and families, than to force them to
> become out-laws; and, from an economical stand-
> point, it is much cheaper to employ and feed them at
> present that they are amenable to law and discipline,
> than it would be to undertake to apprehend them after
> having thrown off all restraint and taken to the bush.[26]

Across the island, and with great purposefulness, the military government allocated funds from public revenues and
allotted positions in public administration for the employment of Cuban soldiers. Thousands of veterans joined the
public rolls as day laborers in public works programs: they
paved city streets and painted public property. They re-
paired country roads, renovated public buildings, and restored the piers and wharves; they cleaned the streets, collected the garbage, and constructed sewers. Thousands of
others, principally former officers, occupied administrative
positions at all levels of national, provincial, and municipal

government, as office clerks, accountants and auditors, post masters and letter carriers, messengers, teachers and policemen.

Public works programs expanded across the island on a mass scale, designed in part to aid in the reconstruction of Cuba, and in part to eliminate the Cuban army and employ the Cuban soldiers. "This system," wrote General Leonard Wood from Santiago in January 1899, "tends to disintegrate the armed Cuban forces wandering about the mountains and put them at work at good honest labor. It not only gives them money but the labor is of such character that it also serves as an education process in the methods of civilization."[27] Wrote Wood five months later:

> The province was orderly and the Cuban Army of between 10,000 and 11,000 men, absolutely disappeared. No bodies of Cuban troops existed under arms in the province. . . . The disbandment of the Cuban forces can be assigned to only one cause—we had been able to give out enough work at fair pay to break up every organization and scatter many of them among the different working gangs.[28]

V The expenditure of public funds in the form of public employment eased the transition to peace for many. It created jobs for countless thousands. This was the minimum condition of order, nothing less than the social overhead of peace in occupied Cuba. That it served also to consolidate U.S. rule was no insignificant consideration. Anything less promised to engender resentment, restlessness, and, inevitably, rebellion. Economic security was the requisite of social peace and both were essential for political order. Efforts by "agitators" and "demagogues" to arouse the local population, Colonel L. H. Carpenter wrote from Puerto Príncipe, "can not induce the people who have work and whose families are provided for to embark in army uprising or adventure that would jeopardize their present condition. If they were out of work and in consequence much discontented, perhaps more could be done with them."[29] Leonard Wood struck a similar note from Santiago.

"The men engaged in this work," he commented, "are in a destitute condition and if they are thrown out of employment are bound to become a disorderly element, in the community: not disorderly from viciousness but from hunger and the necessity existing in their families."[30] Across Cuba, public works and public administration created enclaves of security in an environment of uncertainty. For many the public payroll was the vital margin between subsistence and indigence. Thousands of Cubans found the passage to peace a journey less arduous because of the employment opportunities created by public works programs.

But not all veterans found relief and recovery on the public rolls. In fact, it is not certain that even a majority did. Most of the soldiers were countrymen—farmers, peasants, ranchers, and rural workers. They were anxious to return to the interior, and begin anew the task of reviving the land and rebuilding their lives. Esteban Montejo later recalled that attempts to provide Cuban soldiers with "various government jobs" after the war did not meet the needs of many of his compatriots. "When the army disbanded," Montejo recounted, "the Negro revolutionaries found they couldn't stay in the city and went back to the countryside, to work in the cane-fields and tobacco plantations, anything rather than work in offices."[31]

Public works, to be sure, provided employment, but it was an employment from which most army veterans were excluded. Positions in public administration and jobs on public works projects were located largely in the cities, and did not address the problems facing soldiers returning to the land. Nor was the military government disposed to extend to the rural communities the kind of assistance provided to urban residents. Aid to farmers was limited to a one-time supply of rations, "so that," Leonard Wood explained, "they may be able to go to their farms . . . and have a limited amount of food at hand from which they can be supplied while their crops are maturing." But Wood was explicit: "After the first crop, I think all, or nearly all this assistance, should be brought to an end." Long-term assistance, Wood feared, either in the form of direct financial aid or low-interest public loans, would serve only to encourage indolence and shiftlessness, "and these people have been downtrodden so long that the ambition to work and get ahead has been, generally speaking, pretty thoroughly killed."[32]

VI   This proved one of the more anomalous features of U.S. policy during the military occupation: a refusal to extend assistance to agriculture in an economy predominantly agricultural, floundering in varying degrees of ruin, and upon which the majority of the population depended. These conditions affected all Cubans who derived livelihood from the land, which is say most Cubans —the large planters and the small farmers, sharecroppers and renters, rural workers and squatters.

The U.S. intervention had provided agriculture both immediate relief and timely reprieve. It saved farmers from the continued destruction of war and temporarily staved off economic collapse after peace. As early as January 1, 1899, upon the formal inauguration of United States rule, Governor General John R. Brooke pledged the full resources of the military government to "build up waste plantations."[33] The pledge initially seemed destined for fulfillment. In April 1899 the military government enacted Military Order No. 46, a provision proclaiming a two-year moratorium on the collection of all debt obligations, "whether or not secured by mortgage on real property."[34]

In the weeks and months that followed, the military government promulgated a variety of decrees designed to provide farmers with immediate relief and assist with long-term recovery. Export duties were abolished. Tariff rates on agricultural equipment and supplies were reduced to five percent ad valorem. Internal trade taxes were eliminated. Municipal taxes on all properties "destroyed by war, and in general, those which are not at present actually productive," were suspended.[35]

These were expedient measures, even essential. The moratorium on foreclosures and the suspension of taxes gave farmers a much needed respite. So, too, did the reduction of import-export duties. These measures were designed, however, primarily to forestall imminent ruin. More important, these measures tended to favor the larger producers, principally the sugar planters who faced insolvency at the end of the war. All the farmers, large and small, faced dreary prospects for reconstruction without credit and even more dreadful prospects for recovery without capital. The reduction of tariff rates on agricultural equipment was of little consolation to planters and farmers who could not, in any case, afford to purchase new machines or secure needed supplies. What they needed more, quickly and on a vast scale, was financial assistance, immediately to renew production, and ultimately to settle years of accumulated indebtedness. From the outset of the United States occupation, farmers turned to the military government for assistance to revive agriculture. But direct aid either in the form of credit support or by way of cash subsidies was not part of the United States design for the postwar reconstruction of Cuba. "Many requests have been made by the planters and farmers to be assisted in the way of supplying cattle, farming implements, and money," Governor General John R. Brooke reported in October 1899. He explained why the requests were rejected:

> The matter has been most carefully considered and the conclusion reached that aid could not be given in this direction. The limit has been reached in other means of assistance to the verge of encouraging or inducing pauperism, and to destroy the self-respect of the people by this system of paternalism is thought to be a most dangerous implanting of a spirit alien to a free people, and which would, in carrying it out, tend to create trouble by arousing a feeling of jealousy in those who would not receive such aid. . . . The real solution to this question of furnishing means to those who need this kind of aid is through the medium of banks, agricultural or others; through them and through them alone, it is believed, the means now sought from the public treasury should be obtained. . . . This system would not destroy or impair the self-respect of the

borrower; he would not be the recipient of charity, but a self-respecting citizen working out his own financial salvation by means of his own labor and brain.[36]

Sufficient capital was available—much of it "lying idle"— Brooke insisted, if "capitalists [were] assured as to the future." Recovery was imminent, Brooke proclaimed confidently in October 1899: "In fact, the era of prosperity appears to be at hand, all that is needed is to have capital satisfied as to future conditions, and this being reasonably assured, there can be no doubt but that the fertility of the soil and the industry of the people will work out a happy solution of the problem."[37]

But Brooke's optimism was misplaced. Good times never arrived—not, at least, for large numbers of planters and farmers. Capital remained scarce throughout the early years of the occupation. Even as Brooke predicted the imminence of prosperity, one Treasury Department official in Cuba concluded that "it would be extremely hazardous to loan money in Cuba on any kind of collateral or property."[38]

Several attempts to establish local credit institutions met U.S. opposition. In one case, José Antonio Toscano and Celestino de la Torriente proposed establishing a Banco de Crédito y Territorio Hipotecario to facilitate loans to needy farmers. Another instance involved a proposal by the civil government of Santa Clara to organize a farmers' loan association *(banco pecuario)* to promote local agricultural revival. On both occasions, the military government rejected the petitions, citing the Foraker Amendment prohibition against awarding of franchises and concessions for the duration of the occupation.[39]

Even within the military government, divergent opinions were heard. General James H. Wilson, commanding Matanzas and Las Villas provinces, urged monthly disbursements of $20,000 for each province to serve as a source of loans for small farmers, with no single loan to exceed $400. General Fitzhugh Lee in Pinar del Río similarly proposed the establishment of public agricultural banks to help needy farmers return to production.[40] Both proposals failed to win approval in either Havana or Washington.

The United States' appropriation of state revenues, while refusing to sanction public aid on the one hand, and the control of the licensing of banking enterprises, while declining to ratify new franchises on the other, made a difficult situation impossible. "There has been considerable thoughtless talk in Cuba about making loans to aid agriculturists," Wood proclaimed as the final word. "It is not believed that any such policy is either wise or desirable."[41]

The first toll of the final reckoning was sounded in the spring of 1901, as the expiration date of Military Order No. 46 neared. Very early the military government let it be known that it intended to permit the original debt moratorium decree to lapse. Cubans across the island protested. Provincial and municipal government authorities denounced U.S. policy.[42] Leopoldo Cancio, Cuba's civilian Secretary of Finance in the military government, vigorously protested the lapse of the debt suspension decree. No class, Cancio complained, had been "chastised more by our internal discords" than the farmers. He continued:

It would be a flagrant injustice that the creditor . . . may demand the whole of his credit, as if nothing had occurred, aggregating principal and interest to dispossess the debtor, who, having been expelled from his residence, has seen his properties wasted, his crops destroyed, his cattle confiscated, and his family decimated by famine and disease. . . . The land should remain in the hands of cultivators or of the true agricultural proprietors, instead of going into the hands of speculators or of people but little versed in the management of farms. Our society having been dominated until now by the mercantile classes, that principle was forgotten and after the first war the Mortgage Law, which with some reforms is still in force, was enacted; the expropriations were made on a large scale, and in consequence thereof, a multitude of valuable estates were destroyed among judicial contentions, for creditors in great numbers of cases were content to realize what they could in cash, selling machinery, woods, buildings, and whatever else was of easy alienation until the land was left bare.[43]

This was a position with which the Cuban civil Secretary of Agriculture, Commerce, and Industry agreed. Perfecto Lacosta warned in June 1900, "The precarious situation [of] the great majority of the hacendados and agriculturists of Cuba requires . . . all the possible aid of the State to encourage the reconstruction of the state."[44] Lacosta returned to this theme almost a year later. Lacosta complained only weeks before the expiration of Military Order No. 46, "Up to the present time nothing has been done toward the improvement of our agricultural situation." In one of the strongest criticism of U.S. policy by a Cuban official during the occupation, Lacosta protested the lack of "pecuniary resources . . . for the work of reconstruction and the almost impossibility of obtaining same, in view of the heavy debt with which rural property is burdened, due to the lack of agricultural banks or other institutions of credit which could render immediate assistance on acceptable terms." Lacosta called upon the military government "to remove the obstacles" to the establishment of credit sources and to "use every means at its command to foment and favor [agriculture's] most rapid development."[45]

VII Farmers and peasants everywhere faced extinction. "The lands of this municipality," the mayor of Nueva Paz in Havana province wrote, "represent a taxable income of $236,000, but all are abandoned. Even those which were not completely ruined are in an unproductive state."[46] "At the commencement of the year 1899," wrote Mayor Julio Domínguez of Cruces, Santa Clara, "no lands in this district were under cultivation, with the exception of a few very small farms surrounding the towns, devoted to the cultivation of vegetables and other products for the sustenance of their owners. Misery, hunger, sickness and general discontent prevailed among the people."[47] The *alcalde* of Jagüey Grande in Matanzas reported similar conditions: "All the estates that were the real wealth of this district were destroyed during the war, and where there had been wealth and plenty, nothing remains but poverty and desolation."[48] The census enumerator of Santa Clara, Juan Bautista Jiménez, reported that few small farmers of the province owned even a single yoke of oxen with which to work the fields, and the animals that were available were "leased by capitalists in the cities who charge for the rent fully one-third of the tobacco and corn harvested." Without capital sufficient to purchase oxen, seed, and implements, Bautista Jiménez predicted, without access to reasonable credit, "the old regime in which the proprietor was nothing more than the unpaid administrator of his *finca* will be perpetuated."[49]

The lapse of the April 1899 moratorium provided the occasion to enact a new decree, establishing a fixed term of four years in which to settle all indebtedness. Military Order No. 139 stipulated in May 1901, "From the 1st of June next all classes of creditors remain at liberty to take action and enforce the collection of mortgage credits, on all kinds of property."[50]

Military Order No. 139 promised to visit calamity on all farmers, large and small alike. The war had reduced the number of farms to 60,107 *fincas*, representing a total area of some 900,000 acres, of which some 52 percent was worked by renters. The war had been especially hard on small farmers. So was peace. Between 1898 and 1900, *fincas* were changing hands at the rate of some 3,700 a year.[51] Small farmers had neither the capital to revive agriculture nor the credit to return to work, or the collateral to obtain either. A survey in 1900 revealed that of some 40,000 farms assessed, some 16,000 were encumbered with mortgages totaling approximately $132 million. The vast majority of the mortgages did not exceed $1,500. But prospects in postwar Cuba for liquidating even these small debts were bleak.[52]

Across the island, the reports were the same: destroyed *fincas* and defunct farms out of production and abandoned for want of assistance. The mayor of San Cristobal in Pinar del Río complained that the municipality had "only 5 estates and 33 small farms out of 206 in antebellum days. The owners are exceedingly poor. Their need is oxen and agricultural implements."[53] Of the 395 *fincas* in Placetas, Santa Clara, 391 were destroyed during the war; of the 219 farms in Ceiba del Agua, Havana, 171 were abandoned; only 50 of the 466 farms in San Nicolás, Havana, were in production in 1899, while 111 of 175 *fincas* in Rodas, Santa Clara, were abandoned; all of the 169 *fincas* in Bauta, Havana, were destroyed.[54] "No assistance has been received in this district from the Government," protested the mayor of Consolación del Sur, in Pinar del Río, "not in work animals or in agricultural equipment. . . . There are 693 farms in this district, 630 of which were destroyed during the war."[55]

Agricultural production, the means of subsistence for a population largely rural, was in crisis. It was not only a matter of restoring the land to production, but reviving production to retain the land. After 1898 the prospects for either were not good. Peace and imminent independence had given rise to an atmosphere of general expectation. The ruinous war was over, and the hopes for social justice awaited redemption. This was the first disappointment, from which many others would flow.

4 A Promise Lost

Land as yet in the eastern half of the Island is cheap, and the results attending intelligent agriculture are exceedingly profitable. . . . A man with intelligence and energy and a moderate amount of money to start with, can quickly make for himself something like a section of paradise.

—William Van Horne, 1904

Foreigners . . . are coming to Cuba with the sole object of acquiring at low prices immense parcels of land, and . . . Cuban owners of those lands, either by lack of foresight or rash anxiety to obtain cash, let go of their patrimony. It is easy to notice the considerable number of foreigners, the majority of them North Americans, arriving at Havana and spreading through the territory of the Island with the purpose of taking possession of the land. A day does not pass without news of alienations in their favor counted by miles, or hundreds and even thousands of acres. . . . Should native control be lost, and by the incessant immigration of foreigners and the preponderance given them by a multitude of favorable circumstances our native tongue should also be lost, the most critical hour of our history would have arrived.

—Senator Manuel Sanguily, 1903

I The war had vastly accelerated the disintegration of rural communities in western Cuba, and when it was over the transformation of land tenure systems was all but complete. Farmers and peasants had been subjected to a new round of displacement and dislocation, and for many this time was the last time. Some abandoned the land to serve in the Army of Liberation. Many others were removed from the land and resettled in reconcentration camps. Vast numbers perished. For many survivors, there was no going back. Western Cuba was not the place to begin

anew, certainly not for Cubans who longed for land but
lacked resources. The reconstruction of agriculture proceeded apace after the war, but much of it around the restoration of the latifundia. In the new postwar order of the
west, many found their choices limited to working as hired
hands on the estates or as wage laborers in the cities.

There was a third choice: migration. For many Cubans,
certainly, migration was not an option; it was a matter of
necessity. The thoroughness with which the armies of both
sides plundered the land and punished its occupants during
the war completed the disintegration that began during the
1880s. For some the devastation was total—farms and family had disappeared, communities had dispersed, towns and
villages destroyed. Rural Cuba was in ruins; there were few
incentives for farmers to return to the land. For many it was
easier to move on than it was to go back. Many had no
choice.[1]

The collapse of traditional land tenure systems in the
west during the 1880s and 1890s had set in motion a wave of
migration. Well before the outbreak of war, many Cubans
had begun to move on to other places. Some traveled to the
cities. Some located marginal land sites in the west on
which to eke out an existence. The census supervisor of
Matanzas province in 1899 was surprised "by the discovery
of numerous residents in forests previously uninhabited or
in valleys previously uncultivated."[2] Many were free farmers and peasants; many were former slaves who exercised
their new freedom by moving. The direction in which most
migrated was eastward, where land was still accessible and
livelihood was available.[3]

The data available for internal migration during these
years is incomplete. The published census information does
not permit a distinction between the population movement
before the war from migration during the war. However, a
comparison of the census of 1887 with that of 1899 reveals a
striking pattern of population shifts on the island. The three
western provinces experienced a significant loss of population. Pinar del Río declined from 225,891 to 173,082, Havana
from 451,928 to 424,811, and Matanzas from 259,578 to
202,462—a total population loss of 137,732 people, or approx-

imately 15 percent of the 1887 population in the three western provinces. Much of this decline, certainly, was due to losses resulting from emigration and deaths during the war and in the reconcentration camps. But not all, perhaps not even most. During these years, and under similar conditions, the three eastern provinces registered a significant increase of population: Santa Clara from 354,122 to 356,537, Camagüey from 67,789 to 88,237, and Oriente from 272,379 to 327,715—that is, a net gain of approximately 11 percent. The most dramatic population shifts occurred in the two most dissimilar provinces: a loss of 57,116 people in Matanzas, a 22 percent decline, and a gain of 55,337 in Oriente, a 20 percent increase.[4]

This marked demographic shift concealed an equally remarkable racial dimension. Much of the migration between 1887 and 1899 was by people of color, the majority of whom were no doubt newly freed slaves. The total population of color in the western provinces declined by 16.6 percent. The number of colored males diminished by 25.7 percent. At the same time, the total population of color in Oriente increased by 22.4 percent, while the number of colored males grew by 23.6 percent.[5]

If the population decline in the west was due principally to war deaths, comparable losses should have been registered in the east. In fact, the loss should have been proportionally greater, for the eastern provinces sustained the greatest devastation for the longest duration. If the losses were indeed comparable, this would then make the population increase in the east even more remarkable. The census data do not reveal the total number of people who perished in eastern Cuba during the war, nor the total number of casualties of war between 1895 and 1898. Vast numbers of people, combatants and noncombatants alike, perished in the hinterland and on the battlefields—deaths never recorded in municipal civil registries. Between 1888 and 1899, moreover, Oriente experienced low fertility and high mortality. The province registered 37,663 births and 69,299 deaths. Both figures must be considered as minimums, for no information was provided for seven *municipios*.[6] A profile of fertility and mortality of the six provinces between

1888 and 1899 suggests that the decline of the population of the west and increase of the east was due in good measure to outmigration and inmigration. (See table 1.) According to the census calculations, Camagüey and Oriente registered the most rapid gains between 1887 and 1894, and thereafter remained comparatively stable for the following five years, an estimate that would correspond to migration eastward during the years of emancipation and deepening rural unrest in the west.[7]

Nor can the increase of population between 1887 and 1899 in the east be attributed to foreign immigration. In 1899, the eastern provinces had the highest percentage of native-born inhabitants, with Oriente (95 percent) and Camagüey (94 percent) the highest. At the other end of the scale, Havana (82 percent) and Matanzas (88 percent) were the lowest in Cuban nativity.[8]

II The war did more than complete the transformation of land tenure systems in the west. It created also the conditions to begin the process anew, this time in the east. Throughout the better part of the nineteenth century, Oriente had remained largely impervious to the currents transforming vast regions of western Cuba into the bastion of the sugar latifundia. Sugar estates in the east were by comparison modest family enterprises without ready access

Table 1   Fertility and Mortality in Cuba 1888–1899

	Total Population		Births	Deaths
	1887	1899	1888–1899	1888–1899
Pinar del Río	225,891	173,082	20,882	54,352
Havana	451,928	424,811	n.a.	n.a.
Matanzas	259,578	202,462	49,097	94,422
Santa Clara	354,122	356,537	93,009	150,709
Camagüey	67,789	88,237	21,563	21,186
Oriente	272,379	327,715	37,963	69,299

Source: U.S. War Dept., Office of Director of Census, *Informe sobre el censo de Cuba, 1899* (Washington, D.C.: GPO, 1900), pp. 738, 740–44.

to the west's capital reserves and technological resources, singularly incapable of participating in the post-Zanjón transformation of agriculture. The Ten Years War had all but destroyed the *oriental* planter class. Certainly the sugar estate occupied an important place in the local economy, but the estate in Oriente tended to be more traditional than commercial, more family than corporate. Life on the *oriental* estate was isolated, and self-contained, conferring on its owner more prestige than profit. The sugar estate was smaller and less efficient than its western counterpart. At the end of the nineteenth century, the size of the average sugar estate in Oriente was 13.2 acres, as compared with 58.4 acres in Matanzas.[9] Technological advances had made fewer inroads. Only a small number of Oriente mills were steam-powered, and even the steam-driven mills of the east produced less sugar than those of the west. Of the 198 sugar mills registered in the mid-nineteenth century, only 84 were driven by steam engines, and 61 of these were located in the jurisdiction of Santiago, near the principal port city.[10]

The province was undeveloped. Transportation and communication facilities were scarce and scattered. A total of 59.6 miles of railroad served a province of 16,000 square miles. The provincial road system was woefully inadequate, and what few roads existed were in varying degrees of disrepair. Many were so wretched that most cargo moved by pack train rather than by wagon, and most of these were impassable during the months of seasonal rains.[11] These conditions discouraged the expansion of large-scale commercial production in Oriente. Potentially rich agricultural regions remained isolated, without access to the principal ports of export. There was little incentive and less opportunity to expand sugar production. Many sugar producers had no interest in developing the resources of the land; many more had no means. Hence much of the productive means of the countryside remained free and available to the local population. As a result, an independent subsistence system flourished. These conditions permitted a greater diversity of agriculture, which guaranteed the persistence of a variety of land tenure forms. Sugar was only one of many products cultivated in the east; only nine *municipios* out of nineteen produced sugar on any significant scale. Sugar estates coexisted with coffee *fincas,* cacao fields, banana plantations, fruit orchards, coconut groves, vegetable farms, tobacco *vegas,* cattle ranches, and mines. The balance was distributed across the province: sugar, coffee, and cacao in San Luis, Guantánamo, Manzanillo and Santiago; fruits and vegetables in Holguín and Gibara: tobacco in Mayarí; cattle in Manzanillo, Jiguaní, Campechuela, Bayamo, Palma Soriano, and Holguín; bananas and coconuts in Baracoa; mining in El Caney.[12] The contrast in agricultural production between Oriente in the east and Matanzas in the west was striking (see table 2). An estimated 79.6 percent of the total area of cultivated land in Matanzas was devoted to sugar; only 35.1 percent of cultivated land in Oriente produced sugar. This difference between the two provinces affected everything else.

The effects of this diversity were striking. No other province had a lower population ratio per *finca* than Oriente: Oriente had 15.2 persons per farm, followed by Pinar del

Table 2   **Principal Crops Cultivated in Oriente and Matanzas, 1899**

	Oriente	Matanzas
Sugar	691,000	1,245,501
Bananas	311,172	225,917
Corn	241,565	38,818
Boniato	212,301	95,661
Yucca	129,128	24,989
Cacao	118,216	—
Coconuts	104,884	1,148
Coffee	93,797	2,796
Malanga	20,919	13,372
Yams	18,936	435
Tobacco	11,498	4,674
Rice	7,254	4,128

Source: U.S. War Dept., Office of Director of Census, *Informe sobre el censo de Cuba, 1899* (Washington, D.C.: GPO, 1900), pp. 561, 570–71.
Note: Figures are given in *cordeles;* 1 *cordel* = .10% acre.

Río with 16.6, Santa Clara 22.1, Camagüey 37.0, Matanzas 49.5, and Havana 68.9. The 1899 census data underscored the contrast between the west and east. Not including Camagüey province, where land was given extensively to cattle grazing, Matanzas had the fewest number of farms (4,083) with the largest average acreage (247 acres). Havana followed with 6,159 farms at 135 acres. Oriente, at the opposite end, contained the largest number of farms with the smallest average acreage. Only .5 percent of the farms in Oriente was over 330 acres, comprising only 26.9 percent of the total area of land under cultivation. The average size of the 21,550 farms in 1899 was approximately 80 acres. Table 3 again shows the marked contrast between Oriente and Matanzas. Oriente claimed not only the highest number of individual landowners, but also the highest number of renters, a total of 43,721.

But it was not only that more land was cultivated by more people; striking too was the social character of land tenure. Nowhere else in Cuba did tenure patterns reflect as accurately the racial composition of the island as in Oriente. Afro-Cuban managers, both as owners and renters, operated 41 percent of the farms. This was almost numerical parity with white occupants. A somewhat less striking but no less noteworthy aspect of tenure in Oriente was that 26 percent of the total land in use was under Afro-Cuban cultivation. Set against the total acreage under Afro-Cuban manage-

Table 3   Average Farm Size in Oriente and Matanzas, 1899

	Oriente	Matanzas
Total cultivated acreage	203,914	171,778
Total farms	21,550	4,083
Farms less than 33 acres	20,997	3,198
Farms 34–99 acres	422	521
Farms 100–165 acres	47	156
Farms 166–329 acres	39	112
Farms over 330 acres	45	96

Source: U.S. War Dept., Office of Director of Census, Informe sobre el censo de Cuba, 1899 (Washington, D.C.: GPO, 1900), pp. 554, 567–68.

ment elsewhere on the island, the percentage in Oriente was nothing short of remarkable. Pinar del Río occupied a distant second place, with Afro-Cubans working 11.4 percent of the land, followed by Santa Clara (6.7 percent), Camagüey (4.5 percent), Matanzas (3.8 percent), and Havana (3 percent). Oriente was also well above the national total of 10.8 percent. Put another way, almost 75 percent of the total land owned outright by blacks in Cuba and nearly 50 percent of land worked by Afro-Cuban renters were located in Oriente province.[13] Table 4 shows the distribution of the total number and ownership of farms in Oriente in 1899. The pattern repeated itself, as shown in table 5, in the size and number of the sugar estates and tobacco *vegas* in Oriente. Not including Camagüey, Oriente had the smallest average acreage, the greatest number of sugar estates, and the largest number of white and colored owners and renters farming the smallest tracts of land.

One last aspect of agriculture in Oriente displayed a significant racial characteristic. In the production of coffee and cacao, the principal crops of the small farmer, colored cultivators constituted a decisive majority.[14] See table 6. Similar patterns prevailed in other small-farm agriculture, where 47 percent of the total *malanga* acreage was cultivated by Cubans of color, as was 42 percent of rice and 42 percent of yams *(ñames)*.

Table 4 Tenancy of Land Under Cultivation in Oriente, 1899

	Total No. of Farms	% of Total	Acres Cultivated	% of Total
White owners	3,855	17.8	76,155	37.2
White renters	7,633	35.4	62,465	30.6
Colored owners	2,411	11.2	17,970	8.8
Colored renters	6,372	29.6	35,007	17.1
Other	1,279	5.9	12,317	6.3
Total	21,550	100.0	203,914	100.0

Source: U.S. War Dept., Office of Director of Census, *Informe sobre el censo de Cuba, 1899* (Washington, D.C.: GPO, 1900), pp. 556, 564, 566.

Oriente was a place of parity and proportion, of equity and equality. The ratio of the sexes balanced exactly: 163,845 males, 163,870 females—the only province in Cuba were women actually outnumbered men. Cubans of color constituted almost as large a portion of the population as native whites, and nowhere in Cuba was it higher: 44.7 percent to 51.2 percent. Almost half of all mar-

Table 5 Tenancy of Sugar Estates and Tobacco _Vegas_ in Oriente, 1899

	Sugar Estates		Tobacco Vegas	
	Total	Average Acreage	Total	Average Acreage
White owners	1,021	39.0	85	1.9
White renters	2,044	9.2	330	1.8
Colored owners	301	4.2	26	1.7
Colored renters	1,407	2.7	167	1.8
Other	445	12.1	60	1.0
Total	5,218	13.2	668	1.7

Source: U.S. War Dept., Office of Director of Census, _Informe sobre el censo de Cuba, 1899_ (Washington, D.C.: GPO, 1900), p. 572.

Table 6 Cultivators of Coffee and Cacao in Oriente, 1899

	Coffee		Cacao	
	Area (Cordeles)	% of Total	Area (Cordeles)	% of Total
White owners	23,704	25.3	30,865	26.1
White renters	14,101	15.2	14,488	12.3
Colored owners	32,970	35.1	40,199	34.0
Colored renters	11,006	23.4	29,866	25.2
Other	1,016	1.0	2,798	2.4
Total	93,797	100.0	118,216	100.0

Source: U.S. War Dept., Office of Director of Census, _Informe sobre el censo de Cuba, 1899_ (Washington, D.C.: GPO, 1900), p. 571, Fe Iglesias, "Algunos aspectos de la distribución de la tierra en 1899," _Santiago_ 40 (December 1980), 170–71.

riages were consensual unions, 39,562 out of 80,045. Nowhere in Cuba did more adults live together by mutual consent, fully 30 percent of the total island population living in consensual arrangements (39,562 out of 131,732). At the same time, nowhere in Cuba was the proportion of the married population so low. Thirty years of intermittent warfare had taken its toll, reducing the married population to only 12.3 percent. Oriente contained the youngest population, with the median age of eighteen and the highest proportion of children under the age of fifteen (43 percent).[15] Decades of war had other effects. The Oriente population had the highest level of illiteracy, 73.2 percent, and the lowest proportion of children between the ages of five and seventeen attending school, only 29.4 percent of the total.[16]

IV Nowhere else was more land available than in the east. Land was the principal source of attraction for the migration to the east. Only 22 percent of the total area of the province was in the possession of private farms, and only 11 percent of this total (203,914 acres) was under cultivation.[17] Large parts of Oriente remained undeveloped and unowned. Indeed, the full dimension of these vacant lands was itself unknown. It was known, however, that long after public lands had ceased to exist in Pinar del Río, Havana, and Matanzas, vast expanses of land in Oriente remained in the public domain. Fully more than twice the area under cultivation in 1899, approximately 500,000 acres, was public land, much of it forest and woodlands located in the remote and inaccessible interior regions of the province. Boundary lines were often ill-defined, and in many instances detailed surveys of state lands had never been completed. Thus, estimates of the total area of public land were only approximate, and not a few believed the actual size of the state patrimony to be far in excess of official calculation.[18] The *municipios* with the largest areas of public lands included Guantánamo (160,000 acres), Jiguaní (119,398), Manzanillo (99,000), Baracoa (65,000), El Cobre (27,000), Holguín (24,000), Sagua de Tánamo (19,000), and Mayarí (1,300).[19]

In 1899 Oriente was still a land of apparently limitless opportunity. Oriente developed quickly as the place for Cubans to start anew. This was the promise that lured thousands to the province from all regions of Cuba.

The postwar surge of population in Oriente was nothing short of spectacular. By the time of the 1907 census, the province neared the half-million mark, increasing by more than 127,000—almost 40 percent, from 327,715 in the 1899 census to 455,086 in 1907, and almost a 70 percent increase since the 1887 census. But the overall increase tended to conceal an even more dramatic surge of population at the local *municipio* level. See table 7.

V But Oriente in 1899 was in ruins. War the second time had been particularly ferocious, far surpassing the destruction wrought by the Ten Years War. Towns and villages throughout the interior had been razed, some reconstructed, and then razed again. Agriculture was in decline. Banana plantations, sugar fields, and coffee farms were ruined. The area under cultivation in 1899 was nearly one-third less than before the war, from 290,916 acres in 1895

Table 7 Population Increase in Oriente, 1899–1907

	1899	1907	% Increase
Mayarí	8,504	17,628	107.2
El Caney	9,126	16,215	77.6
Puerto Padre	19,984	34,061	70.4
Manzanillo	32,288	54,900	70.0
Palma Soriano	12,305	20,235	64.4
Alto Songo	12,770	20,553	60.9
Guantánamo	28,063	43,300	54.2
Holguín	34,505	50,224	45.5

Sources: U.S. War Dept., Office of Director of Census, *Informe sobre el censo de Cuba, 1899* (Washington, D.C.: GPO, 1900), pp. 198–200; Cuba Under the Provisional Government of the United States, *Censo de la República de Cuba, 1907* (Washington D.C.: GPO, 1908), pp. 306–08.

to 205,953 acres four years later.[20] The few miles of railroad that did exist had fallen into disuse. Roads and bridges were impassable.

Not all regions and not all residents suffered equally. Many families fled behind insurgent lines, there to find refuge and at least partial respite from the effects of war. Insurgent lines served as the outer defense perimeter behind which new rural settlements flourished. Within many liberated zones, the *pacífico* population dedicated itself to cultivating crops and raising livestock as a source of provisions for the Army of Liberation. It mattered not on whose land these communities took hold, and whether it was privately owned or publicly held. That would become an issue later. For the duration of the war, it mattered only that the land fell within the security of insurgent-held zones.[21]

Outside the enclaves of Cuban-held countryside and Spanish-occupied cities, the war raged in full fury, and nothing or no one standing between the contending armies was entirely safe from the operations of either or both. At the end of the war, vast regions of Oriente province bore stark testimony to the destruction released by almost four years of war. During an official tour of the province in late 1898, Major James H. McLeary, inspector-general of the eastern military department, reported bleak conditions across the province: "The people all along the route are evidently much in need of provisions, that is to say, that have a limited variety." McLeary continued:

> Many of the people appear to be almost destitute of clothing. . . . Taken as a whole, the people who came under my observation cannot be regarded as prosperous, commerce in the towns being entirely dead, and agriculture in the country being at a state of suspended animation. There does not appear ever to have been any such thing as manufacturers. . . . There are scarcely any work animals to be found along the route, a very few horses and still fewer mules and oxen, none of which can be obtained at any price. . . . Houses and fences are burned, fields abandoned and suffered to grow up in guinea grass, and the orchards which for-

mally covered it, are entirely gone. All the fruit trees in this section have been destroyed.[22]

Conditions did not much improve during the early years of the occupation. Farmers who had survived the war now faced collapse in peace. In the region of Holguín and Gibara, local property owners estimated that a credit grant of $100,000 distributed among 500 farmers would suffice to stimulate recovery in the district—that is, about $200 per farmer. In Januay 1900 local property owners appealed to Leoonard Wood for public assistance for agriculture in northern Oriente, explaining, "In the jurisdiction of Holguín and Gibara there are more than 500 small farmers that for reasons well known lack the necessary elements to work the soil, and that with very little help in the way of animals, and implements of agriculture, they could develop the riches of the community at large."[23] Almost a full year later local authorities continued to report conditions of distress and depression. "Agriculture in this municipality," wrote the Mayor of Gibara in November 1900, "is today in the same condition it was on January 1, 1900 owing to the fact that all farms are abandoned for lack of agricultural implements and of oxen and in the few small farms that any cultivation is done it is by hand, producing hardly enough to cover the primary necessities of the farmer."[24]

The conditions in the *municipios* of Holguín and Gibara were typical of conditions in Oriente. In Holguín, some 3,260 *fincas* accounted for an estimated 456,550 acres of land, of which only 14,849 acres were under cultivation in 1899. Similarly, in Gibara, 1,205 *fincas* covered 124,425 acres, of which only 32,355 were engaged in agricultural production in 1899.[25]

Everywhere in Oriente through the years of the military occupation, recovery came slowly, if at all. In July 1900 Mayor Francisco Mastrapa of Mayarí complained of persistent hardship: "The advance of agriculture is slow due to the undeniable poverty of the countrymen who are entirely without indispensable factors, such as oxen, horses and farming utensils whereby they would increase their crops."[26] From the Mayor of Jiguaní came a similar account of distress and despair: "16,000 *caballerías* of this district are devoted to cattle breeding, but these are abandoned because the proprietors of same excepting a very few, have not the necessary resources to reconstruct them. The agricultural progress is very slow, for the same cause of lack of funds to attend to cultivation."[27] And from the *municipio* of El Cobre:

> This municipality is progressing very slowly, and with great difficulty, because the people of this agricultural district . . . can hadly do anything due to the miserable condition in which the war left them. The bad conditions of the roads prevents the farmers from carrying their products to Santiago de Cuba where the market would buy them. The *ayuntamiento* has requested from the Military Governor some assistance to and the reconstruction of this district that produces the best coffee and cacao. . . . The small income of the *ayuntamiento* does not allow it to attend to the reconstruction of the district.[28]

The mayor of Baracoa reported similar conditions:

> This municipality is in a very poor condition due to the lack of money, agricultural implements of all kinds, and animals. There is not one yoke of oxen in this district and so far no agricultural progress has been obtained. The roads are also in very bad condition as they have not been repaired after the war; the communications are very difficult, above all during the rainy season, when the rivers overflow and there is not one bridge to cross them.[29]

Agriculture everywhere in Oriente was in decline. Almost one-third less land was under cultivation than in 1895, a decline from 290,916 acres to 205,953.[30] The average size of the Oriente farm was approximately 80 acres, but the average area cultivated in 1899 was a mere 10 acres, as shown in table 8.

Table 8 Agriculture in Oriente, 1899

	Population	Total Acreage	Acreage Cultivated 1899	Acreage Cultivated (1895)	Fincas Total No.	Fincas Average Acreage	Fincas Average Area Cultivated
Alto Songo	12,770	64,112	9,611	(27,041)	1,515	42.3	6.3
Baracoa	21,944	89,181	22,340	(41,191)	2,110	42.2	10.6
Bayamo	21,193	137,075	14,673	(7,360)	1,373	99.8	10.7
Campechuela	7,369	39,156	9,782	(10,065)	321	121.9	30.4
El Caney	9,126	73,775	2,601	(4,336)	611	120.7	4.2
El Cobre	10,707	136,086	8,540	(10,467)	1,253	108.6	6.8
Cristo	1,194	144	69	(—)	19	7.5	—
Gibara	31,594	124,425	32,355	(42,520)	1,205	103.2	26.8
Guantánamo	28,063	150,032	23,592	(26,911)	1,262	118.8	18.6
Holguín	34,506	456,550	14,849	(43,017)	3,260	140.0	4.5
Jiguaní	10,495	49,712	7,619	(7,455)	863	57.6	8.8
Manzanillo	32,288	87,136	17,361	(23,075)	2,033	42.8	8.5
Mayarí	8,504	19,635	4,885	(6,953)	734	26.7	6.6
Niquero	2,718	6,240	2,744	(4,454)	265	23.5	10.3
Palma Soriano	12,305	55,502	7,398	(25,048)	1,404	39.5	5.2
Puerto Padre	19,984	178,721	13,314	(16,237)	1,119	159.7	11.8
Sagua de Tánamo	5,796	76,349	3,526	(3,316)	628	121.5	5.6
San Luis	11,681	36,131	6,398	(11,261)	1,289	28.0	4.9
Santiago	45,478	22,935	2,260	(3,572)	286	80.1	7.9

Source: U.S. War Dept., Office of Director of Census, *Informe sobre el censo de Cuba, 1899* (Washington, D.C.: GPO, 1900), pp. 198–200, 566.

VI

Two generations of Cubans over three decades had sacrificed much to make Cuba free, but most of all to make Cuba for Cubans. They had pursued Cuba Libre purposefully, and they had paid dearly for their pursuit. They accepted with equanimity the necessity of self-abnegation as the cost of self-determination, and with equal serenity contemplated the systematic destruction of the land they sought to deliver—confident that in the end it would belong to them. Everything else would take care of itself in due time.

Cubans were not the only ones who coveted Cuba, however. North Americans also had designs on the island. Their opportunity also came within reach in 1898. The armed intervention set the stage, the military occupation paved the way, and immediately Cuba was opened to North Americans.

The promise was everywhere, just for the taking. "Nowhere else in the world," one North American investor insisted, "are there such chances for success for the man of moderate means, as well as for the capitalist, as Cuba offers today. . . . I advise the capitalist to invest in Cuba, and seriously suggest to the young and ambitious man to go to Cuba and cast his fortune with those of the island."[31] "It is simply a poor man's paradise and the rich man's mecca," proclaimed the *Commercial and Financial World*.[32] Two former North American consular agents in Oriente reported in 1898, "Land, at this writing, can be bought in unlimited quantities at from one-half to one-twentieth of its value before the insurrection." And they concluded: "For the ordinarily prudent man with some capital, who is willing to work, the island has opportunities for success and wealth through safe and profitable investments, the equal of which can be found in no other place."[33]

It was Oriente in particular that most appealed to North Americans. Here was a spacious province, bountiful in its resources, and prodigious in its promise. The vast expanses of hardwood forests were well known. The mineral potential was generally believed to be almost inexhaustible. Iron, manganese, nickel, and copper were among the most prominent resources awaiting development. The agricultural potential also appeared unlimited, principally sugar, of course, but many other crops, including citrus, vegetables, bananas, coconuts, coffee, and cacao. Moreover, with a comparatively low population density, Oriente exercised the same lure on North Americans as on Cubans. The vision was irresistible, and the timing was propitious: a new frontier at a time when Frederick Jackson Turner was lamenting the passing of the old. It was described variously as "virgin land," the "new California."[34] "Indeed," exulted Leonard Wood in 1901, "the island may be called a brand-new country."[35] Eastern Cuba offered open country in the form of cheap land, and open opportunity for people with industry and ingenuity—for farmers, miners, ranchers, and investors of all types: precisely the kind of people who had settled the last North American frontier.

These accounts of Oriente circulated early during the occupation. No one was a more passionate promoter and persistent publicist of these opportunities than Leonard Wood. First as department commander of Oriente province, and later as military governor of the island, Wood labored indefatigably both as an advocate of U.S. investment and as architect of policies to facilitate that investment. "Taken as a whole," Wood reported in 1899, "the Province of Santiago presents wonderful opportunities for industrious Americans. I know of no portion of our own country from which such great returns can be expected in so short a time as can be obtained in this province of Cuba."[36] Wood wrote persuasively, summoning a vision of a promised land in the tropics. "Tropical fruits all grow in the greatest abundance," he noted, and went into detail about bananas, coconuts, figs, limes, lemons, oranges. "Ordinary 'garden truck' grows with great rapidity and is of good quality." There was vast potential for tobacco, cotton, cacao, coffee, and, of course, sugar: "In this one province alone there are immense underdeveloped areas of the finest sugar land and enough magnificent land unplanted to equal the present total output of the island." Land, vast tracts of it, was available to everyone from speculators to settlers. Much of it was in the form of public land, but much was also in the way of abandoned land, from defunct farms and damaged estates, prices to sell—quickly and cheaply. "A large part of the province consists of lands which have never been reduced to private ownership and may therefore be described as Public Lands," Wood noted. He described the vast forest reserves— "valuable timber, consisting largely of splendid native hardwoods, including much mahogany, have never known the ax and are only waiting for development to become a great source of wealth." And there were the mines: "Santiago's greatest riches are mineral; its vast deposits of oxide of manganese and high-grade iron ore are as rich as any in the world." Investment opportunities were unlimited:

> Capital in large quantities can find remunerative employment in the construction of railroad lines, of which at present there are practically none; in sugar estates and mills, . . . in mining on a large scale, by the consolidation of small contiguous claims, and in the exploitation of large tracts of timber lands by use of logging, railroads, wire tramways, and sawmills. Franchises for street railroads in the cities and for electric lighting, if procurable on equitable terms, should prove inviting to capitalists who can afford to wait a short time for returns on their investments. For the small capitalists, it is believed that no better opportunities for investments which require personal attention and supervision, in small tracts, of coffee and cacao. Land suitable for these crops is abundant and cheap.[37]

"Where else in so comparatively small an area," Wood asked in a published interview, "within such easy access to the markets of the world can such a range of undeveloped wealth be found. . . . If I were a millionaire looking for investment I certainly should bring my money here, knowing what I know of Cuba's 'dormant wealth.' "[38]

But it was not enough to transfer North American capital to Cuba. It was also necessary to transfer North Americans. A central and recurring theme in Wood's eulogy to Oriente was the potential the province offered for homesteading. Wood understood well the politics of population, and realized too that a steady influx of North Americans into

Cuba would ultimately facilitate another objective: annexation. He looked forward to the future when the population of Cuba reached 12 million, made up in the main of "industrious and enterprising planters and developers, a large proportion of whom will probably come from our own country."[39] It was not a prospect without precedent. North American emigration to Texas had more than adequately prepared the way for union. "I do not think annexation would be desireable immediately," reasoned Senator Cushman K. Davis, chairman of the Senate Committee on Foreign Relations in 1897. "If Cuba were free there would be 150,000 American residents on the island within ten years. That itself would ensure conditions which would make annexation desireable."[40] The Columbia, S.C. *State* predicted one year later, "In a year or so there will be a rush to the island like those of the past to Texas and Florida, and in a few more years the majority of the inhabitants will be English-speaking. Then Cuba will be ripe for annexation, and impelled by industrial and economic conditions its people will ask for Statehood in the Union."[41] "The situation in Cuba today is extraordinary," Irene Wright exulted as late as 1910. She continued:

> It constitutes, therefore, a rare opportunity for pioneers, and they are already here making the most of it. They are not, however, the pioneer type of which we read, for they are matched against odds which require another equipment than their storied predecessors elsewhere have carried. . . . Those others who carved the American Union out of the wilderness of North America, wiping Death's Valley and the Great American Desert off the map, have attained the stability of statehood and the prosperity government irrigation fetches; they who labor now in Cuba are striving toward the same ends, to give final shape to that which they have taken in hand. Arrayed against them are the rigors of a southern, not a northern, climate; and the dangers of contact with decadent, not savage, contestants with them for control. . . . At tremendous cost, but surely, they will triumph; and at

the sacrifice of much that is worthy, in itself, of a fairer fate they will erect out of ruin and decay a fabric worthy of them.⁴²

The minimum necessary incentive to encourage North American immigration, Wood understood, was the availability of homesteading opportunities. And nowhere else in Cuba was land more abundant, more fertile, and more available than in Oriente. "Santiago province in general," Wood asserted in 1901, "is good farming-land and offers magnificent agricultural opportunities to settlers. It cannot be said that any part of Cuba has been thoroughly developed. . . . Of all the provinces Santiago probably holds the most of this undeveloped wealth."⁴³ All that remained was to make the information about the land public, its transfer possible, and its development practical.

VII This was the purpose to which the military government committed itself during the occupation: to facilitate North American investment and immigration. Central to both objectives was the easy accessibility of land at attractive prices and in abundant parcels. The first step in this process was a military order revoking the April 1899 moratorium decree. "From the 1st of June next," Military Order No. 139 stipulated, "all classes of creditors remain at liberty to take action and enforce the collection of mortgage credits, on all kinds of properties."⁴⁴ "Nothing has been done to keep money out of the country and prevent reconstruction than the original stay law," Wood wrote in defense of Military Order No. 139. "It would perhaps have been hard to have had an immediate foreclosure, but it would have been very salutary." Permitting the decree to lapse, Wood predicted confidently, promised a "gentle means of bringing the present condition . . . to an end with as little harshness as possible."⁴⁵

No longer guaranteed immunity from foreclosure, and without access either to credit or capital, large numbers of farmers everywhere in Cuba faced expulsion. Landowners large and small, with outstanding debts, suddenly faced the necessity of settling years of indebtedness, or losing the land. Nor could landowners reasonably expect land to serve fully as the medium of exchange for the settlement of debts. The reality was that land values in Cuba had collapsed, falling to a fraction of previously assessed values—that is, below the appraised worth against which loans were previously extended. The land was in ruin and production was in crisis, and landowners lacked either the means to repair the former or a market to revive the latter. "The money secured by mortgages on these estates," reported Wood, "was loaned when the mills were standing; the destruction of the mills has left the estates worth only a fraction of the mortgage. There is no hope of this class of people getting out of the hole."[46]

Depressed land values meant too that the land itself was insufficient collateral to refinance the liquidation of existing loans. Across the island, landowners ceased resisting the inevitable and sold out, often at great losses. In the municipality of San José de las Lajas in Havana province, land was selling for one-fifth of its full value. "Land is sold at $100 to $200 per *caballería*," reported the mayor, "its real value being $1,000 for first class."[47]

The tax policy adopted by the military government, further, facilitated the acquisition of land. Land taxes were levied on farm income rather than farm value. This form of assessment served to encourage land speculation, favoring investors who acquired large tracts of valuable but unproductive land while paying no taxes.[48]

The military government also facilitated the expansion of North American capital into railroad construction. In February 1902, government authorities enacted Civil Order No. 34, modifying railroad laws by removing obstacles to the establishment of new lines and the expansion of existing ones. Investors received official sanction to acquire all land necessary for railroad construction and maintenance. Indeed, the modifications were themselves prepared by railroad investors.[49] "The railroad law has got to be modified," Wood insisted to Secretary of War Elihu Root a month earlier, "or no pronounced development of business in this line can be expected. . . . I want you to feel sure that I am as much interested as anybody in protecting American interests when I can do so without directly violating the law."[50] Vast tracts of land were subsequently subject to expropriation in the pursuit of an enterprise owned almost entirely by foreign capital. Railroad companies during and after the occupation routinely attached property proclaimed necessary for the expansion of railroad construction.[51] The Cuba Company was among the first to avail itself of the new railroad law. It acquired land across Oriente: 50,000 acres for terminals, for construction zones, town and depot sites, and a right-of-way 350 miles in length, and along the way purchased sugar estates, produce farms, and forest lands.[52] The company frequently and effectively invoked Civil Order No. 34. In one contested case, it appropriated some 25,000 square meters of land from the *finca* "El Escorial" in Holguín, and successfully justified its action by the terms of the law.[53]

A month after the enactment of Civil Order No. 34, the military government promulgated Civil Order No. 62. Perhaps one of the most important decrees of the occupation, this order was designed for the purpose of "cleaning up the mess of titles that has entangled the properties" of communal lands *(hacienda comunera)*.[54] For the better part of the nineteenth century, much of rural Cuba had organized around the *hacienda comunera*, a system of communal farming in which ownership of land was distributed in allotments and held in common by communities in the form of shares *(pesos de posesión)*, the equivalent of stock in a corporation. This was one of the prinicpal forms of traditional landholding. The tenure of *posesión* guaranteed an owner *(comunero)* title to a certain portion of the original tract *(merced)*, but not a good and clear title to any specified part of the land. *Pesos de posesión* were a right in the land, to some of it somewhere within the boundaries of the tract. Over the years, *pesos de posesión* underwent constant division and distribution. When an owner died, the assessed value of the hacienda was allocated among heirs. The land itself was not divided, rather each heir obtained a right upon the estate. The estate would pass on to all heirs, becoming immediately communal property. The original land grant remained intact, but the right to the land was distributed in direct proportion to the fixed dollar share. The number of shares in any given tract increased with the passage of time, as each successive owner willed allotments to new heirs or sold portions to new cultivators. Rights to the land multiplied in the course of time, and ownership often became hopelessly confused and continuously contested.

Pesos de posesión were willed, sold, and otherwise transferred without regard to the proportion of land corresponding to each share. Thus, a *merced* of some 6,000 *caballerías* valued at $50,000 in 1800, for example, could be distributed among five heirs at $10,000 apiece, any one of whom could resell all or any part of the *posesión* into smaller units. Over the years, ownership fell into increasingly smaller *pesos de posesión*. Any given tract of land could be owned in *posesión* of hundreds of persons, whose share may have ranged from thousands of *pesos* to only a few. Actual landholdings varied in size, and often did not correspond to the number of *pesos de posesión* held. Holdings were typically designated a *finca,* and to facilitate recognition they were given proper names by owners. Conditions were complicated further by requirements of *posesión*. If an owner failed to work the land for more than a year and a day, others holding an interest in the property could establish a right to the claim by occupancy. All told, those circumstances created a chaotic web of ownership and occupancy.[55] "In many cases," complained the director of the 1899 census, "the area of the *fincas* were found uncertain and contradictory, and were given in many different units of measurement. The occupant was often unknown, and many portions of land were in the possession of occupants on the basis of sufferance, of necessity without defined limits."[56] A special commission examining the *hacienda comunera* in 1901 reported:

> In so far as the real nature, the location and the area and the boundary thereof are concerned, there prevails the greatest confusion which can be imagined. The actual title-deeds of said properties are scarce, doubtful and even unknown. Neither the number, nor the real names, nor the exact location, nor the area of the

greater part of said undivided properties are known. In many instances, not even those who name themselves tenants in common, know if they are really such tenants, nor why they are called tenants in common. . . . On very few occasions do we know what number of "pesos de posesión" correspond to a property, or which the property-holders ascribe to themselves. They . . . are not familiar with the real significance, scope and value of their "pesos de posesión," and in the greater number of cases not . . . one of them knows why he states that he has so many "pesos de posesión" in such a property. Everything in this matter constitutes an entanglement.[57]

Tracts of land grants were rarely surveyed and inevitably boundaries were inexact, unofficial, and almost always unverifiable. Measurement was invariably defective. Distances were often appraised by the sound of a conch shell horn or by the length of time required in travel between two points. Boundaries consisted typically of a forest, hill, stream, marsh, or other natural feature or arbitrary point mutually agreed upon such as a cut in a tree, fallen log or a small creek. And just as often, landmarks disappeared. Sometimes *posesión* was known only in the collective memory of the community, possession recognized as a tradition. When in one litigation in 1909 farmers were asked how they recognized the boundary of their *hacienda*, one *comunero* responded: "The line has been there from time immemorial and has been respected by the co-owners."[58]

It was precisely this ambiguity that made the *hacienda comunera* wholly incompatible with the requirements of large-scale commercial production. Ownership over any tract of land was claimed by large numbers of people holding varying amounts of *pesos de posesión*, thereby making transfer of the entire unit all but impossible. The only recourse was litigation to challenge ownership, and for the vast numbers whose titles were imperfect, incomplete, or otherwise flawed, adjudication was usually the first step toward dislodgement. Valid titles, too, were often challenged, and not infrequently the judicial survey *(deslinde)* so reduced the size of a legal claim as to make subsistence agriculture all but impossible. Court proceedings tended to be blatantly unfair to the *comuneros.* Wrote sociologist Lowry Nelson after several years of field work in rural Cuba:

> The sugar companies purchased land from the peasants where the latter could show a title, but where titles were in question—as so many of them were—recourse was had to the courts. There can be no doubt that the contest in the courts was a one-sided affair in which the companies had the overwhelming advantage. They could employ the best lawyers who knew the loopholes in Cuban land laws. They could if necessary corrupt the officials, high and low with bribes.[59]

Holders of invalidated claims were required to abandon the land, taking with them whatever livestock, crops, and personal property were located within the boundaries of the properties. Immovable property, specifically gardens, planted fields, and orchards, were to be appraised and the owner adequately indemnified.[60]

After the war, *haciendas comuneras* remained an important form of land tenure in the eastern half of the island. In the west, in those regions given to large-scale sugar production, land titles had been cleared and consolidated earlier in the nineteenth century. The *hacienda comunera* was particularly important in Oriente. However vague, *pesos de posesión* represented a legal right to the land. For a comparatively modest sum, farmers could obtain *posesión* and secure the attending right to work some part of the *finca.* This was *minifundista* farming on a large scale and provided a livelihood for generations of small farmers with minimum capital outlay. The communal land system served as the foundation of local agrarian systems. As early as 1901, a special Cuban commission formed to study the *haciendas comuneras* warned the military government of the grave consequences of suppressing communal land tenure:

> It must be taken into consideration that any measure contrary to law which may be adopted would not favor the distribution of the soil among the cultivators

thereof; on the contrary, it would be an incentive for the strong and powerful. In our territorial communities the medium and small owners, people whose succession from fathers to children and during three or four generations have been distributing their title among themselves and who occupy or possess the land which in our rural economy, are the only sufficient for the decorous support of a family.[61]

The promulgation of Civil Order No. 62 announced the demise of the small independent farmer in the east. Under the terms of the decree, a plaintiff seeking to fix the precise boundaries of a tract of land obtained court sanction to undertake a survey of the property in question. The court appointed a special tribunal to examine the *pesos de posesión* held by all *comuneros* to determine the legitimacy of each claim. Expensive judicial surveys, commissioned by the plaintiff, fixed new and detailed boundaries, which were submitted to the court. Attorneys and surveyors petitioned the court to ratify new boundaries and sanction new deeds of titled ownership *(dominio).*[62]

It was a system that favored the large and powerful over the small and powerless. It was especially disastrous in postwar Cuba. To already ambiguous historic conditions of landownership and real estate titles, the war—most of which was fought the longest in the eastern provinces—contributed even further to the confusion. Every uncertain claim was vulnerable to litigation.

The implications were clear. As long as the *hacienda comunera* prevailed as a dominant tenure form in eastern Cuba, the transfer of land would remain hopelessly impractical, if not altogether impossible. Wood early recognized that the *hacienda comunera* obstructed the recirculation of land in Oriente, and he understood, too, the necessity of eliminating this form of ownership before land could pass into the possession of new proprietors. The persistence of the *hacienda comunera,* moreover, effectively precluded the concentration of land. "In some parts of the Province," he wrote during his tenure as provincial commander in 1899, "estates have been granted out of large tracts of land to different individuals, which estates have never been set apart to the individual holders. The result is a sort of tenancy in common." This system made it "difficult to settle, improve and cultivate the land with satisfactory results." The solution was obvious: "Provision should be made for the partition of such tracts and their allotment in severalty to the present owners in common."[63] This was the view, too, of the Merchants Association of New York, and the relation between the *hacienda comunera* and North American immigration to Cuba was established early and directly:

> Nothing of greater advantage could be done by the Government than to make a public survey of the lands. . . . Some equitable and uniform system for defining limits and titles, and thereby removing the present hazard attending land transfers could doubtless be devised and would do much to further the general sale of cheap Government lands to small holders—an essential to the influx of a new and progressive population.[64]

Years later, the Foreign Policy Association would conclude that U.S. land policy during the occupation, specifically Civil Order No. 62, had established "the foundation for modern corporate development, and the present latifundia system which would not have been possible had the old system of land tenure remained in effect."[65]

VIII Eastern Cuba experienced again disruption and dislocation. For decades after the war tens of thousands of Cubans had migrated to Oriente in search of new livelihood and new land. They were not disappointed. That had always been the promise of the east: a place of new beginning, but most of all a new freedom. Through the better part of the nineteenth century, the province had attracted the outcasts who lost themselves deep in the vast expanses of the Oriente interior. And in this, the most Cuban region of all of Cuba, generations of Cubans had found the promise of redemption fulfilled.

The attraction of Oriente increased after the war.

Thousands of impoverished and landless army veterans, mostly Cubans, but Spaniards also, together with the former *pacíficos* and *reconcentrados* from across the island, journeyed eastward to begin life anew in the interior regions of Oriente. Many bought into *haciendas comuneras*. Others settled as squatters, dispersing inland throughout the unchartered expanses of public lands, there swelling the ranks of small peasant farmers.

But after 1899 Cubans were not alone. North Americans also arrived, first in the form of any army of conquest and a government of occupation. They promulgated decrees and enacted laws, thereby tilting the legal system of the new republic to favor other outsiders, also from the United States. They arrived as brokers and vendors, homesteaders and settlers, speculators and investors, and they all came for the same thing: land.

It did not take many to upset the old order of things. North Americans arrived with capital resources well out of proportion to their numbers, and with equally disproportionate advantages in an impoverished economy. They arrived determined to transform the economic purpose and social function of the land from public domain to private development, from communal to corporate, from the family plot to the commercial plantation. They possessed the capital to buy up what land was available and the political connections to make available what land could not be bought outright. They promised to overwhelm and overturn a way of life long immune to outside currents. In this new order of things it was not entirely clear what place Cubans would or could occupy. The signs bode ill. Remarked one North American traveler to Cuba in 1911: "Foreigners own ninety per cent of all the land in Cuba that is worth working, and, since this is the case, the more foreign capital that comes in, the better for the country. In other words, the only outlook for the Cuban is to serve as a hired man."[66]

The results were predictable. Destroyed property and defunct estates failed to revive, becoming easy and cheap acquisitions. In a capital-starved environment, North Americans enjoyed a vastly superior position, and with the resources at their disposal found their expectations readily realized. The laws of the occupation encouraged land transfers and transactions. Cubans had been buffeted back and forth, their homes were destroyed, and their possessions lost. The destruction of entire communities meant more than damage to property. Also destroyed was proof of ownership in private copies of deeds and documents, in public records and official depositories. *Ayuntamientos* and *municipios* across the east experienced the worst of the war. Public buildings were reduced to rubble. In some *municipios* of the Oriente, the loss of public records, property titles, and land registries was total. The municipal records of Baracoa, Banes, Las Tunas, and Jiguaní were completely destroyed.[67] "All the records of the *ayuntamiento* disappeared during the war," reported the mayor of Jiguaní in 1900; "the district was entirely destroyed."[68] Where record collections were not destroyed, they were removed. Many real estate records were in the custody of local registry offices, the contents of which were included in the archival materials that evacuating Spanish authorities returned to Spain. Records that could not be transported were often simply destroyed. "The destruction of the records of this office by Spanish troops on their evacuation of this town," complained the mayor of Mayarí, "prevents the recording of the number and condition of *caballerías* of land under cultivation."[69]

These conditions cleared the way for new land transfers and transactions. Postwar impoverishment, the scarcity of the resources to stimulate agricultural recovery, and the expiration of the foreclosure moratorium portended problems—for Cubans. Civil Order No. 62 provided the legal basis through which to overturn traditional forms of tenure and tenancy in the east. Confusion over property titles, unclear land boundaries, and uncertain ownership all but invited litigation and served to facilitate the alienation and consolidation of communal land. The promulgation of Military Order No. 62 had especially devastating consequence in the east, where the *hacienda comunera* prevailed but where proof of ownership had perished during the war.

Several developments converged in a fateful combination. Many Cubans could not prove ownership of land, whether in the form of *posesión* or *dominio*. On the other hand, many who could demonstrate title could neither secure the means to revive agriculture nor to settle outstanding debts. Whatever form the predicament assumed, the results were the same: Cubans were losing the land. The process began immediately at the end of the war. When North American real estate speculators overran the island in search of new land and old estates, Cuban landowners were prepared to deal. "The Spaniards want to sell because they want to get out," commented one writer in January 1899. "The Cubans must sell because they cannot afford to keep."[70] Well-financed North American syndicates and land companies retained teams of attorneys, foreign and Cuban, and descended on rural communities to press new title claims, challenge existing property deeds and boundaries, assess new land value and taxes, and inaugurate judicial surveys. Land agents and land surveyors swarmed over what remained of local archives and municipal registries in search of information useful to prove that existing titles and claims were flawed or defective. Claims centuries old were scrutinized for the slightest irregularity to permit a legal challenge. It was a cumbersome process, but not difficult.[71]

Vast tracts of land in Oriente passed under North American control. Much of the early and extensive expansion occurred in the regions of Manzanillo to the south and Puerto Padre–Holguín–Gibara in the north. In 1901, the Cape Cruz Company purchased the estates of "Aguas Grande," "Limoncito," and "San Celestino," a total of 16,000 acres in Manzanillo. That same year, investment broker Joseph Rigney acquired control of the "San Juan" and "San Joaquín" estates and the sugar mill "Teresa," also in the region of Manzanillo.[72]

North American control over land in the north also expanded rapidly during these years. In 1899, the newly organized Cuban-American Sugar Company acquired 70,000 acres of land in Puerto Padre. The Cuban-American *central*, "Chaparra," soon became one of the most productive mills in Cuba. By far the most extensive land tracts in Oriente were acquired along the northern coastal zones of Banes, Antilla, and Mayarí by the United Fruit Company. In the region of Banes and Antilla, United Fruit acquired an estimated 225,000 acres. Nearly 75 percent of the municipality of Banes and almost half of Mayarí were acquired by United Fruit. The Nipe Bay Company, a United Fruit subsidiary, expanded on 130,000 acres in Mayarí, south of Nipe Bay. Within a decade of independence, almost the entire Oriente north coast, from Baracoa on the east to Manatí on the west, passed under the control of foreign sugar producers.[73]

North American real estate companies acquired title to extensive tracts of land and ownership of countless numbers of estates that were either defunct or in default. These were among the earliest expressions of the colonization schemes, projects in which U.S. land companies acquired property in Cuba and resold tracts and subdivisions to North American settlers, colonists, and farmers. Most were similar to the Taco Bay Commercial Land Company. Incorporated in Boston, the syndicate acquired vast tracts of land in Oriente. In 1904, the company purchased the "Juraguá" estate. An extensive plantation west of Baracoa, some 20,000 acres in size, "Juraguá" before the war had successfully produced bananas, coconuts, and sugar. During the war, it had suffered extensive damage, and by 1898, it was in debt and without sufficient capital to resume prewar production levels. Under the auspices of Civil Order No. 62, the Taco Bay Company acquired the property with assurances to prospective buyers that all existing liens and mortgages were cleared up "by the best legal talent, Messrs. Runcia and Lamar of Havana."[74]

Throughout the early years of the republic, North American real estate and land speculators acquired enormous tracts of land in Oriente, without serious opposition. One New York company purchased 180,000 acres along the banks of the Cauto River in Oriente. Another syndicate acquired 50,000 acres on Nipe Bay for the purpose of establishing a winter resort.[75] Other land transactions in eastern Cuba included:

Illinois Cuban Land Company, incorporated in Hoopes-
ton, Illinois, acquired Paso Estancia, a 10,000-acre
tract in central Oriente.

Cuban Development Company, based in Detroit, acquired the 12,500-acre Vista Alegre estate in the region of Victoria de las Tunas in Oriente.

Las Tunas Realty Company, incorporated in Youngs-
town, Ohio, purchased several estates around Victoria de Las Tunas in Oriente.

Cuban Agricultural and Development Company, incorporated in Pittsburgh, purchased over 135,000
acres of land around the region of Guantánamo.

Cuban Realty Company, incorporated in New Jersey,
purchased 15,000 acres in western Oriente.

Potosí Land and Sugar Company, based in Cincinnati,
acquired title to property in the region of Victoria de
las Tunas.

Buena Vista Fruit Company, based in Boston, purchased 3,000 acres of citrus land in central Oriente.

Eastern Cuba Development Company, acquired 1,000
acres near Victoria de Las Tunas.

In addition to real estate companies, North American
missionaries and church organizations also quickly established their presence in Oriente. The Methodist church was
among the most active, and by 1907 the Methodists had
acquired some $150,000 worth of property, much of which
included some of the finest tracts of agricultural lands in
Guantánamo, Holguín, and Mayarí—a total of thirty across
the island. The Society of Friends arrived in Cuba and acquired some $30,000 worth of property in Puerto Padre. The
Baptists purchased land throughout Oriente and developed
a total of forty-five sites, including churches, schools, and
offices. The Episcopal church established their missionary
headquarters in Ensenada de Mora. By the end of the decade,
Seventh Day Adventists and the Church of the Brethren had
also established their presence in eastern Cuba.[76]

These developments announced the onset of ambitious
colonization schemes, the first wave of immigration from
the United States that many believed would lead to a vast

North American presence on the island and culminate in annexation. In the early 1900s, thousands of North American families emigrated to Cuba to establish agricultural colonies. The Colonization Company of Minneapolis acquired the 6,000-acre estate of Palmarito in the Cauto Valley in 1906. Two Swedish-Lutheran colonies were established, one in Mayarí and the other at Bayate. A colony of Finnish-Americans purchased a 1,000-acre tract east of Omaja. The Cuba Polish Company of Toledo established a Polish-American colony on some 1,000 acres near Victoria de las Tunas. By the early 1900s, U.S. colonists had established thirty-five agricultural settlements throughout Cuba. In Oriente, settlements were made in Bartle, Las Tunas, Omaja, Cacocún, Holguín, Palmarito, Pedernales, Sabanaso, Guanamo, Mir, Paso Estancia, Bayate, and Ensenada de Mora.[77] By 1905, some 13,000 North Americans had acquired title to land in Cuba worth over $50 million. "Americans own more land in the province of Santiago, I am told," the U.S. Minister in Havana reported in 1904, "than in any other province of the Island, their holdings amounting to something more than a million acres."[78] Estimates of the magnitude of North American property holdings in Cuba varied, and all tended to be impressionistic. The impressions were that it was considerable. In 1906, one writer estimated North American ownership of and at 4.3 million acres, some 15 percent of the total land in Cuba.[79] Another estimate calculated that 60 percent of all rural property was owned by foreign companies, with another 15 percent owned by resident Spaniards, and Cubans reduced to 25 percent.[80] In 1909, sugar magnate Manuel Rionda used different figures, but arrived at similar conclusions. "Spaniards I dare say own 30/40% of the property—Americans 25/40%. So the Cubans, the real Cubans, do not own much."[81]

U.S. Mining companies also increased their holdings in the east throughout the latter nineteenth century and the early years of the twentieth. The principal mineral deposits in Oriente included iron, manganese, copper, and lead, distributed in two principal regions in the north and south. The southern region was located largely in the districts of El Caney, Firmeza, Daiquirí, Ponupo, El Cristo, and Bayamo.

These mines were controlled by the Juraguá Iron Company (Pennsylvania Steel and Bethlehem Iron Company), Spanish-American Iron Company, Sigua Iron Company, Cuban Steel Ore Company, and Ponupo Manganese Company. In the north, the mining zone was located largely in Mayarí and owned almost entirely by the Spanish-American Iron Company.

Mining operations expanded rapidly after the war. During the occupation, the military government actively promoted North American mining interests, issuing a total of 218 concessions, 134 of which were located in Oriente province.[82] Mining companies also increased their control of the land. The 21 claims of the Juraguá Iron Company in El Caney totaled an estimated 1,140 acres of land. In 1905 the Spanish-American Iron Company acquired 28,000 acres of land in Mayarí. Spanish-American Iron, the largest holders of iron property, owned a total of 134,569 acres of surface rights and an additional 150,986 acres of mining rights. In all, 436,560 acres of land was distributed among approximately 2,000 mine operations.[83]

X Among the newest casualties of the peace were the old casualties of the war. Thousands of peasants and farmers, many of whom were *comuneros*, were displaced and dispossessed. Without proof of *posesión*, the loss was permanent.[84] The process of consolidation of land, and the inevitable demise of the small farms, began almost immediately after the war.

But the decline in the number of *fincas* did not fully encompass the magnitude of the crisis unfolding in Oriente. It also signified the displacement of even more farmers and peasants who settled the land. These included vast numbers of squatters who faced immediate expulsion, without recourse. Thousands of Cubans, since the closing decades of the nineteenth century, had migrated to the east and settled on unworked and/or unclaimed lands. Soldiers from both armies, and from both major wars, had moved onto whatever land was available—public lands, unclaimed coastal keys, and countless abandoned estates. Not a few settlements in Oriente after the war were entirely squatter communities. Leonard Wood wrote in late 1899:

> During the war many of the estates in the interior were abandoned and have become overgrown. Their owners are either dead or in foreign ports or living in towns, too poor to attempt any work tending to reclaim and re-establish their estates. The result has been and is that many persons have settled on these estates, as well as on different portions of the public domain, and have remained in undisputed possession for several years. Their removal will be attended with considerable difficulty and hardship and probably with considerable disturbance, as the individuals who have made these irregular settlements are largely soldiers of the late Cuban Army. . . . At present they find themselves without means and without homes. Many of them were formerly slaves. Others are the descendants of people who have never owned or had a permanent home. Some are poor people who were formerly tenants on the larger estates.[85]

Wood's allusion to "irregular settlements" underscored the emergence of a new social reality in Oriente. Although de facto occupation of the public domain had long been one of the principal means of obtaining possession of land, after 1898 more squatters were crowding onto less available land, and expecting to obtain grants. In 1898, Inspector General James H. McLeary described one such flourishing squatter community settlement in El Cristo: "None of the people who live at Cristo claim to have title to their lands. They are mere squatters, but expect to receive the lands from the government at some time in the future."[86]

Equally important, after the war squatters were moving onto abandoned but privately owned property. Across eastern Cuba squatter settlements emerged on these sites, and in many instances they assumed the proportions of small towns and villages. Wrote Irene Wright traveling in 1910 through one such site in the Cauto valley: "The town of Palmarito is itself a squatters' settlement, lacking all right to exist, but existing sturdily just the same, to the extent of thirty houses or thereabouts, of frame, composition and concrete, built in two rows paralleling the railroad tracks. . . . Scattered over the tract are the small country estates of other squatters."[87]

Settlements of this type were not new. Indeed, many towns and villages in Oriente traced their origins to similar antecedents; however, after 1898 many squatters' communities developed on private property. Many were estates rendered unproductive by the war and abandoned by their owners, who were unable to revive agriculture either during the conflict or immediately after its end. Many landowners faced the daunting prospects, too, of dislodging large numbers of squatters who had settled on their property, a process that involved lengthy and costly judicial proceedings, while all the time the land remained beyond their control, and debts piled up. It was easier to sell out.

The land acquired by North American interests, hence, often came occupied with squatters. The new owners immediately sought to eject their unwelcome tenants. The Ferrer family sold estate lands containing the squatter settlements to the Cauto Produce Company (1903) and the Swedish Land and Colonization Company of Minneapolis (1906). After several years of litigation, most squatters were forcefully removed, and the land sold in parcel tracts to North American colonists and farmers.[88] The Paso Estancia hacienda in central Oriente, an estate of approximately 10,000 acres, was acquired by the Illinois Cuban Land Company and cleared of squatters to make way for forty North American homestead families.[89]

XI As long as land was plentiful, or cheap, the issue of contested *pesos de posesión* and squatters settlements could be ignored. The cost of resolving conflicting claims held by *comuneros* and squatters, typically requiring expensive judicial surveys and attorney fees and protracted litigation, often exceeded the value of the land in question. In the early twentieth century this began to change. Land values increased and land supplies diminished. Cubans across Oriente were losing the land, and in many cases it mattered little whether or not they possessed legal claims. The alienation of peasant lands occurred unevenly. It proceeded most rapidly along the coast, in those *municipios* with the best ports, where highways, railroads, and communication systems were most advanced, specifically Puerto Padre, Gibara, Holguín, Banes, and Mayarí in the north and Manzanillo and Guantánamo in the south. It was slowest in the interior. Many zones in Oriente remained in the early years beyond the easy reach of commercial development due to a lack of transportation facilities.

Internal migration began almost immediately with the inauguration of the republic. Displaced farmers and peasants migrated inland to the interior foothills, valleys and zones believed beyond the immediate reach of the capitalists and colonists from the north.[90] In fact, there was no escape.

5   Deferred Hopes Denied

A complete state of agitation exists in the province of Santa Clara, hard times being felt and there is a general feeling of inquietude. The increase of the number of bandits is alarming, many armed gangs traversing various parts of the province, and their work is having considerable effect. Several kidnappings have been committed within the past fifteen days for the purpose of demanding ransom.
—Supervisor of Police, Havana, September 1900

We need assurances that the banditry of the past will not continue in the new Cuba. Otherwise, the republic will begin in worse condition than the colony ended.
—*Diario de la Marina*, March 12, 1902

I The war of 1895 did not end banditry in Cuba. Rather, it confused the issue, making it more difficult to distinguish bandits, and all but impossible to define banditry. The difference between a patriotic gesture and a criminal act lost all meaning during the conflict. Nor were Spanish authorities inclined to make such distinctions. They routinely characterized all Cubans in arms as outlaws and all Cuban military operations as outrages. The Cubans responded in kind, and typically denounced the acts of the Spanish army as criminal depredations. But it was the guerrillas, the name given to the irregular corps recruited locally and attached to units of the Spanish army, that Cubans consistently denounced as murderers and marauders. Cubans made finer distinctions, too, for there were indeed persons who took advantage of war to pillage for personal gain. They were known as *plateados*, freebooters who stole indiscriminately and caused havoc across the countryside. Many were army deserters, some were outcasts of various sorts and longtime fugitives. The Cuban army command reserved its most severe punishment for *plateados:* summary execution. Early in the war, General Máximo Gómez ordered Cuban field commanders to exterminate *plateados* in every district under the control of the Liberation Army.[1]

While the end of the war simplified the task of identifying banditry, it also contributed to conditions reviving banditry. The release of 50,000 soldiers into the devastated countryside added new pressures on the shattered rural economy. Meanwhile, tens of thousands of *reconcentrados* were leaving the cities. At about the same time, hundreds, maybe thousands of Spanish soldiers—no one knew how many—had chosen to remain in Cuba after the war, and they also traveled inland.

They returned to the land, vast numbers of hopeful cultivators, only to find the farms in ruin and the prospects for revival bleak. The prospects of wage employment were no more promising. Commercial agriculture and industry everywhere in Cuba were in crisis. The sugar mills were slow to recover from the effects of the war. Most did not. "The sugar estates," General George W. Davis wrote from Pinar del Río in early 1899, "only found in the eastern part of the Province, are all destroyed and the owners of these estates cannot give employment."[2]

Cuba was in transition, again: from war to peace, from colony to republic. Cubans were in transit, again, all returning home: from exile to homeland, from the cities to the countryside, from the mountains to the plains. Few found home as they remembered it, if they found home at all. The *reconcentrados* who left the cities, the *pacíficos* who descended from the mountains, and the discharged soldiers found their former world in a shambles.

The prospects were especially daunting for the soldiers of liberation. Peace found the soldiers destitute, a condition they had struggled in arms to escape. They had sacrificed much in behalf of Cuba Libre, for many, everything. They had won, but lost everything in the process. Their country was occupied anew, their government was again administered from abroad. Allocation of resources and benefits was controlled by the United States, who used this power prin-

cipally in the pursuit of North American interests and sec-
ondarily, if at all, in behalf of Cuban interests. Nothing
could have prepared Cubans for the impoverishment that
their success had caused them. They returned to an economy totally unprepared to receive them. They had been
promised land for their service in behalf of Cuba Libre, but
received nothing. Although indigent veterans repeatedly
appealed to authorities to make good on commitments
made in the name of Cuba Libre, there is no evidence that
these requests were ever met.[3]

Outlawry offered one remedy. Lawlessness increased in
rural Cuba, signaling, once more, unrest in the countryside.
The ways of war persisted. Even before the Liberation Army
disbanded, many soldiers had returned to a fugitive existence. Plantations reported an increase in pilfering; merchants and shopkeepers complained of rising thefts and
robberies.[4] Patriots became bandits. Cuban General Porfirio
Valiente explained in late 1898, "Most of them were good
soldiers during the war, but many have since been virtually
bandits out of sheer hunger as they could not get rations
because they were armed and refused to disband."[5]

Postwar banditry differed markedly among regions. The
differences were portentous. In the western provinces, the
principal areas of prewar lawlessness, banditry was short-
lived, outlaw bands were smaller.[6] The decline of banditry
in the west signaled the restoration of social peace. The
effects of war and the displacement of the reconstruction
camps during the 1890s completed the process begun by the
sugar revolution of the 1880s. Within a year of peace, order
prevailed throughout the western regions. "Now it may be
surely said," wrote one rural guard commander in late 1899,
"that there are no more bandits in . . . the three provinces of
Pinar del Río, Havana, and Matanzas."[7]

Conditions were different in the east. Lawlessness spread
rapidly in Oriente immediately after the war. Arrests in the
east were well out of proportions to those in the more
heavily populated west. In August 1901, the west reported a
total of 307 arrests to 587 in the east, and a month later 323 in
the west, 451 in the east.[8] Local observers noted these differences. "The banditti question in the province," cabled one

correspondent from Santiago de Cuba in mid-1899, "is assuming much more serious proportions. In spite of the fact that there have been many arrests, . . . including the principal leaders, the number of outlaws is increasing instead of diminishing."[9] Leonard Wood reported similar conditions. "There has been . . . some brigandage in different parts of the province due to no particular cause other than idleness and viciousness. Most of the men engaged in this work were old hands at it, and have returned to it naturally since the end of the war."[10] He later recalled: "At the end of the war, many restless and disorderly spirits . . . resumed irregular and lawless lives, and to such an extent did they carry their depredations that they became a serious menace to public order, life, and property."[11]

Numbers alone portended problems. Most of the returning soldiers came from the east. More than half the soldiers in Pinar del Río at the end of the war were easterners.[12] At the same time, the majority of Cuban army units were disbanded in the eastern half of the island. The First Army Corps was stationed in Santiago, the Second Corps was located in Manzanillo, the Third Corps in Camagüey, and the Fourth Corps in Santa Clara. A total of 35,000 officers and soldiers out of 50,000 reentered civilian life in the east.[13]

Certainly much of the lawlessness in the east was attributable directly to conditions created by the war. Many bandits were *plateados* during the war, or worst yet, the despised guerrillas, and for the latter especially there was no possibility of returning home. They were marked men, and the recurring unsolved murders of former guerrillas was one of the enduring features of political life in the early republic.[14] But these were not the only outcasts who took up permanent residence outside the law in Oriente. Cuban deserters who were not held in much greater esteem than the guerrillas, and had no place to go, also found sanctuary there.[15] Not all these outcasts, certainly, were transformed into brigands. Others vanished into the impenetrable back country, to eke out a living through subsistence farming.

Some Cubans who turned to banditry were former soldiers honorably discharged, and immediately destitute. And so many of them took refuge in the east simply because most of them came from the east. They were first to enroll in the cause and they had endured personal privation the longest, and their communities had been disrupted the most. They gave more to free Cuba than they expected to receive from free Cuba, and they received even less than they expected. Nothing could have prepared them for the cruel denouement of the cause that began with such lofty purposefulness.

The massive demobilization of Cuban soldiers in the east, together with the destruction of the area, had fateful results. Cuban authorities warned the military government that conditions in the east required a different approach. Rafael Portuondo, president of the Executive Committee of the Cuban assembly, urged Governor General John B. Brooke to allocate special funds to the east:

> The difference in amounts to be paid to privates . . . is based on the following considerations: the men who have served the longest are those who have suffered most and are in more need in proportion to the time they have been deprived of gaining their sustenance and that of those dependent upon them; in the Oriental Department where, in my judgment, it is more difficult to relieve the conditions of our soldiers, as there the proportion between the number of soldiers and non-combatants is greater than in other Districts, and is precisely where there is the greatest number of 1895 soldiers, and because the rural population of that region comprises two thirds of its inhabitants and its agricultural wealth has either been destroyed or injured.[16]

II The process of transition began in eastern Cuba immediately after the war, and these developments would change the east as they had transformed the west. Banditry was symptomatic of crisis, and already, as early as 1899, all signs pointed to disruption. Oriente was in transition.

Much of the postwar lawlessness assumed the form of attacks on country stores, holdups, and extortion. The larger *fincas* were attacked, and cattle rustling became widespread.[17] Banditry gave expression to mounting rural unrest in several key *municipios* in Oriente. Those experiencing the most serious lawlessness had suffered greatly in the war and were slow to recover. Holguín registered 3,260 *fincas* with a total area of 456,550 acres, of which only 14,849 were returned to cultivation in 1899. Puerto Padre counted 1,119 *fincas* of 178,721 acres, only 13,314 of which were under cultivation in 1899. Similar patterns existed in the other *municipios:* 32,355 acres out of 124,425 for the 1,205 *fincas* in Gibara; 4,885 acres out of 19,635 for the 734 *fincas* in Mayarí. These *municipios* also included some of the largest populations in the province, the result of early postwar migration: Holguín, 34,505; Manzanillo, 32,288; Gibara, 31,594; Puerto Padre, 19,984.[18]

These were the *municipios,* moreover, in which North American capital and sugar production expanded most aggressively immediately after the war. Thus, the Cuban search for land was simultaneous with the foreign acquisition of property. They arrived at the same regions at about the same time. The Cubans never had a chance.

Banditry after 1899 became uncontrolled lawlessness. Military intelligence estimated the existence of several thousand bandits operating in hundreds of small groups. In the region of Holguín, Puerto Padre, and Gibara on the north coast, the North American district commander reported in June 1899 periodic armed encounters with bandits numbering into the hundreds. Banditry flourished further east in the region of Mayarí and Baracoa, as well as in the southern zones around Manzanillo and Santiago. A total of eighty-four fugitive bands were known to operate in Oriente: fifty-two in the region of Santiago de Cuba, thirteen around Manzanillo, and nineteen near Holguín. Most bands ordinarily operated in groups of three or four, but were known to combine forces to mount major operations against large sugar estates and railroads.[19] In Holguín alone, more than 250 court cases were pending in 1899. One local judge reported, "It is certain that the increase in crime had been extraordinary this year in Holguín, as a result of the last war and the great development of brigandage in that region."[20]

"The whole country is filled with desperate characters," commented one traveller returning from the east, "many of them former officers and members of the Cuban army, who commit every outrage and who are ready for any sort of deviltry."[21]

III Responsibility for order in Cuba after 1898 passed to the United States, and from the outset, banditry cast a shadow over the occupation. Lawlessness served to prolong rural uncertainty and insecurity, thereby delaying postwar reconstruction and disrupting economic revival. That persons and property continued vulnerable to disorders into the period of North American rule had an early demoralizing effect on planters and producers. "People were afraid to go into the country," Colonel L. H. Carpenter reported from Camagüey in 1899, "and make any start with cattle or in other directions without being assured protection."[22] The army local commander at Holguín reported, "The general attitude of the people seems to be abject fear of the bandits which was alleged as the reason they could not cultivate their fields to obtain subsistence."[23] To the east, in Mayarí, a bandit band of some seventy men had, in the words of the local military chief, "reduced this section to fear."[24]

Banditry in postwar Cuba also challenged North American authority. From the outset, the United States had justified its presence in Cuba largely for the purpose of restoring order and peace to the island. President William McKinley proclaimed in his war message of April 1898 that the United States sought "to secure in the island the establishment of a stable government, capable of maintaining order and . . . insuring peace and tranquility and the security of its citizens."[25] The military occupation was also justified in the name of order. Pledged General John Brooke upon assuming power as governor general:

> I deem it proper to say that the object of the present Government is to give protection to the people, security to person and property . . . and to afford full protec-

tion in the exercise of all civil and religious rights. To this end, the protection of the United States Government will be directed, and every possible provision made to carry out these objects through the channels of civil administration . . . in the interest and for the benefit of all the people in Cuba, and those possessed of rights and property in the island.[26]

Like the Spanish before them, the North Americans were obliged to demonstrate the efficacy of their presence, both and at once as a means of justifying colonial rule and obtaining political support. Nowhere would default of that mission stand in sharper relief than in the failure to provide security to persons and property. A government committed publicly to restoring order and promoting prosperity unable to end disruption could not long expect to obtain either the confidence of producers or the collaboration of the propertied. The presence of bandits operating boldly and at will served in more than symbolic ways to undermine the credibility of U.S. administration.[27]

North American authorities responded to conditions of lawlessness early in the occupation. Like Spanish military authorities before them, U.S. commanders gave local rural guard units principal responsibility for the suppression of banditry. The rural guard met a number of needs. It was conceived originally at a time of mounting pressure to disband the Cuban army, thereby offering an ideal method through which to hasten the dissolution of the insurgent force. Cuban officers received analogous rank in the rural guard, often retaining authority over many of the same men they had commanded during the war. The rural guard was also seen as a means through which to relieve postwar employment pressure. "I deem it a matter of the utmost importance," warned General J. C. Bates from Santa Clara early in 1899, "that a system of rural guards should be organized and be in operation before the Cubans disband; and I strongly urge that we go to considerable expense to employ a large number of the Cubans as guards. . . . We should give employment to about two thousand Cubans, many of whom are in my opinion very liable to give us serious trouble unless we take care of othem."[28] General Francis V. Greene struck a similar note, and urged the establishment of a local constabulary out of the Cuban army "at the earliest possible moment, otherwise there is danger that the force may disintegrate and turn into brigands."[29]

But most of all the rural guard was designed to provide stability and security in rural Cuba. Outlawry was in the outlands, out of the easy reach of North American authority. In fact, the United States found itself oddly ill fit to discharge the very task for which it justified the occupation: rural pacification. North American troops were unacclimated to the weather, unacquainted with the terrain, uncertain about local custom, and unfamiliar with the language. Military authorities realized this early in the occupation. "Knowing the physical character of the remote parts of this Province, as I do," reported Major John A. Logan, provost marshal in Santa Clara, "I can easily see that a great amount of men and money would be necessary to apprehend the smallest band of . . . outlaws. That this can be done by our troops, is impossible; that in the end natives will have to be employed; how much easier and better to employ them in the beginning and leave no excuse for such transgressions as are bound to come from the disbanding of any great number of the present Cuban forces."[30] Leonard Wood in Santiago struck a similar note:

> The American private soldier, ignorant of the language and susceptible to all the diseases incident to the climate is not available for many duties which can be performed successfully by men speaking the language, belonging to the country and immune to the climate. The average American private soldier does not understand the customs of the people, his amusements and recreations are few, the result is many small misunderstandings with the natives, not all of them serious, but sufficient to keep up slight irritation.[31]

But there were large implications to "small misunderstandings" and "slight irritation." In early 1899, the United States found itself stalled in a frightful guerrilla war in the Philippines, and suddenly affairs in Cuba assumed a different light. Henry Adams wrote from Washington in February 1899, "The thought of another Manila at Havana sobers even an army contractor."[32] In the opinion of Senator Joseph B. Foraker, "the moment the American soldiers pull the trigger on the Cubans, if they ever do, the—well, the mischief will be to pay generally and the administration at Washington will have to pay it, and I predict there won't be funds enough for the purpose."[33] General Fitzhugh Lee in Cuba agreed: "If by accident or bad management an exchange of shots took place anywhere between the Cubans and American soldiers, resulting in many of the former falling into ranks again, the country might have a guerrilla war on its hands and our troubles multiply."[34]

Early in the occupation Cubans were assigned to the front line of rural pacification. They were familiar with the terrain and the people. But most of all, they enforced the authority of the occupation government at minimum political risk to the United States. Cubans pursued Cubans, and whatever happened in the course of that pursuit could not be attributed directly to the North Americans. "Let the Cubans kill their own rats," Wood prescribed tersely.[35] "These native regiments would embody the restless and wild spirits which have been engaged in the recent war and again, anyone at all familiar with people of this sort understands fully how much more readily and gracefully they submit to authority enforced by their own people than by a people of absolutely alien blood."[36]

IV The rural guard gave chase everywhere and, it seemed, endlessly. But the task was daunting, and it constantly strained the guard's resources and resolve. Repeatedly during the occupation, North American military advisors complained of fatigue and frustration in the rural guard. The complaint of the district commander in Holguín in 1899 was repeated with increasing frequency elsewhere: "The present force is completely run down by hard service."[37]

Early attempts to suppress banditry met with uneven success. Under the direct command of North American military advisers, the rural guard patroled interior regions, investigated complaints, and gave chase to outlaws as conditions warranted. But the arrest of bandits was one matter, prosecution quite another. Many cases never reached the courts. Complainants changed their minds, witnesses changed their stories. Friends and family of defendants let it be known that all persons party to the government case would be subject to swift reprisals, and on more than one occasion witnesses for the prosecution met violent deaths.[38] The moral was not lost: testifying against an accused bandit was all too often a fatal act. This was a moral also clear to court officials; *fiscales* and judges were also subject to threats of reprisal.

But the actions of local judicial authorities were not always motivated by fear. In the Holguín and Gibara regions, court magistrates formed part of a larger network that included local bandits and rural communities arrayed against North American authority and its armed adjunct, the rural guard. Its source was ambiguous, and its goals unclear. During the first year of the occupation, district military chiefs repeatedly complained to provincial command headquarters of the "sympathy shown and aid given the outlaws by certain civil officials."[39] "It was very difficult to obtain evidence," protested one United States military advisor in Holguín, "the reason being given that the court would soon set free the bandits who would then take revenge. . . . The mail at Holguín was at this time and has been ever since filled to overflowing, and we could not hear of any one in the Department having been tried. . . . No bandit has yet so far as I know been convicted by the Court."[40] Judge Juan A. Calderón of Holguín and his brother Agustín Calderón of Gibara were among the most conspicuous local magistrates in their defiance of U.S. authority. Their conduct was described by one officer as "reprehensible and criminal," with the added complaint: "It is notorious that Juan Calderón did release bandits from jail without trial, so that the efforts of authorities in endeavoring to put down lawlessness were for some futile."[41]

North American efforts to end rural lawlessness were often thwarted. Court magistrates frequently ordered imprisoned fugitives released for lack of evidence to convict or lack of will to prosecute. One remedy available to the U.S. officials was obvious, if admittedly only partial: dismiss the pusillanimous few who obstructed justice, and replace the fainthearted *fiscales* and magistrates with attorneys who prosecuted with vigor and judges who sentenced with vengeance. Leonard Wood did precisely this. He periodically purged judicial officials, including the Calderón brothers, who were anything less than implacable in their prosecution of bandits.

But efforts to control banditry were hampered at other points. It was not certain that the rural guard fulfilled its charge, particularly when operations involved the pursuit of former soldiers of the Liberation Army. Available field reports are scattered and incomplete, but they suggest that the rural guard was most effective when operations involved the pursuit of guerrillas, *plateados,* and deserters, and least effective when the objects of pursuit were army veterans. Rural guard Captain Wilfredo Betancourt, reporting efforts to capture bandit Enrique Mesa, a former officer in the Cuban army, addressed the issue directly: "The situation [is] critical in Manzanillo territory in the persecution of the bandit Enrique Mesa. The greater number of men in my company are very young, and the few older ones are opposed to the capture of Mesa because they think they should not capture a comrade."[42]

There was another problem: outlaws were frequently protected by the rural population. Complained Betancourt of the failure to capture Mesa: "The complete silence in which the campesino families are in is another one of the causes that make his capture almost impossible—it is impossible to get one single disclosure *(confidencia)*."[43] These conditions were encountered throughout the province during the occupation. As late as February 1902, only months before the U.S. evacuation, the rural guard chief of Oriente, Lieutenant Colonel Juan Vaillant, reported extensive popular support for bandits. To the actual number of bandit chieftains, Vaillant speculated tersely, "has to be added the vast numbers of spies or accomplices upon whom they rely."[44]

These developments underscore, too, the early estrangement between the rural guard and the rural population. The rural guard was an agent of the occupation, designed principally to meet the needs of property owners—in Wood's terms, the "producing classes." This mission defined the essential character of the Cuban armed force. It could be argued that this purpose was in the best interest of the vast numbers of small farmers, peasants, and agricultural workers who returned to the land; it was less clear that it was in the best interest of the squatters, drifters, and migrants who moved about the fringes of legality.

The rural guard represented property interests. Recruits into the rural guard, particularly the officers, were selected on the basis of social criteria, racial considerations, and ideological compatibility. From the outset, North American authorities allied the rural guard directly with property owners. Enlistment qualifications included literacy, good character, and excellent standing in the community—the latter two attributes corroborated by persons of adequate social standing. Applicants were required to provide letters of recommendation from at least two well-known citizens of good repute—"preferably property owners," stipulated the North American military advisor.[45] The military government demanded that all new recruits were expected to "present certificates of good character from individuals— preferably plantation owners; well known to be men of unquestioned integrity. . . . It would be advisable to obtain as many of the men as possible from those recommended by plantation owners as it is for the protection of rural estates and maintenance of order in rural districts that this guard is being organized."[46] Planters frequently interceded directly with the government officials to obtain the appointments and assignments of particular officers who had been uncommonly solicitous of the needs of property owners.[47]

The organization of the post system also conformed to the needs of property. Rural guard posts were often established at no expense directly on the property of large landowners. Planters provided land of sufficient size to permit drill and exercises, grazing land for livestock, free building materials, access to drinking water, construction of roads serving the detachment, and the establishment of a communications network to connect the smaller posts with provincial headquarters.[48] By 1905, the vast majority of rural guard posts were situated on private property. Of the 288 stations, only 28 were owned outright by the state. The balance was either rented privately or donated rent-free by municipalities and property interests, including the Chaparra Sugar Company, the Juraguá Iron Company, and the United Fruit Company.[49]

The rural guard also soon developed into the principal instrument of eviction of small cultivators. Across Oriente the appearance of the rural guard usually meant trouble for rural communities. They were correctly associated in the popular imagination with forced removal of peasants, farmers, and squatters. It was easy to conclude that the rural guard was in league with property interests. Indeed, that was its purpose. A social chasm of enormous proportions developed between the rural guard and the rural population. The realization that the rural guard represented interests in conflict with the best interests of farmers and peasants bound rural folk to the protection of their own interests against the armed agents of those who threatened them.[50]

V The country people's refusal to cooperate in the capture of bandits, together with the court's unwillingness to convict captured bandits, prompted North American military authorities to adopt alternative measures. It became expedient simply to murder bandits immediately upon capture, as the Spanish had done. Suspects were executed under the sanction of *ley fuga:* attempted escape thwarted by alert, and accurate, armed escorts.

Summary execution became an early feature of occupation justice in Oriente. "My authority is absolute," Wood exulted privately to his wife in late 1898, "even to life and death if I choose to use it."[51] Instructions to execute bandits at the site of capture originated at the top of the provincial command with Wood himself, if not in the form of expressed pronouncements then by way of explicit prompting. Wood proclaimed in 1899, "I issued [an order] that the brigands be brought in dead or alive, preferably dead."[52] This served, in fact, as a standing directive for district military commanders. "It looks as if bandits had quit for a time;" Captain Francis Moore instructed the U.S. advisor to the rural guard in Puerto Padre, "if such is the case, in your section let the troops and Rurales rest. If the bandits continue depredations hang all you catch, using Rurales supported by regular troops."[53] "Brigandage existed on a large scale," explained Major V. Harvard of Holguín, "under the leadership of well-known chiefs, that it was absolutely necessary to use immediate, strong and effective measures to stamp it out, that half, temporizing measures would have been worse than worthless."[54]

The rural guard served their commanders well. Recounted one traveler in Oriente in 1899:

> As soon as it becomes known that a man is a desperate character, or that he has been guilty of any outrageous offense, his name is placed upon the blacklist. This is turned over to . . . Captain Gallano, who proceeds to hunt the criminal down. Usually a machete and a pair of spurs are brought back by the gendarme as evidence that no further trouble may be expected from the parties under the ban.[55]

In his official report of 1899, Wood explained the large number of bandit deaths due to "resisting attempts to arrest them."[56] This was the official position, and was repeated frequently in field reports.[57] But it was not necessary always to justify the death of captured bandits. In remote and out of the way places, fugitives were executed and their bodies left for others to find. Thus one field report from Holguín in September 1899: "Three bandits, in addition to four of night before last, hung last night in Auras and Tunas vicinity by unknown parties."[58]

This practice of summary execution did not pass unchallenged. Local Cuban authorities often protested North American law enforcement procedures. Judge Agustín Calderón issued several summons in 1899 to the local rural guard commander to appear in court to answer for the rash of hangings in Holguín. The orders were ignored, and in-

stead Calderón was removed by the military government.[59]
Two years later, a judge in Santiago de Cuba ordered the
arrest of two rural guards for the murder of an alleged bandit.
Once more, North American military authorities thwarted
the Cuban court system. The local U.S. military advisor
appealed to the adjutant general's office in Havana: "This
action of the court will greatly injure the guard and I respect-
fully request that order of court be suspended." The court
order was ignored.[60] Tensions between the rural guard and
the courts mounted. As long as the action of the rural guard
received sanction from the military government, it was
above the law. Judicial authorities were openly critical of
the rural guard, and questioned the value of its purpose.
"The Rural Guards," complained Judge Antonio Rivero of
Holguín, "are scarcely of any service on account of their
small number; besides, they are, as a general rule, incompe-
tent and display very little zeal in the discharge of their
duties."[61] In July 1899, Judge Juan A. Calderón denounced
the "terror" in Holguín and Gibara, referring not to bandits
but to the rural guard. Calderón protested the summary
execution of prisoners, alluding specifically to an incident
involving two suspects known to have been captured alive
and murdered en route to prison.[62]

These charges worked their way to the upper reaches of
the military government. Wrote General James H. Wilson,
military governor of Matanzas: "Both [Governor General
John] Brooke and [Adjutant General Adna] Chaffee tell me
that Wood is in very deep water. They knew personally that
he has been hanging a lot of people without trial. . . . Chaffee
says that Wood told him in person that he was having
alleged *bandetti* killed without trial."[63] Wrote Brooke in
secret and guarded admission of summary executions in
Oriente:

> That brigandage existed in the Province of Santiago is
> an admitted fact; that very vigorous measures were
> necessary to suppress it, is also true; but that men
> should have been hung without due process of law,
> cannot be said to have been necessary. The hanging of
> men seems to be a fact, though there is no direct

evidence on this point, yet there seems to be little, if any doubt that it is true. There does not, however, appear to be any evidence that it was done by soldiers.[64]

These practices had long-term implications. Under the training and tutoring of North American military advisors, the newly organized Cuban rural guard learned that it was appropriate and adequate to dispense summary justice without the formality of judicial review. It was a procedure that was to give permanent character to rural justice.

6 Resisting the End

Rural property here has experienced serious modifications and many peasant families have seen their *fincas* and *pesos de posesión* disappear in the mesh of judicial nets. It is necessary to have justice, and to obey the laws, but not to trample the hapless farmer and take away from him what his grandparents transmitted to his parents and what his parents have bequeathed to him. The poor farmer has no guarantees.
—*La Lucha*, March 12, 1912

The Cuban never willingly sells his land, never sells it until necessity compels him to do so.
—H. DeLisser, *In Jamaica and Cuba*, 1910

Looking at the material life of our people, with such a large number of them poor, and with a large number of families who lost all they possessed in our desolating wars, we prefer that the lands of the State, destined today for private parties, to be in turn transferred to powerful foreign corporations, should be divided into small *fincas* and given to Cuban farmers, whether veterans or not, and thus increase our rural population, creating at the same time a new foundation of riches for the country, the strong bulwark of the nation for the moral and economic defense of our independence.
—Emilio Núñez, President, Veterans Association, 1912

I Transactions and transfer of land in Oriente proceeded rapidly during the early years of the republic. The form of land tenure was changing, so was the character of land tenants—all at once, from public to private, from minifundia to latifundia, from communal to corporate, from Cuban to foreign. Railroad construction proceeded apace, and accelerated both the transfer of land and the transformation of land use. The expansion of railroad facilities opened the interior to foreign markets, and more and more Cuban agriculture turned to production for export. As interrelated developments, the Cuba Company line connected Santiago with Santa Clara in 1900. Two years later Santiago was connected directly to Havana, completing the rail linkage of all six provinces. Provincial railroad expansion followed quickly thereafter. In 1905, Alto Cedro was connected to Nipe Bay, giving rise to the new port city of Antilla. A year later, a rail link joined Cacocún with Holguín. Rail service was also established between Martí in Camagüey east through the Cauto Valley to Bayamo, Palma Soriano, and San Luis. Shortly thereafter Bayamo was linked with Manzanillo.[1]

The process thrived on its own success. The expansion of railroads opened new land, and previously undeveloped land passed into large-scale commercial production. Sugar estates and mining expanded. Real estate speculators and land developers acquired some of the most productive properties in Cuba, and everywhere in Oriente North American agricultural colonies flourished.

An inexorable, and fateful, cycle ensued. Land along coastal zones came under the control of the sugar latifundia early. It mattered little whether it became corporate-owned land (administration cane) or *colono*-owned estates; the results were the same. Farmers and peasants were displaced, and they withdrew deeper onto the interior *sabanas* or higher into the foothills of the northern and southern mountain chains.

The case of one land litigation in Palma Soriano in early 1912 sets in relief much of what was occurring elsewhere in the province. In 1911, the Canadian Realty Company purchased from the Illinois Land Company the 10,000-acre "Paso Estancia" estate. Upon assuming possession, the Canadians discovered an estimated 300 squatters, described by the English vice-consul, W. Mason, as "a whole lot of negro squatters who had their homes but no apparent mode of living except charcoal making from the woods there." Canadian Realty obtained a local court judgment ordering their expulsion, but squatters refused to move, charging that the judge had been bribed. In early 1912, the Canadians appealed to provincial governor Rafael Manduley for assistance. Reported Mason:

> If these squatters were industrious and labouring men,
> the Company would easily settle with them to allow
> them to rent, but the whole are loafers who never do a
> day's work and live on robbery and their presence on
> the property prevents their selling their lots to any
> purchasers who know that in purchasing, he is saddled
> with three or four of these rascals who are constantly
> threatening him and stealing his produce.[2]

In early May, on the eve of widespread disorders, armed forces moved to dislodge the squatter communities from "Paso Estancia."[3]

The loss of land coincided with an increase of population, and the combination of the two portended hard times. To be sure, the effects of these developments were everywhere different. Some of the larger *municipios* were initially unaffected. But not all *municipios* in Oriente could accommodate both decreasing land supply and increasing population growth. A crisis was in the making that would eventually affect all of Oriente, but it was experienced first in the southeastern region of the province, in the cluster of the five contiguous *municipios* of Alto Songo, El Caney, Guantánamo, San Luis, and Santiago. These *municipios* were quite unlike any other region in Cuba. Nowhere else was the total percentage of the Afro-Cuban population so high. Over the two census cycles of 1899 and 1907, people of color constituted a distinct majority population:[4]

	1899	1907
Alto Songo	74.9%	71.8%
El Caney	52.8	53.1
Guantánamo	68.0	67.5
San Luis	70.6	68.9
Santiago de Cuba	57.9	55.6

Southeastern Oriente had long served as a refuge—in the late nineteenth century for runaway slaves before emancipation and free slaves afterwards, in the early twentieth century for veterans as well as victims of the war.[5] In fact, outcasts of all social types over three generations had found opportunity in the region. The *municipios* were located largely within the impenetrable high country, within or near the foothills and valleys of the Sierra Maestra mountain range—"a *terra* incognita," wrote one geographer in 1907, "unexplored, undescribed, and unmapped."[6] It was broken land, irregular, a succession of rising terraces, intersected by countless small valleys. It was also bountiful and productive.

II The province had suffered much from the war, especially the southeastern section. The central valley stretched from the Cauto in the west to Guantánamo on the east, and included the towns of Palma Soriano, San Luis, El Cristo, La Maya, Dos Caminos, and Tiguabos. Some of the most severe and sustained military operations occurred in the central valley as both armies fought for control of the principal road system of the province *(camino real)*, one of the most contested stretches of territory in the eastern campaign. For the Spanish it served as the vital corridor through which to move the provisions necessary to maintain its garrisons in southern Oriente. Its defense was central to the Spanish presence in eastern Cuba. For these reasons, it was a special object of Cuban military operations. Towns along the *camino real* were variously and routinely besieged, isolated, raided, and invaded. Much of the agriculture and ranching in the surrounding countryside ceased. The cities became wholly dependent on Spanish relief convoys. Sometimes they arrived, sometimes they did not. At the end of the war, much of the region was prostrate. Wrote the mayor of San Luis:

> The condition of this municipality in January 1900 was lamentable because many families from the country were compelled to live in the city, in the most miserable situation, not being able to commence agricultural labor, due to the absolute lack of money and

agricultural implements. In 1899 . . . there were hardly any oxen in this district. . . . About only 20 farms were under cultivation in January 1899 because all the rest were entirely destroyed by the war and the zone of cultivation was very small.[7]

For the better part of the nineteenth century, the southeastern economy had remained substantially unchanged: some sugar cultivation, some ranching, also some mining, logging, and fishing, but mostly small farming, and much of this coffee and cacao. In Alto Songo a population of 12,770 worked some 1,516 *fincas*, most of which were devoted to coffee, cacao, corn, fruits and vegetables, sugar, and pasture. In El Caney, with a population of 9,126, the majority of the 611 *fincas* registered in El Caney in 1899, and much of the farm land, was located in the zones to the north and the south, with the greater part of the latter in the foothills of the Sierra Maestra. They were devoted largely to coffee, cacao, corn, and livestock. The central regions of El Caney, specifically the towns of El Cristo, Daiquirí, and Demajayabo, were the center of iron and manganese mining dominated by the Spanish-American Iron Company and the Juraguá Iron Company. The *municipio* of Guantánamo lay almost entirely within the Guantánamo Valley, a horseshoe basin bordering on the Caribbean and enclosed on all other sides by the Sierra Maestra and Sagua-Baracoa mountain ranges. A population of 28,063 worked 1,262 *fincas*, most of which produced coffee, cacao, and sugar. The *municipio* of San Luis counted 1,289 *fincas* and a population of 45,478 engaged principally in the production of sugar, fruits, and livestock.[8]

The population surge in Oriente between 1899 and 1907 was especially pronounced in the southeast. Three of the five *municipios* registered a population growth significantly above the 40 percent total increase in the province. Alto Songo rose from 12,770 (2,814 families) to 20,553 (3,963 families), a 61 percent increase. In several towns and villages within the *municipio*, specifically Jarahueca, Loma del Gato, Socorro, and La Maya—the principal coffee and cacao zones in Alto Songo—the population almost doubled in size. The population of El Caney increased 78 percent, from 9,126 (1,743 families) to 16,215 (3,147 families). Guantánamo experienced a 54 percent increase, from 28,063 (6,596 families) to 43,300 (9,804 families). Even higher increases were recorded within the municipality, including Palma de San Juan (351 percent), Indios (279 percent), Isleta (208 percent), Sigual (180 percent), Bano (162 percent), and Caridad (123 percent). Only in San Luis and Santiago de Cuba did the population growth fail to surpass the overall provincial increase, the former increasing by 22 percent, from 11,681 (2,344 families) to 14,212 (2,990 families) and the latter 18 percent, from 45, 478 (10,292 families) to 53,614 (12,163 families).[9]

Several developments appeared to be occurring at once. After some years of declining fertility, the region experienced a sudden and spectacular increase in the birth rate. As was occurring everywhere in Cuba, stability and security returned to the lives of *orientales*. The women were released from reconcentration camps; the men returned from the army. This had particular significance in Oriente. Most of the soldiers returning to civilian life originated in the east, and it was to the east they returned, and the southeast in particular. Some towns in Alto Songo provided as much as 80 percent of their male residents to the army, comprising half the original invading column.[10] That so much of the war had been fought in the east, moreover, and that so many of the soldiers from the east had served away from home for the duration of the western campaign, combined to make both the number of marriages and births in Oriente during the war the lowest of Cuba:[11]

	Marriages	Births
1894	565	3,481
1895	368	2,144
1896	212	1,269
1897	126	811
1898	142	974

After the war, married soldiers returned to their wives, single soldiers returned to marry. A population surge soon followed. In 1899 alone, the number of marriages in Oriente increased to 471, while births reached 2,829.[12]

Fertility increased everywhere in Cuba. Between 1899 and 1907, the population under five years of age increased by 162 percent, from 130,876 to 342,652. Oriente province registered an even slightly higher increase of 164 percent, from 32,156 to 84,788. The increase in the southeastern region was also significant, with three of the *municipios* well above the national and provincial average:[13]

	1899	1907	%
Alto Songo	1,348	4,145	207.5
El Caney	644	2,793	333.6
Guantánamo	2,349	7,101	202.3
San Luis	1,115	2,824	153.3
Santiago de Cuba	3,017	7,249	140.3

These developments had one further implication. The population increase in Oriente occurred through the combination of both high fertility and low mortality. Between 1907 and 1916, Oriente province had the lowest death rate in all of Cuba, 10.07 per 1,000.[14] The most significant increases were registered within the dependent age population, specifically groups under the age of fifteen and over sixty-five. The 1907 census indicated that 40 percent of Oriente's total population (185,270 out of 455,086) was under fifteen years of age, with another 10,598 over the age of sixty-five.[15] Within the population of color, further, more than 41 percent was less than fifteen years of age (81,177 out of 196,092), and 5,669 over sixty-five.

The estimated increases by 1912 were even more telling. The average annual population increase in Oriente was approaching 16,500, while the annual death rate for these years averaged approximately 5,000. By 1912, the percentage of the total population under fifteen years of age had reached almost 50 percent (302,265 out of 608,078). The population of color registered a similar proportion, with 112,000 out of 225,000 under the age of fifteen.

The high postwar fertility meant a large number of dependents per adult. As table 9 indicates, not only did the number of families increase, but also the average size of families expanded.

III   The burgeoning postwar population added new pressures on limited resources, but most of all pressure on land. By 1907, the population density of southeastern Oriente was among the highest in Cuba. With one exception, all the *municipios* were above the national average of eighteen inhabitants per square kilometer. Santiago de Cuba counted seventy-eight inhabitants per square kilometer, San Luis twenty-nine, Alto Songo twenty-two, and El Caney twenty-one.[16]

Only Guantánamo stood below national average, with eight inhabitants per square kilometer. But other develop-

Table 9   Family Size in Southeastern Cuba, 1899 and 1907

	Persons per Family			
	1–2	*3–5*	*6–10*	*11 and over*
Alto Songo				
1899	802	1,128	719	168
1907	711	1,688	1,371	193
El Caney				
1899	428	688	475	90
1907	702	1,322	979	234
Guantánamo				
1899	2,005	2,829	1,488	164
1907	2,671	4,309	2,558	266
San Luis				
1899	527	909	747	96
1907	677	1,280	947	86
Santiago de Cuba				
1899	2,830	4,637	2,381	254
1907	3,536	5,333	2,970	324

Sources: U.S. War Dept., Office of Director of Census, *Informe sobre el censo de Cuba, 1899* (Washington, D.C.: GPO, 1900), p. 510; Cuba Under the Provisional Government of the United States, *Censo de la República de Cuba, 1907* (Washington D.C.: GPO, 1908), p. 203.

ments were transforming the largest southeastern *munici-pio*, and suggested trends elsewhere in Oriente. Everywhere in Guantánamo small farms and communal lands were disappearing. Sugar production increased and land concentration expanded.

More and more land passed under the control of fewer owners. Across the Guantánamo valley, the sugar estates consolidated control over the land. By 1912, the valley was dominated by ten sugar mills, all foreign. The "Soledad," "Isabel," and "Los Caños" were owned by the Guantánamo Sugar Company. Guantánamo Sugar, incorporated in 1905 in New Jersey, owned outright an estimated 55,000 acres of land in the *municipio*, as well as the majority stock of the Guantánamo Railroad. The "Santa Cecilia" estate was the property of the Santa Cecilia Sugar Company, which was incorporated in Maine in 1904 and owned more than 12,000 acres in Guantánamo. Other estates included the "Santa María," owned by the Santa María Sugar Company (United States); "San Miguel" and "Esperanza," property of Oriental Cubana (France): "San Antonio," owned by St. E. Montlue (France); "Confluente," property of Confluente Sugar Company (Spain); and "Romelie," owned by Brooks and Company (England).[17]

Sugar cultivation expanded everywhere in the southeast. In San Luis, older mills "Santa Ana" and "Union" and the new mill "Borjita" increased sugar production. In Alto Songo, the "Almeida" estate expanded cultivation.

The expansion of the sugar system foretold the extinction of small *fincas* and the expulsion of farmers. It was occurring in varying degrees everywhere in Oriente, but it was happening especially fast in the southeast, with the fastest rate of population growth in Cuba. The decline in the number of small *fincas* in the region was striking:[18]

	1899	*1905*
Alto Songo	1,515	477
El Caney	611	518
Guantánamo	1,262	1,154
San Luis	1,289	100
Santiago de Cuba	286	124

Between 1905 and 1911, further, the number of *fincas* in Guantánamo had declined from 1,154 to 419.[19]

The increasing population density told a similar story from another perspective and the signs were no less ominous. The peasant population was increasing, the land available for subsistence farming was decreasing. A vicious cycle ensued, one of land hunger, rising land prices, and usurious debts. More and more people were crowding onto less and less land. Every parcel of land converted to sugar production meant a corresponding loss of land available for subsistence agriculture and small-scale commercial production.

Farmers and peasants also faced the loss of livelihood. The expansion of sugar into Oriente during the early 1900s meant the introduction of cheap contract labor from the West Indies, at wages normally impossible to sustain Cuban workers and their families. Since the establishment of the republic, sugar producers had sought to use workers from neighboring islands. In 1906, the Guantánamo Sugar Company recruited 500 Puerto Rican laborers to work the cane fields.[20] Thereafter, sugar producers turned increasingly to Jamaica and Haiti. The first significant wave of Jamaicans and Haitians arrived for the 1911–1912 harvest, as 2,000 workers entered Santiago de Cuba to work on the expanding cane fields.[21]

Cuban unemployment was on the rise, in some instances dramatically. By 1907, more than 20 percent of the total male population over the age of seventeeen was unemployed. This included 16.7 percent in El Caney, 18.0 percent in San Luis, 19.2 percent in Alto Songo, 20.6 percent in Guantánamo, and a staggering 35.1 percent in Santiago.[22]

Other telling trends provide additional insight into the developing rural crisis. Between 1899 and 1907 the percentage of Afro-Cuban men engaged in agriculture declined from 40 percent to 35 percent, while the number of Afro-Cuban women was reduced to half. Both developments reflect the decline of family agriculture as the number of small *fincas* and *haciendas comuneras* disappeared. Wage employment, on the other hand, increased. These years recorded an increase in the proportion of Afro-Cuban men in manufacturing and Afro-Cuban women in domestic service.[23]

Hardship was not confined to those who lost their land. Depression occurred simultaneously with dispossession. The value of the small farmers' principal cash crops, coffee and cacao, was in decline. Low prices for cash crops reduced the ability of small farmers to meet past financial obligations or contract new ones. Many simply could not make it, and many failed. By 1911, Cuban coffee production had declined to the point where it could meet only a quarter of the local demand, the balance provided by imports from Puerto Rico.[24] The following year witnessed the lowest production of coffee at the lowest prices in a decade.[25]

At the same time, consumer prices were rising. Farmers' earnings were diminishing, while the cost of life was increasing. By 1912, the price of basic foodstuffs had reached an eight-year high, increasing an average of 60 percent since 1904, as shown in table 10. The income on which households were required to subsist was becoming increasingly inadequate. Despair stalked rural families as men failed to discharge their responsibilities as providers.[26]

Even nature seemed to conspire against the hapless farmer. In 1909 and 1910 a series of devastating hurricanes battered the island, causing extensive damage to agricul-

Table 10   Price of Basic Foodstuffs in Cuba, 1904 and 1912

	1904	1912
Rice	$ 3.00	$ 4.70
Lard	10.50	17.85
Salt	1.94	2.63
Flour	6.88	7.67
Chick peas	7.86	8.60
Beans	3.85	4.75
Peas	4.80	5.55
Olive oil	8.00	12.50
Vermicelli	4.50	5.25

Source: Cuba Review 10 (October 1912), 16.

ture. A drought followed, and caused further havoc. "And now the countryside is nearly impoverished," commented one local observer.[27] The outlook was bleak. "The drought has prevented the raising of small crops," reported the U.S. minister in April 1910, "and it seems certain that there will be a good deal of real destitution during the coming summer. All this will contribute to a general discontent."[28]

The size of peasant plots was dwindling and the *haciendas comuneras* were disappearing. The implications were clear: the next generation would be landless. In the course of a very short space of time, Cubans of color were experiencing a sudden and steep descent into destitution. They faced the grim prospect of ending in worse conditions than those in which their parents began. The loss of self-sufficiency portended the default of a promise. Generations of Afro-Cubans had found land and livelihood in the east. They were confronted not simply with the failure to fulfill their expectations, but with the forfeiture of expectations fulfilled. Afro-Cubans were facing the collapse of their world, and they had nowhere else to go.

IV Developments in southeastern Oriente were simultaneous with mounting and related discontent elsewhere. The deteriorating condition of people of color in Oriente was not dissimilar to that experienced by all Afro-Cubans. They had not fared well in the new republic. In fact, in many cases, their condition had actually deteriorated. Their contribution to the cause of Cuba Libre was well out of proportion to their numbers, but their compensation from free Cuba was disproportionately low. They had been promised political equality and social justice, but received neither. "During the colonial days of Spain," Arthur A. Schomburg wrote during a visit to Cuba in 1905, "the Negroes were better treated, enjoyed a greater measure of freedom and happiness than they do to-day. Many Cuban Negroes curse the dawn of the Republic. Negroes were welcomed in the time of oppression, in the time of hardship, during the days of the revolution, but in the days of peace . . . they are deprived of positions, ostracized and made political outcasts. The Negro has done much for Cuba. Cuba has done nothing for the Negro."[29]

The effects were striking. Afro-Cubans were underrepresented in elected office, and appointed positions, the armed forces, and the civil service. Cubans of color made up 30 percent of the total population, approximately 610,000 out of 2 million. Census information in 1907 is only suggestive concerning the status of Afro-Cubans in the public life of the republic, but it suggests a consistent pattern. Three census categories clearly identifiable as public positions were teachers, soldiers and policemen, and government functionaries *(funcionarios de gobierno)*. Cubans of color were underrepresented in each:[30]

	Whites (Cubans & Foreigners)	Cubans of Color	%
Teachers	5,524	440	7.9
Soldiers and policemen	6,520	1,718	26.3
Government functionaries	194	11	5.6

In all three categories, foreign whites (828 teachers, 1,135 soldiers and policemen, and 68 government functionaries) numbered nearly as many or more than Afro-Cubans.

A profound sense of betrayal settled over the Afro-Cuban community. Black political leaders had initially joined the established political parties. Although individual Afro-Cuban politicians achieved some notable success, conditions never improved for blacks in general. Appeals to white political leaders and elected officials fell on deaf ears. As early as 1902, Afro-Cuban political leaders met with new President Tomás Estrada Palma to protest the shabby treatment of blacks in the new government. The small number of blacks in the rural guard and police, Generoso Campos Marquetti complained, and the discrimination of blacks in the civil departments of government, underscored the neglect "towards a race that had valiantly spilled its blood in defense of the Cuban cause." "The truth is, Mr. President," he protested, "this is not what we expected from the Revolution and things can not continue like this."[31]

In 1907, several ranking black political leaders took the first step toward a portentous political realignment. They withdrew from the established political party system to organize a new movement, first in the form of the Agrupación Independiente de Color and later into a full-fledged political party, the Partido Independiente de Color. The new party advocated honest government, improved working conditions, and free university education. But its principal concerns centered on issues of race, specifically demands for increased representation of Afro-Cubans in elected office and public positions, including the armed forces, the diplomatic corps, the judiciary, and all civil departments of government.

The formation of the Partido Independiente de Color challenged the existing parties for control of the black vote. This challenge was particularly serious to the ruling Liberal party, for its status as a majority party depended directly on the Afro-Cubans' support. The Liberal administration of José Miguel Gómez (1908–1912) did not hesitate. In 1911, the government enacted the Morúa Law, a measure designed to outlaw the organization of political parties along racial lines.[32]

V Political tensions mounted, social discontent deepened. The Partido Independiente de Color directed attention to a wide range of injustices. Afro-Cuban political grievances reminded all Cubans of color that race was as much an unsettled issue in the republic as it had been in the colony. But Afro-Cuban political objectives found little endorsement and less enthusiasm among vast numbers of people of color in Oriente. The effort at political organization in Oriente was short-lived and ill-starred. Most of the 200,000 people of color in Oriente, approximately 40 percent of the electorate, looked on indifferently. Indeed, the *independientes* failed to secure even the minimum number of signatures required to nominate candidates in the 1908 provincial elections.[33]

In fact, the source and substance of Afro-Cuban grievances in the republic were varied; significant social distinctions existed within the population. The new party tended to represent the interests of Afro-Cuban politicians, former ranking officers of the Liberation Army, professionals, and intellectuals, generally representatives of black petite bourgeoisie—those Cubans who aspired to gain entree into the political system, through either elected positions or appointed posts. The *independientes* directed their attention to institutional racism, to formal practices of racial discrimination that obstructed their participation in the public life of the republic they had helped create. The party charter addressed itself almost exclusively to political matters; it addressed grievances to government authorities and the leaders of the ruling political parties.

These were issues of only marginal concern to Oriente's Afro-Cuban farmers, peasants, and rural workers. At the time of the party's formation, they were in serious crisis and preoccupied with urgent matters of survival. It was not that they were unsympathetic, but their lives were in disarray, their communities in despair. Lawlessness was on the increase, announcing the onset of social disintegration. "There exists at Guantánamo, and the surrounding country," reported the U.S. consul at Santiago, Ross E. Holaday, "a state of lawlessness that is calculated to cause considerable apprehension among the good citizens." Traveling through Guantánamo in 1910, Holaday learned that resident foreign businessmen had "received letters demanding money, and threatening to burn their property, or take their lives, or that of some member of their family, if they refused to comply with the demands of the unknown writer."[34]

Disorders in 1912 coincided with the onset of the *tiempo muerto*, and the immediate sources of the disturbances were no less compelling than the long-term ones. In a very real sense, they were the same. The peasants and farmers were losing their sources of livelihood even as they lost their claims on the land. It was not only that there was no work during the *tiempo muerto*; there was no adequate work during the harvest, traditionally the time of full employment. *Tiempo muerto* had always brought on hard times, but times got harder as the opportunity for subsistence agriculture declined. The U.S. minister wrote fully two years before the uprising, "The result is that when the crop is over there are many idle persons left in the country districts with practically no means of support. The majority of these are improvident negroes, not well to do at any time, but especially 'hard-up this year.' "[35]

VI Disorders broke out sometime in May.[36] Newspaper accounts in 1912 were not clear, but what was certain was that conditions had intensified. Disorders were no longer sporadic and short-lived incidents, but more akin to spontaneous and sustained outbursts of collective despair.

The uprising began as an armed movement designed to force the Gómez administration to repeal the Morúa law. The purpose of the *independiente* leadership was never clearly defined or well publicized. In a published newspaper interview in late May, party leaders Evaristo Estenoz and Pedro Ivonet announced their intention to provoke U.S. intervention as a means to topple the Liberal government if the Gómez administration refused to abrogate the Morúa law. "They want equal rights with whites," the correspondent concluded tersely, "or they will put an end to the Republic."[37]

But the movement quickly became something larger. Political grievances ignited social protest. They were not unrelated, but they were separate. Afro-Cuban politicians demanded a place in the republic, and mobility. Afro-Cuban peasants demanded a place on the land, and permanence. Not for unrelated reasons, they were failing at both. But the origins of these grievances in 1912 were sufficiently distinct as to make the sources of rebellion different.

The uprising, such as it was, lasted through the early part of the summer. It spread swiftly—spontaneously, it seemed. Disturbances occurred in every province of the island, but they were the most extensive in Oriente, chiefly in the southeast. The rebellion spread rapidly by word of mouth from town to town, without the separate bands concerting a common action. Many of the original insurgents were party rank and file.[38] Their political grievances were real, and by 1912 despair and frustration ran deep and wide among the *independientes*. But the party rank and file were not the only participants, nor even the majority. The uprising baffled observers: no pronouncements, no proclamations, no palpable purpose. "It [is] highly improbable," commented U.S. Minister Arthur M. Beaupré in May, "that the negroes at the head of the Independent Colored Party would be capable of engineering a movement of this scale. The negroes now in revolt are of a very ignorant class."[39] Several weeks later, Beaupré wrote again: "I can only say that the entire situation is surrounded by a pronounced element of mystery. It is quite impossible to determine who is responsible for the present movement, what are the intentions of the negro leaders or what danger there is of disturbance in Havana and other provinces."[40]

It soon became apparent that this was no simple political disorder. Something more was stirring. One North American military observer discerned an important distinction between the *independientes* in arms and other Afro-Cubans in the field. The disturbance in Alto Songo, Major Henry C. Davis reported in June, was caused "by small bands of men whom it appears difficult to identify as revolutionists; they are acting rather as outlaws and I am of the opinion they are nothing but bands organized to steal."[41] The U.S. consul in Santiago had a better understanding of the character of the uprising, and its implications. Wrote Ross E. Holaday:

> That there is much danger to be apprehended on account of the present disturbed political condiiton admits of no doubt because, however good may have been the intentions of the leaders of this movement not to destroy or take life, the mere fact that their thousands of irresponsible followers are continually obliged to live by pillaging and to continually evade authorities of the law will, if allowed to continue, result in anarchy and a complete overthrow and derogation of organized society under the law throughout the province. The leaders will not be able to control them or their actions for any considerable period of time and they will not hesitate in a short time to destroy property.[42]

What occurred in eastern Cuba in 1912 was only marginally related to the armed movement organized by the Partido Independiente de Color. The *independiente* protest set in motion a larger protest, and the countryside was set ablaze. Disorders quickly assumed the proportions of a peasant jacquerie: an outburst of rage and the release of a powerful destructive fury directed generally at the sources and symbols of oppression. As a genre of peasant movements, the jacquerie of 1912 possessed a formless and desultory character. It was a popular outburst, born of social distress and directed not at government but at local social groups, committed to the destruction of the new order of things and the restoration of traditional ways. They rebelled against specific conditions and local sources of abuse. They were without a program of reform, without defined policy, without organization, without formal leadership.[43]

The protest gave expression to collective rage, and for all its spontaneity and apparent ambiguity of purpose, it was not without method. The yearning for the old ways was the source for the destruction of the new ones. It was an outcry against injustice, and sought at once to destroy the dispossessors and expel the expropriators immediately, in one surge of violence and destruction. They attacked property, especially foreign holdings, mostly sugar property.

These were veterans of the war of liberation: they had once before waged successful war with fire, and they used it with great effect. "It is daily becoming more apparent," reported the U.S. consul in Santiago, "that those in revolt are not insurgents but incendiaries who may destroy in an hour property representing millions of dollars in value and that has taken years to construct."[44] All principal sugar mills in Guantanamo reported damages. Nearly $100,000 worth of standing cane on the "Esperanza" estate was destroyed. The "Santa Cecilia" mill reported extensive damage to the company railroad lines. The "Limones" estate was torched and 2,500 tons of cane went up in smoke. The "Romelie" mill was attacked several times. Several buildings of the "Confluente" mill complex were destroyed. The manager of Fidelity Commercial and Trading Company in Guantánamo reported, "[The rebels are] burning up our cane, buildings, stealing our horses and cattle and sacking three of our stores."[45]

Property was attacked everywhere in Oriente. Company stores were sacked and livestock stolen. Railroads made easy targets; tracks were destroyed, rail bridges were burned, railroad stations were razed.[46] Trains were halted and held up, sometimes derailed first. Telegraph wires and telephone lines were cut. Mining companies were attacked.[47] The larger coffee estates were torched, such as the "Olimpo" *cafetal* in Alto Songo.

Country stores, the *bodegas* and *cantinas*, largely Spanish-owned, also suffered high losses. Spaniards were the merchants and shopkeepers, and collectively this rural burgher class took in 70 percent of the wages paid to local laborers. As local financial agents, lending money and providing credit, they frequently charged usurious interest and moved easily into the supporting role of villain as mounting indebtedness pushed peasants and workers ineluctably into indigence. One traveler of Spanish merchants wrote in 1911, "They are money-lenders in the small districts and furnish the farmers, at exorbitant rates of interest, with the means of raising and marketing their crops."[48] Perceived as one more source and symbol of oppression, rural *bodegas* and *cantinas* were plundered everywhere. Shops and stores were sacked in Guantánamo, San Luis, Santiago, La Maya, El Caney, Alto Songo, El Cobre, Daiquirí, Palma Soriano, and Holguín. The attackers made off with money, machetes, tools, arms and ammunition, clothing, supplies, and food, then razed the shops.[49]

The insurrectionary torch was also applied to towns and villages: the towns of La Maya and Jarahueca in Alto Songo were all but totally destroyed. Insurgents sacked Caney del Sitio in the *municipio* of Palma Soriano, razing a good part of the village and seizing and estimated $100,000 in money and merchandise. Palma Soriano, San Luis, and El Cobre were threatened more than once.

The attacks against the towns were not solely for plunder, and property was not attacked randomly. A far more important purpose impelled the insurgents; farmers and peasants had lost their lands in litigation in the courts and had been bested by documents and depositions. The new order of things was duly recorded in municipal registries, and every successful incursion into municipal centers resulted in the destruction of the local archives and records offices. They fell upon public records purposefully, and not as wanton acts of destruction. At every opportunity, public buildings were razed. It was a particular type of destruction, and together the acts suggested method and meaning. The gesture was at once symbolic and substantive, an instrumental act designed to destroy the documents that had despoiled them of their lands. The burning of deeds, surveys, and titles served as more than an outlet for pent-up frustration. Also, and quite rationally, it destroyed the documentary evidence of the new order of things. The first building destroyed in La Maya was the land registry office. The archives of Tacamara, San Juan, and Bijarú in the *municipio* of Holguín were destroyed. The records of San Ramón de las Yaguas in El Caney were saved only because a local judge had removed the documents before the destruction of the registry office.[50]

Reports from the disaffected regions underscored the economic sources of the disturbances. "Whatever may have been the immediate object of the threatened uprising of the blacks," reported one North American naval officer, "its real cause was due to the existing economic condition of the blacks."[51] One marine brigade commander arrived at a similar conclusion, if in slightly different terms: "So called rebels [are] malcontents and men out of employment, fighting in order to loot and riot without cause or justification."[52]

An estimated 10,000 Afro-Cubans participated in the uprising, largely in southeastern Oriente province. The assault was against property, not persons. The Cuban press, for all its lurid accounts of the "race war," attributed few deaths to insurgents. Rebels did not engage government troops; on the contrary, they sought to avoid all contact with the army. The insurgents, *La Lucha* editorialized as late as June 27, "have limited themselves to fleeing every time they see a glimpse of the yellow [army] uniform, without offering even one serious battle."[53] At another point, *La Lucha* accurately if unwittingly underscored the character of disorders.:

Robbery, looting, and fire are the weapons with which they fight; that is to say that it is a war against property and private wealth, not a war for a political ideal nor to overturn a government: . . . across all parts, rural shops and stores sacked and burned, bridges destroyed, and sugar mills under the power of the torch of the rebels who exact money under the threat of death and destruction.[54]

The extent of the popular support given to the insurgents is not clear. Not a few observers believed they enjoyed widespread sympathy from the noncombatant population.[55] The U.S. minister reported learning that "many of the so-called peaceful elements are in more or less open sympathy with the rebels and may at times join forces with them."[56] "Given the enormous extension of the vast zone," *La Lucha* reported in June, "the most dangerous insurgents are not those in the woods, but those who are pacific in the villages, who by day gather intelligence concerning the movement of the armed forces, pass it on to the insurgents, and by night join them to plunder and pillage."[57] The Cuban army command apparently concurred, and in early June, the government suspended constitutional guarantees for all of Oriente and ordered all noncombatants out of disaffected zones.[58] Reconcentration camps reappeared in Oriente. For the second time in two decades, thousands of peasant families were forcefully removed from the countryside, and contending forces lay siege to the productive capabilities of the land. The parallel was not lost on Theodore Brooks, the English vice-consul in Guantánamo: "The methods employed by the Cuban military against the Negroes far exceed in severity and cruelty those employed by General Weyler, of which the Cubans complained so bitterly when used against them."[59]

VII Order was restored at a terrible cost. In late May, the United States landed marines in Oriente province to protect North American property. Released from the responsibility of garrison duty, the Cuban army undertook a ruthless pacification. The armed forces killed indiscriminately: by decapitation, by hanging, and by firing squads. Military authorities let it be known, one observer in Palma Soriano reported, that the army "was cutting off heads, pretty much without discrimination, of all negroes found outside the new town limits."[60] "They have lopped off the heads of probably some six thousand negroes in this province," reported one North American resident in Guantánamo, "and the rest as a whole have had the fear of God drilled into their souls."[61] "It is reported by parties coming from San Luis," cabled the U.S. consul from Antilla, "that prisoners falling into the hands of the government forces are shot down or beheaded unmercifully without any form of trial, my information being that not a single prisoner was allowed to escape alive at that place."[62] British vice-consul Brooks in Guantánamo described similar conditions as late as July: "During the last two weeks the Government campaign had degenerated into a hunt of defenseless Negroes and a very large number of the latter have been virtually assassinated, being dragged from their homes and cut to pieces with machetes, or shot."[63] One navy officer later reported:

> Since the withdrawal of the constitutional guarantees several negroes . . . have been hanged, presumably by the soldiers, but no one believes that these negroes were really rebels. As a rule the bodies are left hanging to the trees, or left lying by the roadside, no effort being made to bury them or to fix the responsibility for the executions. The execution of innocent negroes may have served the purpose of intimidating the disaffected ones.[64]

When it was all over, the final casualties revealed the magnitude of the carnage: murder, massacres, and mass graves everywhere in Oriente. Race and gender converged in deadly combination: black men were killed summarily.[65] Nor were security forces inclined to make distinctions between black Cubans and black foreigners. Scores of Haitian contract workers also fell victim to government repression.[66] Few prisoners were taken, and only in the larger

provincial towns. The government reported modest casual-
ies: two rural guards dead, a few wounded.[67] By the end of
the summer, peace returned to Oriente. Just in time, too, for
preparations for the 1912–1913 *zafra* were about to begin.

7 Farewell to Hope

There in the jungles of Oriente, father was my teacher. . . . I was his assistant in healing the sick and wounded. Haitians and Jamaicans would come to us with terrible machete wounds, inflicted as they fought to open breaches in the forests. . . . That was when we lived in the house of cedar, and the mountains burned to make way for sugar, and the beat of the bongos came to us from the immigrants' shacks.
                    —Teresa Casuso, *Cuba and Castro,* 1961

From the height of Turquino peak [Sierra Maestra], Oriente appears as if it were one immense canefield.
          —Carlos Martí, *Films cubanos. Oriente y Occidente,* 1915

A fire set by incendiaries broke out yesterday in the canefields of the American Sugar Company plantation near Baire and about 1 million *arrobas* of sugar cane were destroyed. Various burnt candles were found scattered over the field, thus demonstrating beyond any doubt that the fire was an incendiary one.
                    —*The Havana Post,* February 22, 1914

We were so poor there were days we didn't eat. . . . Our problem was that we had no land to work and no way of making a living. Things were so bad for us that my folks migrated from place to place in search of a way to better their situation. . . . We kept wandering over highways and byways for almost a year trying to find a place to make a living. . . . But we had nothing. It was desperation that drove my folks on, looking for somebody to give them a piece of land.
                    —Armando Cárdenas, *Neighbors,* 1978

The events of 1912 were portents, stirrings of discontent everywhere on the increase. They announced the approaching end of a way of life, not only for Afro-Cuban peasants in Oriente, but for all peasants in Oriente. A decade after independence, eastern Cuba was undergoing rapid social and economic change. It was not occurring everywhere at once. A variety of diverse agricultural activities survived into the twentieth century, and although the sugar latifundia had expanded their control over land, traditional tenure forms persisted. Coffee *fincas,* cacao farms, tobacco *vegas,* ranches, banana fields, fruit and vegetable farms and forests flourished in different regions of the province. So did *comuneros,* renters, private farmers, and squatters.

This was changing, although the events of 1912 suggested that change had affected some districts and some Cubans much more adversely than others. Grievances were not clearly articulated, only acted out, and the meaning of those actions was left to others to explain. The explanations advanced at the time, as well as later, failed to appreciate adequately the sources of events or interpret their significance correctly. The issue of race blurred the meaning of the uprising. The uprising of 1912 was seen as one in a series of many political protests in the early republic. Class was subordinated to race, the social was eclipsed by the political. Even sympathetic renderings did little more than to put a more favorable light on the same story line.

The emphasis on race had one other effect, if not function. The portrayal of the uprising as the work of disgruntled black politicians and, concomitantly, the view that the protest was a race war, served to divide the peasantry along racial lines. The rebels were mainly black, but it was not clear that the source of the rebellion was entirely racial. Not that the issue of race was unimportant—on the contrary, the *independientes'* protest underscored the fact that growing numbers of dispossessed peasants were of the same race. And, indeed, with the preponderance of people of color in southeastern Oriente facing indigence, it was not unreasonable for many to perceive race as the source of their plight. It also offered a basis of unity for black peasants. However, Cuban authorities also had compelling motives to represent the uprising as a race war. The view of the protest as a *guerra de razas* gained currency, then and thereafter. The construct served to unify the white majority across class lines. It set black peasants apart from white peasants and facilitated repression. The conditions that drove black peasants to rebel in 1912 were present everywhere in Oriente. However, perception of the uprising principally as a *guerra de razas* directed by the Partido Independiente de Color allowed white peasants to interpret the dispute as a political one and the cause a racial one—neither one of which had very much to do with them. Far-reaching changes were overtaking eastern Cuba. Although it was not immediately apparent, 1912 was the first collective response to those changes.

II War broke out in Europe in August 1914, and immediately the rich European beet fields were transformed into the desolate battlefields of the western front. Beet sugar production collapsed. Between 1914 and 1918, the international supply of beet sugar declined almost by half, from 8.3 million tons in 1914, to 5.8 million tons in 1916, and 4.4 million tons two years later.[1] The decrease in the world supply of sugar led to an increase in sugar prices: 2.05 cents per pound in 1914, 2.74 in 1915, up to 3.41 in 1915, and 4.74 in the following year.[2]

Almost fifty years after European producers had reaped the benefits of war in Cuba, Cuban producers turned war in Europe to their advantage. International conditions served once more as a powerful incentive for the expansion of Cuban production, and the most promising site for this was the east. Certainly it was rich land. "Western Cuba, old, tired out," Manuel Rionda reported to his New York office, "lands are not as good as Eastern new lands."[3] Moreover, nowhere else in Cuba was more land available for new production. New sugar companies, largely North American, appeared across the eastern provinces. Old estates, *haciendas comuneras,* and family farms passed into sugar cultivation. Larger producers absorbed smaller ones. Mills expanded at the expense of small *colonos.* Large *colonos* expanded at the expense of smaller farmers and peasants.[4]

Consolidation of sugar properties placed more and more land under increasingly fewer owners. As early as 1912, the Atlantic Fruit Company began sugar production on some 40,000 acres of newly acquired land along the north coast.

The Santa Cecilia Sugar Company and the Guantánamo Sugar Company expanded their operations in the southeast. In 1914, the Manatí Sugar Company inaugurated operations with the acquisition of 76,500 acres of sugar land and fifty-one miles of railroad. Two years later, the International Commercial Company acquired more than 33,000 acres near Paso Real. The Cuba Cane Sugar Corporation launched by far the most ambitious enterprise of the period. Organized in 1916, Cuba Cane did not establish new mills but assumed direction over and consolidated management of existing estates. Within a year, Cuba Cane had acquired seventeen fully equipped mills, owning outright 353,000 acres and leasing on a long-term basis an additional 194,000 acres. In 1916, the Cuban-American Sugar Company acquired some 325,000 acres, eight sugar mills, two refineries, and 225 miles of railroad. The United Fruit Company added an estimated 100,000 acres to its holdings on the Oriente coast. The Nipe Bay Company increased its holding by 127,000 acres. In Niquero, the New Niquero Sugar Company rounded out its expansion at 31,000 acres while leasing an additional 9,000.[5]

Cane fields spilled out of the traditional sugar regions of the west and into new land in the east. In 1899, sugar cultivation in Oriente accounted for approximately 69,000 acres of land. By 1918, an estimated 825,750 acres were planted with cane, and another 2.3 million acres held in corporate reserve.[6]

The movement eastward began during the U.S. occupation and gained momentum in the years thereafter. The Reciprocity Treaty of 1903 gave producers in Cuba a guaranteed market in the United States at preferential tariff rates. The expansion in the east after 1903 was nothing less than spectacular. Old mills were reorganized, new mills were organized, but most of all new fields of cultivation expanded. In 1899 the three eastern provinces had the lowest percentage of area owned by *fincas* and the smallest percentage under cultivation. (See table 11.) Between 1899 and 1918, a total of two new mills were established in the west one in Pinar del Río and one in Havana. During the same years, a total of forty-two new mills commenced operations in the

eastern provinces: seven in Santa Clara, fifteen in Camagüey, and twenty in Oriente. Of the thirty-five new mills in
Camagüey and Oriente, a total of twenty-four were North
American.[7] The effects were telling. Table 12 shows that the
expansion of sugar production in the east increased dramatically both in absolute tonnage and as the percentage of the
total Cuban output. Even as the western producers increased their production more than twofold, their share of
the total output decreased to less than one-third. The total
percentage of the eastern provinces conceals the spectacular
increase in Camagüey and Oriente, whose share of total
output for these years increased from 2.71 percent to 19.82
percent, and 13.55 percent to 24.18 percent, respectively.
Within two decades, Camagüey and Oriente accounted for
almost half of the island's total output.

During these years, the largest available reserves of public
land passed into sugar production. Miles of rich timber
forests were wantonly leveled to increase the acreage of
sugar cultivation: by logging, by fire, by dynamite—by
whatever way was quickest. Cuban production of cedar and
mahogany declined dramatically, from 10.4 million feet and
10.2 million feet in 1914 to 561,000 and 161,000 in 1919. The
total value of Cuban timber exports declined from $1.2
million in 1914 to $17,083 in 1919.[8] "All the trees have been
removed ruthlessly," Irene Wright commented of Nipe Bay
Company operations in Mayarí, "and, in some cases obvi-
ously unnecessarily, till cane fields cover the country like a

Table 11   Agriculture in Cuba, 1899

	% in Farms	% Under Cultivation
Havana Province	45.6	5.8
Matanzas	41.4	6.6
Pinar del Río	33.8	4.3
Santa Clara	30.6	4.0
Camagüey	29.2	.4
Oriente	22.0	2.4

Source: U.S. War Dept., Office of Director of Census, *Informe sobre el
censo de Cuba, 1899* (Washington, D.C.: GPO, 1900), p. 554.

smooth unwrinkled blanket."[9] Teresa Casuso recalled these years in Oriente a long time later:

> I remember, in Oriente, the great impenetrable forests that were set aflame, whole jungles that were fired and razed to the ground to make way for the sugar cane. My parents were in despair for that lost wealth of beautiful, fragrant tropical wood—cedar and mahogany and mastic, and magnificent-grained pomegranate—blazing in sacrifice to the frenzy to cover the countryside with sugar cane. In the nights the sight of that flaming horizon affected me with a strange, fearful anxiety, and the aroma of burning wood down from so far away was like the incense one smells inside churches.[10]

Much to the bewilderment and confusion of rural communities, small landowners, farmers, and peasants found themselves subjected to a new round of displacement and dispossession. The eastward expansion of the zones of sugar cultivation adversely affected all other forms of agriculture in Oriente. The value of cane land soared. Property selling for $250 per *caballería* in 1914 sold for $1,000 in 1916.[11] This created impossible conditions for small cultivators, especially coffee and cacao producers. Capital was scarce. Banks refused to extend credit to coffee growers, except under usurious rates of interest often as high as 5 percent monthly. The results were not long in coming. Coffee and cacao farms

Table 12   Sugar Production in Cuba, 1901–1918

	Western Provinces		Eastern Provinces	
	Pinar del Río Havana Matanzas	% of Total	Santa Clara Camagüey Oriente	% of Total
1902	449,518	44.94	550,747	55.06
1906	610,317	42.65	820,674	57.35
1912	924,534	37.86	1,517,446	62.14
1918	1,251,290	31.19	2,720,541	68.81

Source: José R. Alvarez Díaz, et al., *A Study on Cuba* (Coral Gables, Fla.: University of Miami Press, 1965), p. 234.

failed, and ultimately passed into sugar production. As early as 1914, the Association of Coffee Producers in Santiago predicted the failure of fully two-thirds of the 2,000 farms in Oriente.[12] Producers' worst fears were proven wrong—the collapse was worse than they had anticipated. By 1919, coffee *fincas* had decreased to less than 200.[13] Coffee and cacao production had totally ceased in nine Oriente *municipios*, including Santiago de Cuba, Mayarí, Holguín, Banes, Gibara, Puerto Padre, Victoria de las Tunas, Campechuela, and Niquero. Coffee plantations, such as "El Olimpo" in Alto Songo and others in Palma Soriano, were attached directly to sugar plantations.[14] Pasture lands, too, were converted to sugar. Peasants and farmers were being eliminated faster than at any time in living memory. The decline in the number of *fincas* in Oriente was striking. The available data are incomplete, but what there is suggests the magnitude of the collapse of independent farms. Between 1899 and 1905, the total number of *fincas* in Oriente diminished by almost half. In some *municipios*, as shown in table 13, the decline was calamitous. This trend gained momentum in the years that followed. The 594 *fincas* in Bayamo in 1905 dwindled to 280 in 1911. During the same period, the 1,154 *fincas* in Guantánamo were reduced to 419; the 2,113 *fincas* in Holguín declined to 639.[15] Those who clung to farming were driven to search for new land deeper in the inhospitable mountain reaches rimming the province, away from traditional transportation routes and local agricultural markets.[16]

Everywhere in Oriente the *hacienda comunera* was disappearing. Within a decade of independence, the vast majority of communal lands had been consolidated into private estates. Between 1903 and 1905, a total of 120 *haciendas* were in various stages of reorganization.[17] In 1907, all the 30 *haciendas comuneras* registered in Holguín were tied up in judicial surveys preliminary to reorganization, as were the communal properties of Puerto Padre, Gibara, and Mayarí. "There is every reason for believing," one real estate broker wrote in 1907, "that within the next four years all the land within this province of Santiago de Cuba will be held in private ownership."[18] In 1914, one traveler through Oriente denounced as a "national shame" the despoiliation of peasant lands:

> The land is owned in common. The cultivators do not have an exact notion of their property rights, nor of the extension of their property, nor of its value, nor of a way to ratify their claims. Among those peasants backwardness is institutionalized. Their language has traces of speech centuries old, that goes back to the era of the *conquistadores*. In that indomitable and wild region man must struggle constantly to produce anything more than the daily necessities of life. And it is

Table 13 *Fincas* in Oriente, 1899 and 1905

	1899	1905
Alto Songo	1,515	447
Baracoa	2,110	1,346
Bayamo	1,373	594
Campechuela	321	n.a.
El Caney	611	518
El Cobre	1,253	606
El Cristo	19	n.a.
Gibara	1,205	543
Guantánamo	1,262	1,154
Holguín	3,260	2,113
Jiguaní	863	681
Manzanillo	2,033	1,086
Mayarí	734	274
Niquero	265	n.a.
Palma Soriano	1,404	453
Puerto Padre	1,119	585
Sagua de Tánamo	1,289	100
Santiago	286	124
Total	21,550	10,854

Sources: See U.S. War Dept., Office of Director of Census, *Informe sobre el censo de Cuba, 1899* (Washington, D.C.: GPO, 1900), pp. 572; Cuba, Provincia de Oriente, *Memoria sobre el estado de la provincia y sobre los trabajos realizados por el gobierno y el consejo provinciales durante el año fiscal de 1904 a 1905* (Havana: Librería e Imprenta "La Moderna Poesía," 1906), p. 167.

clear that the *oriental* mountain man is in no condition to contest more intelligent persons, who live in the cities, and are rapidly appropriating all the national territory.[19]

In some zones the loss of land was virtually total. Not only did they lose land sufficient to live off, they lost land adequate to die on. Years later a longtime resident of Mayarí recalled the early years of the United Fruit Company:

> Those were the days when people were run off their own lands—though they had papers dating back to colonial days to show it was theirs—because corrupt officials would sell the land to La United. They began their measurements of huge tracts with just a millimeter off at the start, but when the line was extended to a distance that little millimeter widened out to become whole towns and farms. You may ask yourself what a pass we had come to that eventually we had to beg La United for a tiny bit of land to have a cemetery![20]

The war in Europe dealt small farmers and rural workers one last blow: it disrupted Cuban exports to European markets, particularly to Germany. The effects were felt first in the tobacco sector, as the collapse of the market for Cuban cigars plunged the industry into crisis. But tobacco was not alone. A large number of smaller agricultural activities suffered, visiting new hardship on all rural communities. The United States consul in Manzanillo reported in 1915, "As the war has fully stopped all shipments to Europe of those commodities exported to German markets, such as tobacco, honey, bee's wax, palma leaf and woods, the consequence is direful for the people in the interior whose main support consisted in the sales of these staples to the country merchant who, in turn, sold them to the exporters in this city."[21]

III Dislodged as independent farmers, an entire sector of the population found itself also displaced as a labor force. They were losing their land and their livelihood to foreigners. It began early in the century, and it never let up. Competition for jobs intensified. Some of this was the result of rising population pressures, but more was due to the importation of cheap foreign labor. Vast resources of the province passed under the control of foreign capitalists determined to depress wages and maintain a cheap labor market. The three principal sources of employment—sugar, railroads, and mining—all resorted to low-paid foreign workers, either in the form of seasonal contract laborers or permanent settlers. In 1901, the Cuba Company dispatched agents to Venezuela and Spain for the purpose of "inducing and assisting" 2,000 workers to emigrate to Cuba to work on railroad construction.[22] Spanish immigration increased dramatically after 1902, reaching almost 130,000 by 1907. Spaniards moved into strategic sectors of the labor force, particularly in the mines and along the railroads. Eighty percent of the 11,000 workers who built the Cuban Central Railroad were Spaniards, most of whom were secured by company agents in Havana. Similar conditions prevailed in the mines: almost 90 percent of the 1,603 miners in Oriente in 1907 were Spaniards.[23] These trends persisted as late as 1919, when almost 75 percent of the miners and 60 percent of railroad workers were foreigners.[24] "Ninety percent of the laborers on the plantations and mines of Cuba are Spaniards," one mining official estimated in 1911. "They make good workmen, far better than the natives of Cuba. In fact, the Cubans will not work as laborers."[25] There was always adequate reason for employers to justify the use of foreign labor. A joint petition of the principal mining interests in 1901 urged the military government to adopt a policy of unlimited immigration:

> The activity in road building and other government work, the opening of a large plantation at Banes, the pushing of the railroad work by the Cuba Company, the opening of new mines, and the lesser enterprises which are starting up throughout the province, in addition to the increased activity of the sugar plantations and other established industries, have created a demand for labor altogether unprecedented in this part of the Island and very greatly in excess of the supply.
> On account of the severity of the labor in the mines

and the fact that the Cubans will not do this class of work, the mining companies are always the first to suffer, and this year, more than ever before, the discrepancy between supply and demand in the labor market is resulting in great detriment and loss to these companies.

In a little more than a month, the Spanish-American Iron Company has lost over 60 percent of its mining force: a similar condition obtains at the mines of the Cuban Steel Ore Company, and the Juragua Iron Company has also been a heavy loser. These companies are willing and anxious to relieve the situation in any way possible. They would gladly import men for the work if there could be any assurance that the men would remain, but experience of many years, during which the Juragua and Spanish-American companies have spent upwards of $60,000 in bringing men to this province, has proven that it is impossible to hold them at the mines. Contracts with this irresponsible class cannot be enforced and the men rapidly spread over the province, only a small benefit accruing to the company in return for its expenditures. . . . To raise the rate of wages would only complicate without relieving the situation.[26]

However, it was not until the early 1910s, as sugar cultivation increased dramatically, that new demands for labor set the stage for the next series of developments. The expansion of the zones of cultivation outpaced the availability of cheap labor. This was not a new problem. During the early 1900s, the expansion of United Fruit Company operations had encountered labor shortages. The north coast had lost much of its population during the war, so that when sugar production commenced, United Fruit found itself without an adequate supply of cheap labor. The problem was partially remedied in 1906 when United Fruit received government authorization to introduce Canary Islanders as permanent settlers through the port of Gibara. United Fruit abandoned the colonization scheme several years later in favor of short-term contractual arrangements with West Indian workers.[27]

What was different a decade later in Oriente, and especially after 1914, was the rapidity of sugar expansion. The construction of new mills and the cultivation of new land outpaced the population. Field labor abandoned the cane fields for higher wages in clearing the forests in the eastern zones. Many found better employment in the construction of new factories and the remodeling of old ones.[28] The hundreds of thousands of acres of new land that had been converted to sugar production set in sharp relief new labor needs of the province. As early as 1912, sugar growers estimated that production could be increased by an additional one million sacks annually if cheap labor requirements were fully met.[29]

Immediately a vicious cycle ensued. Sugar expanded into new zones that producers claimed were incapable of meeting local labor requirements. But this was only part of the problem, and perhaps not even the bigger part. In fact, sufficient numbers of Cuban laborers were available for work, but not sufficient numbers to depress wages. The rapid expansion of sugar in the east had the immediate effect of creating a high-cost labor market. Wages began to increase, particularly during 1916 and 1917, as wartime production was gaining momentum. "Labor situation is viewed with concern," reported the trade weekly *Facts About Sugar* in 1916. "It is pointed out that laborers' wages have been advanced three times during the past twelve months, with further increases predicted if the high levels of prices hold."[30] Within a year, the editors' worst fears had come to pass: "How serious the situation is, is indicated by reports from the eastern provinces that wages there have now reached the point where ordinary hoe hands are receiving $3 a day, and in some instances, where the work has been contracted for, as much as $5."[31] The trade weekly published by Willet and Gray issued a similar report: "Some districts report labor scarcity and wages as high as $1.50 to $2.50 a day have been paid."[32] Nor was the wage scale in Oriente a source of concern only to local producers; high wages in the east affected producers in the west. Wages everywhere increased. Producers in the west were obliged to maintain a competitive wage scale or face the prospect of losing workers to the eastern fields. Wrote Manuel Rionda several years later:

> In former times the plantations in the Eastern section could afford to pay higher prices for cutting cane, and this coupled with the fact that their cane being on lands that produced more tonnage per acre and, therefore was larger in size, a man was able to cut more cane than in the Western plantations where the cane being smaller one blow of the knife did not cut as much as it would in a cane field of an estate in the Eastern end of the Island. The higher wages and the bigger cane attracted the laborers to the Eastern estates. . . . The Western estates increased their scale of wages and while their cane was not as good as in the East, the laborers preferred to remain there near the large cities and, consequently, the Eastern plantations did not have the advantage of the stream of labor working as in former years.[33]

Foreign contract workers would not only meet local labor requirements but also depress local wages.

The system of contracting laborers from Jamaica and Haiti began in 1912, after eastern producers experienced difficulty in completing the 1911 harvest. The prospects for the 1912 *zafra* were worse, for three large sugar mills were preparing to commence new operations: "Morón" in Camagüey, "Delicias" in Puerto Padre, and "Manatí" in Las Tunas. The three new mills alone, producers argued, would create a demand for an additional 10,000 cane cutters. Nor did this include the new operations launched by several smaller mills, including "Río Cauto" (Bayamo), "Ermita" (Guantánamo), "Borjita" (San Luis), and "América" (Palma Soriano), which required another 3,500 workers. The requirements of eastern production had increased from 4,500 cane cutters in 1902 to 21,000 in 1913.[34] The influx of West Indian workers increased accordingly, from 2,000 in 1912 to 3,458 in 1913. The number of West Indians rose dramatically after 1914: 4,500 in 1915, 12,000 in 1916, 18,000 in 1917, 19,000 in 1918, and 35,000 in 1919.[35]

There was one other grim reason for the increased need of West Indian labor after 1912. "There is a shortage of labor," reported the U.S. consul in Santiago in August 1912, "which is attributed to the fact that a great many of the people who formerly lived on these coffee estates and worked there were killed in the recent rebellion."[36]

In addition to the recorded influx of foreign contract laborers, many tens of thousands more were suspected to have entered the island illegally. No one knew precisely how many West Indians entered eastern Cuba unlawfully, but illegal immigration assumed serious proportions. And unlike regular contract arrangements, whereby workers normally returned to their homes upon the completion of the harvest, illegal migrants often remained in Cuba permanently. In fact, Cubans were losing control over their coasts. As early as 1912, Antonio Masferrer, the chief administrator of Santiago customs, publicly warned about the uncontrolled illegal migration of West Indian workers. "The coasts of Oriente are in a state of abandon," Masferrer complained. "This lack of vigilance has permitted clandestine immigration, some 10,000 individuals of color from Jamaica, Santo Domingo, and Haiti."[37] Again and again, Cuban gunboats intercepted vessels attempting to land Haitians and Jamaicans on deserted Oriente coasts. In April 1916, in one instance, a ship carrying 600 Haitians was seized in waters outside Santiago. Local authorities estimated that in the month of April alone, an estimated 2,500 Haitians and Jamaicans had entered Cuba clandestinely.[38]

Oriente was in the throes of social unrest, and the mass influx of contract labor was at once cause and consequence of these conditions. Cheap Antillean laborers displaced Cubans from the local labor market. Work was scarce, and when it could be found, the pay barely sufficed to support a family. Thousands of Cuban farmers and peasants, owners of private farms, holders of *pesos de posesión*, and renters, found themselves unable to subsist on depressed wages.

The arrival of West Indians in such great numbers contributed further to the disruption of Oriente society. Isolated communities, for generations impervious to outside influences, were suddenly subjected to a wave of foreign migration totally without precedent. Foreign languages, strange customs, and new religions swept through the province, undermining the region's long tradition of cultural stability. "Customs peculiarly Cuba's are very scarce," wrote Irene Wright from Oriente as early as 1910. "The language Cubans speak is invaded by an increasing host of half-naturalized words and phrases. The population suddenly released from colonial conditions has not found itself as a Cuban people or constituted a nation with an identity of its own."[39]

IV These were years, too, of a renewed and extraordinary population surge. Between 1899 and 1907, the Oriente population had increased from 327,715 to 455,086, a 38.8 percent increase. Between 1907 and 1919, the population of the east recorded a 60.6 percent increment—from 455,086 to 730,909.[40] By 1919, Oriente had become the most populous province in Cuba. In two decades, the population had more than doubled. In some *municipios* the increase in population was especially striking. (see table 14). The popu-

Table 14   Population Increase in Oriente, 1907–1919

	1907	*1919*	*% Increase*
Palma Soriano	20,235	49,531	144.7
Niquero	6,387	14,186	122.1
Victoria de las Tunas	14,358	34,102	137.5
Sagua de Tánamo	8,398	15,499	84.5
Campechuela	8,095	14,895	84.0
Bayamo	26,511	45,961	73.3
Jiguaní	13,327	22,693	70.3
Alto Songo	20,553	34,278	66.7
Mayarí	17,628	28,792	63.3

Sources: Cuba Under the Provisional Government of the United States, *Censo de la República de Cuba, 1907* (Washington, D.C.: GPO, 1908), p. 346; Cuba, Bureau of the Census, *Census of the Republic of Cuba, 1919* (Havana: Maza Arroyo y Caso, 1920), p. 434.

lations density also increased, from 12.3 inhabitants per square kilometer in 1907 to 19.8 in 1919. The increase in density in specific *municipios* served to set the rate of population growth in relief. Population per square kilometer is displayed in table 15.

The age structure of this population also reveals some striking features. By 1919, the population of Oriente was the youngest of all Cuba, with an average age of 21.3 years. Almost 47 percent of the population was under the age of fifteen (342,925 out of 730,909)—the highest percentage of young dependent population in all Cuba. A high proportion of this population consisted of young, geographically mobile, unmarried men. Over 60 percent of the native white and colored male population between the ages fifteen and twenty-nine was single (159,743 out of 260,471).[41] During these years, too, the postwar baby boom generation was preparing to enter a labor market that offered diminishing prospects for gainful employment. Almost 20 percent of the native male population, both white and colored, was of economically productive age—between fifteen and nineteen.[42]

Cubans in Oriente were approaching adulthood at a time of bewildering change. Families were in crisis. The loss of land and lack of livelihood, proletarianization and pauperi-

Table 15   Population Density in Oriente, 1907 and 1919
(per sq. km.)

	1907	1919	% Increase
Puerto Padre	6	30.5	408.3
Palma Soriano	11	26.6	141.8
Guantánamo	8	14.2	77.5
Jiguaní	8	13.6	70.0
Bayamo	7	11.8	68.5
Alto Songo	22	35.9	63.1
Holguín	14	21.2	51.4

Sources: Cuba Under the Provisional Government of the United States, *Censo de la República de Cuba, 1907* (Washington, D.C.: GPO, 1908), p. 197; Cuba, Bureau of the Census, *Census of the Republic of Cuba, 1919* (Havana: Maza Arroyo y Caso, 1920), p. 294.

zation, occurred at the same time. Families had increasingly less to leave their children—less land, fewer *pesos de posesión,* few material goods. And in the newly emerging market economy, parents had fewer relevant skills and crafts to pass on to their daughters and sons. Increasingly, members of peasant households abandoned the land and sought wage work to supplement family income. These developments announced the decline of the peasant family household as an independent unit of production and subsistence. Family members were now required to find outside employment as individuals for wages. The transformation was as dramatic as it was stark: from one generation to another, peasant families saw their children spill into the swelling ranks of the rural proletariat. It was, to be sure, not irrevocable; there was considerable movement between the peasantry and the proletariat. But the trend was fixed, as peasants lost effective control over the means of production. More and more, basic necessities, food and nonfood alike, had to be purchased with cash or on credit. And more and more, the stability of households depended on steady wage employment.

The loss of land affected both men and women, pressuring all members of the family to locate outside sources of income. Increasing numbers of men, women, and children wre uprooted, transformed into itinerant workers in search of temporary work of any kind. More women entered the labor market in Oriente. Peasant women no less than men were being proletarianized. The data is scanty but suggestive. Large numbers of women became domestics, almost three times as many in 1919 than in 1907—from 2,962 to 8,293. The number of women in the Oriente cigar factories increased from 21 in 1907 to 115 in 1919, a development that bode ill for both sexes. Women were employed at lower wages, thereby allowing manufacturers to depress wages for men. The number of men employed in the cigar factories declined from 3,495 to 2,985. In 1907, agriculture accounted for the employment of 735 women; in 1919 there were 2,985. What was particularly striking about women in agriculture was their shifting marital status. Almost 90 percent of women agriculturists in 1907 were married, legally or consensually; in 1919 this proportion declined to 40 percent. In this one occupation, hence, as peasant households declined and men sought outside wage income, single women in increasing numbers entered the labor market.[43]

The rise in the number of women in agriculture also underscored the breakdown of traditional sex roles caused by the deepening impoverishment of independent farmers. The participation of women in the rural labor force increased as the household lost access to the means of production. Women had to go to work because households were without sufficient land to subsist.[44]

Moreover, other forces were at work to compel women to leave the home in search of outside income. Those occupations traditionally identified as "women's work," sewing and needlework, were in decline. This was a significant development, for stitchery, which could easily be done in the home for additional family income, was compatible with child rearing and subsistence agriculture. The increase in cheap textile imports more than any other factor accounted for the decline of household sewing. Domestic manufacturing faced new competition from foreign industrial products, and all but collapsed. By 1918, textile imports made up 13.5 percent of Cuba's total imports, second only to foodstuffs. The amount of money spent on foreign textiles increased from $13.7 million in 1908 to $45.7 million in 1919.[45] The effects were telling. While the total population of women in Oriente increased by 55.7 percent between 1907 and 1919 (221,350 to 344,796), the percentage of seamstresses declined by 39.3 percent (from 2,174 in 1907 to 1,139 in 1919), while the proportion of dressmakers diminished by 47.4 percent (436 in 1907 to 229 in 1919). The number of women launderers also declined by 71.3 percent. Women were displaced from these jobs by foreign men, whose numbers as launderers increased from 55 to 595. In the descending wage hierarchy, foreign men were used to depress the wages and displace from work Cuban women.[46] By the end of the decade, women had become a reserve labor force, to be engaged or ignored as the vagaries of the market economy dictated.

One other line of work attracted women in increasing numbers: prostitution. Rural dislocation and destitution occurred at a time of sugar prosperity, with the sudden rise of boom mill towns filled with thousands of West Indian male contract laborers, distant from home with disposable income. The equal sex ratio of 1899 had shifted dramatically in 1919, when Oriente had the second highest male-to-female ratio in Cuba: 56 percent male, 44 percent female.[47] And even this ratio told only part of the story. As shown in table 16, in the principal sugar zones, the imbalance of postadolescent males to females of childbearing age was nothing short of astonishing. Company towns sprang up across Oriente, concentrating transient male populations in an atmosphere of boom prosperity: in Palmarito, Jobabo, Chaparra, Barajagua, Antilla, Cacocún, Norte (Holguín), Oeste (Banes). Prostitution flourished, brothels prospered.[48]

V Life in Oriente had become incomprehensible. Everything was changing, quickly and permanently. Cubans lost the land, and could not find work. The proportion of the native white male population engaged in agriculture declined from 38.0 percent in 1907 to 29.5 in 1919. Unemployment increased. Unemployed white native males increased from 4.9 percent in 1907 to 9.4 percent in 1919; for colored males, unemployment rose from 3.7 to 5.6 percent. In 1919, Oriente had the highest unemployment rate in Cuba.[49] "The labor situation has been and is rather acute," wrote one sugar producer in Guantánamo in 1914,

Table 16   Adult Population of Childbearing Age in Oriente, 1919

	% Male	% Female
Palma Soriano	67.8	32.2
Victoria de las Tunas	66.3	33.7
Puerto Padre	62.3	37.7
Mayarí	61.9	38.1
Guantánamo	59.3	40.7
Holguín	59.1	40.9
Banes	57.0	43.0

Source: Cuba, Bureau of the Census, Census of the Republic of Cuba, 1919 (Havana: Maza Arroyo y Caso, 1920), p. 417.

"and may become very serious. . . . The laborers are very badly in need of wages as there had been no work of any kind here for many months. . . . There have been a number of *'mitins'* in the Plaza at which fiery speeches have been made. . . . It has been reported by people who should know that burning of cane fields is also planned."[50]

In this time of crisis, the necessity of stable wage employment for marriage and independent household formation created uncertainty and insecurity. A family economy based on marriage depended on possessing the means of support, which traditionally meant land. The effects of less available land and fewer opportunities for livelihood were registered in delayed marriages. The trend was particularly evident among native males, and especially striking among black males. In 1907, men of color in Oriente were marrying younger than blacks elsewhere in Cuba. Twelve years later, the trend had been reversed, as shown in table 17. They were marrying later than the national average, or not marrying at all. The pattern for the population at large reflected a similar trend (see table 18). Conjugal unions were also in flux. The percentage of the total number of people legally married increased from 17.0 percent (77,374 out of 455,086) in 1907 to 18.4 percent (135,019 out of 730,909) in 1919. However, the percentage of consensual unions was in decline, from a total 11.0 percent (50,393 out of 455,086) in 1907 to 9.0 percent (66,485 out of 730,909) in 1919.[51]

Table 17   Married Black Males in Oriente, 1907 and 1919
(in percent)

Age Group	1909		1919	
	Oriente	Cuba	Oriente	Cuba
21–24	23.5	23.0	16.3	17.2
25–29	54.0	49.1	35.3	36.4
30–34	67.5	61.9	52.7	53.8

Sources: Cuba Under the Provisional Government of the United States, *Censo de la República de Cuba, 1907* (Washington, D.C.: GPO, 1908), pp. 432–33; Cuba, Bureau of the Census, *Census of the Republic of Cuba, 1919* (Havana: Maza Arroyo y Caso, 1920), pp. 541–42.

Even as consensual unions were in decline, illegitimate births were increasing. Vast numbers of mobile young men wandered across the countryside in search of work as itinerant laborers, following the harvest of maturing crops and migrating in and out of mill towns and provincial cities. These conditions contributed to the sharp rise of births out of wedlock. The number of illegitimate children had always been high in Oriente—consistently the highest in Cuba. In large measure, this was due to the proportionally higher rate of consensual unions, children which were classified by census enumerators as illegitimate. In 1899 22.6 percent of the total population of Oriente (74,329 out of 327,715) was

Table 18   Marriages and Consensual Unions in Cuba, 1907 and 1919
(in percent)

	15–20 Yrs.		21–34 Yrs.	
	1907	1919	1907	1919
White females (native)				
Married	17.2	19.7	50.6	59.1
Consensual union	4.9	5.8	20.0	18.0
Colored females				
Married	10.3	10.4	27.8	35.7
Consensual union	6.9	9.1	29.2	34.3
White males (native)				
Married	1.3	1.9	38.5	45.6
Consensual union	0.6	0.6	13.2	13.8
Colored males				
Married	0.8	1.0	23.6	19.7
Consensual union	0.7	1.1	20.7	15.7
Totals				
White females (native)	18,715	21,772	23,516	34,747
Colored females	15,718	17,613	20,869	28,698
White males (native)	16,113	19,554	23,444	31,622
Colored males	13,456	19,689	20,006	41,205

Sources: Cuba Under the Provisional Government of the United States, Censo de la República de Cuba, 1907 (Washington, D.C.: GPO, 1908), pp. 431–32; Cuba, Bureau of the Census, Census of the Republic of Cuba, 1919 (Havana: Maza Arroyo y Caso, 1920), pp. 540–42.

born out of wedlock. An estimated 61.8 percent of the total
[46,004] consisted of Afro-Cubans. The proportion remained
constant in 1907 at 21.7 percent (98,768 out of 455,086), 61.1
percent of whom were Afro-Cuban (60,444). In 1919, however, the total percentage increased dramatically, constitut-
ing more than 35 percent of the population (255,496 out of
730,909). This overall increase notwithstanding, the Afro-
Cuban proportion remained consistent at 61.9 percent
[158,243].[52]

Related, and also symptomatic of the crisis, was the general increase in fertility in Oriente during these years of
dramatic socioeconomic change. The incentive for childbearing increased because children served as a means
to augment family income and make ends meet. At a very
young age, children could assume a number of useful
chores, in and out of the home. Between 1914 and 1919, the
population of Oriente surged. Nowhere in Cuba was the
percentage of children five years of age and younger as high:
17.9 percent of the total population, 18.4 percent of the
native white population, and 17.4 percent of the population
of color.[53] Years later, Sara Rojas recalled her childhood in
Oriente with ten brothers and sisters. The family worked a
small parcel of land while the father worked for wages at the
nearby sugar mill. The role of the children was crucial:

> *Papá* worked as a cart driver on the Miranda *central.*
> All of us had to help out on the farm because he didn't
> have time to look after it by himself. When I was little,
> the girls in the family worked like men. . . . My eldest
> sister, Agustina, assigned the chores. We got up at
> daybreak and went down to the cattle corral to fetch
> charcoal or firewood for breakfast. . . . We all helped
> —one would fetch firewood, another would carry wa-
> ter, and so on. We, the eldest, would hoe the corn and
> beans. That's the hardest chore of all for a child be-
> cause you have to work under the hot sun. . . . After-
> ward we'd go to get the calves, feed the pigs, and gather
> cane for the cattle. At harvest time, when there wasn't
> much cane, we'd rake the cane fields to gather fodder.
> Besides the farm work, we swept, washed dishes,
> washed and ironed clothes, ran to the stores on er-

rands, and looked after the small children. All day long we worked—they sure made full use of us![54]

The increase in the overall population in Oriente between 1899 and 1919 concealed an entirely different demographic drama occurring at the local level. The increase of population in Oriente was not evenly distributed. The expansion of sugar not only appropriated the land, it also expelled the cultivators. Considerable numbers of towns and villages in *municipios* experiencing the greatest increase actually suffered sharp losses of population. Between 1899 and 1907, Puerto Padre, the site of early sugar expansion, experienced a 70 percent population increase, from 19,984 to 34,061. This growth, however, concealed a population decline in almost all the communities outside the mill towns (see table 19). This process contined elsewhere throughout the following decade. Indeed, between 1907 and 1919, several towns situated in the new regions of expanded sugar cultivation in eastern Cuba disappeared altogether. Former coffee and cacao producing communities in Gibara, Mayarí, Holguín, Puerto Padre, and Baracoa registered significant losses. Fully

Table 19 Population Distribution in Oriente, 1899 and 1907

	1899	1907
Arenas	1,119	896
Caisimú	1,653	706
Cauto del Paso	1,500	984
Manatí	1,064	519
Maniabón	995	792
Ajo de Agua	1,157	1,123
Oriente	2,471	1,246
Palmarito	1,072	890
Playuelas	1,038	907
Yarey	1,231	839

Sources: U.S. War Dept., Office of Director of Census, *Informe sobre el censo de Cuba, 1899* (Washington, D.C.: GPO, 1900), pp. 198–200; Cuba, Bureau of the Census, *Census of the Republic of Cuba, 1907* (Washington, D.C.: GPO, 1908), pp. 401–03.

one-third of Baracoa's twenty-three towns and more than half of the fourteen towns in El Cobre lost population. The *municipio* of El Caney registered a 7 percent population loss. Similar losses occurred in Alto Songo, Bayamo, Guantánamo, and Jiguaní.[55]

VI The traditional world of generations of *orientales* was crashing suddenly in their midst, without apparent reason. The limited land resources were already insufficient to support the Oriente population, and even less able to absorb the demographic growth registered in the 1910s. The sugar latifundia had arrived to Oriente, fully four decades after the agrarian upheavals of the west, and with similar effects. Family farms were expropriated. Squatters were expelled.[56] *Haciendas comuneras* were extinguished. Wrote Lowry Nelson:

> The expansion brought new insecurity to the owners in the communal haciendas. While such rights were not always of very great value in actual gain to the individual, they were recognized as legal, and large numbers of peasants enjoyed a measure of economic security in their *pesos de posesión*. But the demands for additional sugar lands brought about the sale and the consequent subdivisions of most of the remaining haciendas. Thus a new group of landless farm people were created.[57]

By displacing farmers and peasants, thereby ending self-sufficiency and depressing wages through the importation of cheap labor from the West Indies, the sugar system depressed living standards everywhere in Oriente. A community made up largely of self-sufficient farmers and peasants was reorganized into a society consisting largely of dependent rural workers, frequently working for foreign corporations, eating foreign-produced foods, living often in company towns, and buying from mill stores.[58]

Land in eastern Cuba ceased to produce for the local population and became instead the preserve of products destined for foreign markets. The expansion of sugar signified the extension of market relationships over a larger area, and the replacement of subsistence farming by production for export markets. This development, together with the surge in population growth, suggested another and no less ominous trend: the expansion of sugar at the expense of local agricultural production. Food supplies on a per capita basis decreased progressively, placing new strains on food resources. The result was predictable: an increasing scarcity of subsistence crops compounded by the decline of cash crops to provide the money with which to purchase the food that no longer could be produced locally. At the same time, with the rise of the boom mill towns, a large market for foodstuffs and consumer products suddenly appeared just as suddenly as farms and farmers disappeared.

Orientales were losing the capacity to feed themselves. "The villages are coming under the siege of the canefields," commented one writer traveling Oriente in 1915. "What will we eat? In Santiago, during the early hours of the evening and on a central street, a young woman in miserable condition approached me, and extending her hand explained: 'Alms, for God's sake, neither my children nor I have eaten today.' There is hunger in the city, there is hunger in the countryside. . . . Every day there are fewer farm plots *(sitios),* every day fewer *fincas,* every day fewer *haciendas.* The powerful fruit companies do not even permit the picking of a banana—in Cuba, where fruits were the natural property of all! The powerful fruit companies do not allow for pigs, do not allow for chickens."[59]

The loss of control over the economic purpose of land, further, increased Cuban dependency on foreign food imports. Between 1914 and 1916, food imports increased in dramatic terms:[60]

	1914	1916	% Increase
Meat	$11,269,163	$18,427,137	63.5
Cereals	15,393,569	26,151,554	69.8
Fruits	722,057	1,247,812	72.8
Vegetables	5,602,017	10,362,443	84.9

Between 1914 and 1919, further, the total value of imported foodstuff almost tripled, from $46.8 million to $134.4 million.[61] The total food imports passing through Santiago alone increased from $7.8 million in 1914 to $9.3 million in 1915.[62] "The small Cuban population," one observer commented, "cannot produce $300 or $400 worth of sugar per capita and at the same time produce its own food."[63] The loss of self-sufficiency occurred, moreover, almost simultaneously with a new series of relentless price increases, especially for food. Between November 1916 and October 1917, the average price of basic foodstuffs and commodities in several representative company stores increased significantly. (See table 20.)

VII Tension deepened across the province. The signs of mounting discontent were everywhere visible.

Crime increased. During the early 1910s, Oriente reported the highest incidence of violent crime in all of Cuba.[64] These were years too of increasing incidents of banditry. Outlawry had continued in desultory fashion during the early years of the republic. For many, life outside the law had become a permanent way of survival. Bandits were wanted men, most of whom had first descended into criminality as an alternative to indigence. Their ranks were periodically augmented during occasions of political instability, when partisan protest erupted into armed protest. They initially formed part of the anonymous rank and file of the political parties, and long after their political chieftains had made peace with the opposition, they were still fugitives. They were led into the field, and left there, to make out as best they could. Many never returned.[65]

But lawlessness in the early republic, as in late colonial times, mostly gave expression to rural unrest and announced profound change in the interior. As a result of the dislocations caused by the expansion of the sugar system, once again banditry erupted across the countryside, this time in the east. Something approaching open warfare erupted in the interior. An estimated fifteen outlaw bands operated in Santa Clara, the most prominent of which include José ("El Oso") Muñoz, Saturino Liriano, Marcel Cepero, Maximiliano Garay, Damián Barroso, Secundino ("Cundingo") Vélez, Severo Lazo, and the most famous bandit of the period, Inocencio Solís. Bands in Camagüey were led by Tomás Valero Báez, José M. Martínez, Abraham Fundora, Santiago Alfonso Rivera and, the only known woman bandit of the period, Elena Martínez. The principal outlaw bands in Oriente were led by José ("Cholo") Rivera, Rafael Valera, and Urbano Guerra.[66]

Bandit activities centered, once more, on the assault against property and property owners. The kidnapping of planters and plantation administrators as well as members of their family was common. The most celebrated cases during the early 1910s included the kidnapping of landowners Juan Mina, Pablo Bravo Jiménez, Tomás Arrechea, José Rabell, and Pedro Díaz. Children of property owners were also kidnapped, including the children of Emilio Almanza,

Table 20   Price of Basic Foodstuffs in Cuba, 1916 and 1917

	November 1916	October 1917	%
Rice	$ 4.60	$ 7.75	68.4
Flour (200-lb. sack)	10.25	15.00	46.3
Bacon	21.00	33.00	57.1
Beef	15.00	18.00	20.0
Hams	28.50	37.00	29.8
Lard	17.00	22.00	29.4
Potatoes	5.00	7.25	45.0
White beans	10.00	15.50	55.0
Codfish	15.00	19.50	30.0
Olive oil	12.50	23.25	86.0
Salt	2.75	3.25	18.1
Soap	7.25	10.50	44.8
Coal (metric ton)	8.75	15.75	80.0
Sewing twine	48.00	54.00	12.5

Source: Robert B. Hoernel, "Sugar and Social Change in Oriente, Cuba, 1896–1946," Journal of Latin American Studies 8 (November 1976), 235.

Joaquín Mesa de la Pera, Amador Cabrera, and Gregorio Marañón. All were released after the payment of ransom.

Property was attacked. Incidents of arson increased, and cane field fires in particular. Arson was one of the principal problems attending every *zafra*. Arsonists destroyed millions of *arrobas* of cane every year.[67] "I cannot understand," sugar manufacturer Manuel Rionda pondered, "why we have so many fires in the plantations east of Santa Clara and so few in the western section of Cuba."[68] Estates were routinely threatened with arson in exchange for tribute.[69] Sugar mills in disaffected zones became armed camps during the *zafra* in anticipation of increased bandit attacks. Bandits raided railroad lines and stations, held up mail carriers, robbed *bodegas* and *cantinas,* and plundered company stores. Cattle rustling increased. "The cattlemen in the Bayamo district," reported the U.S. consul in Santiago, "complain of losses on account of a band of thieves who, it is alleged, have settled in that community and live by stealing a few head of cattle at a time from the ranches."[70] Travel into the interior was hazardous, and few planters of means traveled without an armed escort. "The bandits are bad and a proof of the incapacity of the Government," complained Manuel Rionda to his New York office in 1911. "In Tuinucu, we have men under arms, which was never found necessary before. This was on account of threatening letters from bandits. When I rode to 'Francisco,' I took four guards!"[71] "A rein of terror exists among the wealthy planters and mill owners," protested the *Havana Post* in 1913, "who are afforded no protection by the government against the outlaws' depredations."[72] By November 1914, banditry had reached sufficient proportions to prompt Secretary of Gobernación Aurelio Hevia to pledge publicly new energetic measures to combat the prevailing wave of lawlessness.[73] Two years later on the eve of the 1916 *zafra,* the government announced a new plan for the suppression of outlawry. Reported one Havana newspaper: "The General Staff of the Army has completed a plan . . . providing for close vigilance through each province in order to completely rid the country districts of bandits. . . . The new plan of cooperation formulated by the army provides for such a close and rigid patrol of the countryside that bandits who attempt to ply their trade this year will fare badly."[74]

Signs of growing rural unrest took other forms no less telling. Many rural communities defended their lands tenaciously. They asked for legal relief and legislative remedy. They appealed to elected officials, hired lawyers, and applied to the courts—and they lost again and again. They took direct action, too. On occasion they would obstruct judicial surveys, destroying surveying excavations and marking posts.[75] They attacked survey teams. It soon became customary for the courts to provide survey crews with an escort of rural guards.[76] Displaced peasants demonstrated and protested. In June 1913 the villagers of Birau in the *municipio* of Mayarí clashed with local authorities during a demonstration to protest the loss of land to the Spanish-American Iron Company.[77] In October 1914, an estimated 4,000 peasants marched in protest against local government in Baracoa denouncing the alienation of their land. The judicial survey of the *hacienda* "Montecristo" was nearing completion, and all signs pointed to the expulsion of hundreds of peasant families who worked the estate as *comuneros*. An armed confrontation between the demonstrating peasants and the armed forces was avoided only after local authorities pledged to seek legal means through which to prevent the loss of peasant lands.[78] A year later, peasants in Banes demonstrated against evictions by United Fruit.[79] On January 1916 farmers and peasants who had served in the Liberation Army convoked an emergency meeting of the Provincial Assembly of Veterans in Santiago. At a highly emotional meeting, they denounced the loss of their land and called upon the government to revoke Civil Order No. 62 and ratify titles of lands worked by the peasant veterans.[80] Several months later, a group of farmers in Guantánamo petitioned the *fiscal* of the Supreme Court for assistance in retaining their land.[81] In July 1917, farmers and peasants marched in Santiago to protest a series of expulsions from their lands.[82]

Appeals to government authorities for relief were without effect. In fact, public officials were themselves often the principal beneficiaries of the sugar boom. The stakes were so high that corruption and bribery flourished—for land titles, property franchises, favorable judicial surveys, and favorable court decisions. Officials in all branches of government and at all levels, with access to public franchises, state subsidies, and official dispensations and waivers, were themselves transformed into wealthy landowners and prosperous sugar producers. Orestes Ferrara, the Liberal party leader and president of the House of Representatives, owned several sugar estates, as did Gerardo Machado, Secretary of Gobernación (1908–1912) and Charles Hernández, director-general of Post and Telegraph (1912–1920). Many held official positions in some of the largest sugar corporations. President Mario G. Menocal (1912–1920) managed the "Chaparra" sugar estate owned by the Cuban-American Sugar Company in Puerto Padre; through two terms as president, he served on the Cuban-American board of directors. Orestes Ferrara and Liberal senator Antonio Sánchez de Bustamante sat on the board of directors of the Cuba Cane Corporation. Ferrara was a major stockholder in the Confluente Sugar Company, a corporation with vast holdings in Guantánamo.[83] Liberal Seantor José Miguel Tarafa held shares in the Central Sugar Company. Miguel Arango, the Liberal party vice-presidential nominee in 1920, was a major stockholder of the Manatí Sugar Corporation and administrator of several Cuba Cane estates in Oriente. Luis Fernández Marcané, a Liberal senator from Oriente and chairman of the Senate Committee on Immigration, was the Cuban legal counsel for the United Fruit Company. In some of the *municipios* in which the larger mills were located, including Victoria de las Tunas, Puerto Padre, Mayarí, Gibara, and Banes, there were few municipal government officials who were not somehow associated with or dependent on the local sugar company. The mill administration was an important constituency, a source of campaign funds, an employer of friends and relatives, an important source of tax revenue, and a powerful economic presence in the community. It was a political force to be reckoned with, and most local officials made their peace with the corporations on the most advantageous terms.[84]

VIII 1916 was an election year in Cuba. The Liberal opposition candidate Alfredo Zayas was the popular
favorite, and by all accounts was expected to
triumph easily in the November balloting. Conservative
President Mario G. Menocal lacked the popularity of his
rival, but was not without advantage: he was the incumbent. His government commanded the army, controlled
the courts, and counted the ballots. Menocal used all three
with great effect, and easily obtained a second term.[85]

Liberals reacted to the electoral fraud immediately.
Within months the party leadership committed itself to
armed protest and the overthrow of the Conservative government. The Liberal plot was quite simple: a seizure of
military installations in Havana, followed by army support
in the provincial capitals.[86] But the conspiracy was uncov-
ered in early February 1917, forcing Liberals to move pre-
maturely and hastily. They failed in Pinar del Río, as well
as in Havana, Matanzas, and in most of Las Villas. They
were briefly successful in Camagüey. In Oriente, however,
they scored their most dramatic success. Mutinous army
chieftains seized control of the regimental command in
Santiago de Cuba. Insurgent army commanders captured
the city, displaced Conservative officials, and installed a
new provisional Liberal government. Several key *municipios*, including Campechuela, Guantánamo, Bayamo, Holguín, Mayarí, and Baracoa, also came under the control of
the insurgent Liberals.[87]

That the plot failed in Havana, however, meant that it
had failed altogether. Most of the army remained loyal, and
the United States quickly proclaimed its support for the
incumbent Conservatives. As the rebellion entered the
second month, the hopelessness of the Liberal cause increased. In early March, government forces scored a major
military victory over the main insurgent unit, taking prisoner some 200 ranking Liberal leaders.[88] The political protest waned, and lost the active support of party members.
Some Liberals surrendered in exchange for guarantees of
personal safety; others abandoned the field for exile
abroad. By early spring, hundreds of Liberals had found
safety in the United States, Jamaica, Mexico, Haiti, and the

Bahamas.[89] After March the protest no longer posed a political threat to the government.

IX Through capture, death, and exile, the Liberal political protest came to an inglorious end. Civilian leaders who had organized the movement, together with ranking army officers who had joined the movement, made their peace with the government and abandoned the field. Liberals and Conservatives settled their differences and peace soon returned to the body politic.

However, the political dispute between the ruling parties served as the spark to ignite the mounting social unrest in rural Oriente into open warfare. Long-smouldering resentment erupted into rebellion. As in 1912, the social merged easily and indistinguishably with the political, and ultimately transcended it. The Liberal protest had aroused to action thousands determined to avenge more than electoral fraud. They brought to the armed protest a complexity of grievances that were only marginally related to the political dispute. As early as February 1917, the French consul in Santiago reported the interior "filling with guerrillas difficult for the insurrection leaders to control."[90] Indeed, very early Liberals lost control of the armed bands that took to the field after February. Any hope of control ended as Liberals surrendered, leaving in the field armed bands free to attack targets entirely of their own choosing for reasons fully of their own making. "The Liberals do not want to fight," an observer remarked in late March, "they do not want to kill or destroy, but being under-officered the men who have private grievances against some of the plantation owners or managers have avenged them in spite of the influence of their officers. The destruction of property is done a great deal by private individuals not by the revolutionists."[91] A similar account came from Eduardo de Ulzurrán, the administrator of the Manatí Sugar Company property on the north coast. Ulzurrán had conferred with Liberal leaders in late March who gave him "repeated assurance that they would not attack Manatí, that it was not their purpose to destroy property and that they wanted

to protect the interests of all foreigners." However, Ulzurrán cautioned, danger was still imminent: "At present I do
not believe that the great peril lies in attacks from the
regular rebel forces—on the contrary, that the great danger

is from the small bands of marauders who have already
commenced to pilfer and commit depradations of all
sorts."[92]

By early spring 1917, by which time most ranking Liberals had abandoned the armed movement, the transformation was complete: the political protest ended, the social
protest began. The U.S. consul in Caimanera reported in
late May, "The revolutionary forces operating in this province have now degenerated into groups of bandits headed by
by notorious characters having no political significance."[93] Manuel Rionda made a similar observation in
mid-March: "This destruction cannot be put down by
force of arms. Militarily the revolution is finished now, but
the small bands keep going around and burning!"[94] All
semblance of political organization disappeared as the
armed bands roamed across the countryside at will. "We
did not ask for any [government] protection before," the
assistant manager of the Miranda Sugar Company cabled
the New York office, "while the Liberals were organized
and under recognized leaders, but now the situation is
different—for the rebels are scattered throughout the
country and we fear the small bands that come across our
property may do us some damage."[95]

Liberals also realized they had released social forces they
could not control. In the end, their political differences
with their upper-class adversaries were considerably less
than their social differences with their allies. They had
good reason to seek an end to the rebellion. Too many
ranking members of the party held substantial interests in
the very sugar properties that were under siege in eastern
Cuba.[96] With sugar prices steadily rising through early
spring and the *zafra* well under way, the continuing disorders, now given directly to the destruction of property,
threatened both the completion of the 1917 harvest and
preparations for the 1918 crop. Orestes Ferrara, one of the
key organizers of the abortive Liberal plot, quickly dis-

sociated himself from the insurgency. The revolt, Ferrara declared through his attorney in New York, Martin W. Littleton, had "gone crazy and was destroying property right and left."[97] As long as the revolution was "purely political," Littleton informed the State Department, Ferrara did not disguise his sympathy and support for the Liberal cause. "Now that the revolution has come to a point where it will end in anarchy," Littleton explained, "he is very much opposed to it because anarchy means the ruin of individual rights and property, and he is a large holder of property himself."[98]

Political protest again provided the occasion for peasant protest. Peasants and rural workers were again in rebellion. Many specific causes provoked the uprising, most of them related to the break in the precarious equilibrium between the sugar producers and the rural communities. The balance between the land and subsistence had been shattered by the expansion of the sugar system, and peasant survival was severely compromised. They had petitioned and protested, they had demonstrated and marched, they had pleaded with elected officials and appealed to legal authorities—all without effect.

An estimated 10,000 insurgents—the "ignorant and incapable class," in the words of the U.S. consul—had taken to the field.[99] They dispersed into scattered armed bands operating in Santiago, Baracoa, Mayarí, Alto Songo, Guantánamo, and Manatí. "The insurgents have broken up into small bands of from twenty-five to a hundred," cabled the consul in Santiago in mid-April, "and have no hesitancy in raiding and plundering wherever and whoever it suits their fancy."[100] A correspondent in Havana reported a similar development: "They are splitting up into smaller bands, retiring into the hilly country and increasing their operations of burning, robbing and destruction of property with greater activity."[101] As the *tiempo muerto* neared, new recruits joined the protest. In May, observers speculated that there would be a "continued increase in the drift of the laboring classes to the ranks of the bandits and revolutionary force."[102] In May, too, naval intelligence reported that the revolutionary movement was gaining ground.[103]

The insurgents laid siege to property—sugar estates principally, but also mines, and railroads. In the northern districts alone, over 100,000 tons of cane were burned. With one exception, every railway station between Antilla in the north and Santiago in the south was destroyed. Most of the bridges were wrecked. *Cantinas* and *bodegas* were looted.[104] They attacked archives and local record depositories, again. The municipal archives in Alto Songo were totally destroyed.[105] They attacked foreign farmers. One group of North American citrus colonists in Oriente petitioned Washington for assistance in the face of new developments in the province. "For nearly two months," the petitioners wrote, "the rebel forces were held in restraint by rebel chiefs that were our neighbors, and we owe it to their efforts that our colonies were left undestroyed at the time. After the government 'successes' in the southern part of the Province, large hordes of rebels invaded our territory. The leaders lost control and our business places, farms and homes have been raided or burned, our horses and cattle have been carried away or killed."[106]

Growing attacks on property inevitably involved North American interests. As the protest continued into early spring, confidence in Havana's ability to restore order in Oriente gave way to a mixture of apprehension and impatience. The U.S. consul in Caimanera urged Washington to deploy a permanent military garrison in eastern Cuba, asserting: "The Cuban Government forces are now confronted with the difficult problem of dealing with bandits who still continue their operations of pillage and destruction of property."[107] In mid-May, the State Department concluded that the Cuban government was incapable of ending the disorders. The only certain means through which to inspire confidence among the planters and provide minimum assurances of safety to the sugar crop, Consul General Henry H. Morgan reported in May, was to send "Marines to the province to cooperate with Cubans [and] with authority to pursue and destroy rebel bands where ever located."[108] In fact, marines had landed at several points to protect North American property in Guantánamo, Ermita, El Cobre, Daiquirí, Baracoa, Banes, and Santiago. At least on three occasions at Ermita, El Cobre, and Daiquirí, U.S. armed forces engaged rebels in combat.[109] In June, Morgan urged again the landing of a permanent United States "armed force into the country as it is the only force the rebels respect and fear."[110] A third request was made later in June: "No confidence whatever can be placed in the Cuban troops, for they are not competent to control the situation."[111]

Disorders continued throughout the summer of 1917. In June, the *New York Times* correspondent in Havana reported learning that the armed protest continued unabated in the "mountainous regions of Oriente province."[112] As late as July 31, the U.S. vice-consul in Antilla reported the existence of "mountaineers" near the towns of La Maya and Alto Songo, well armed, some with new rifles, and all with plenty of ammunition.[113] In August the first contingent of a permanent detachment of marines arrived in eastern Cuba, officially for the purpose of warm climate training. "The United States Government intends sending to Cuba 10,000 troops," wrote Manuel Rionda, "ostensibly for training, but in reality to preserve order during the harvesting of the sugar crop. We may all be satisfied and make a peaceful and successful crop."[114] For the duration of 1917, marine "practice marches" were organized around the pursuit of armed bands in the eastern interior.[115] Gradually disorders diminished. The marines remained until 1922.

Not all armed bands disappeared, however. Survivors receded deeper into the mountain folds of the eastern wilderness, there to remain as communities of outcasts and fugitives in much the same fashion as the *cimarrones* had survived in the nineteenth century.[116] Periodically, in the years that followed, the capital press published brief back-page accounts of the results of army encounters with bandits who remained at large after the 1917 uprising. In December 1917, the bandit chieftain "Nando" Guerra eluded a government ambush. In January 1918, Justo and Enrique Hernández were captured and summarily executed by a rural guard patrol. In January 1920, Augusto Puente Guillot met his end at the hands of the rural guard unit in

Boniato.[117] Ultimately, the capital press lost interest in reporting the fate of the bandit survivors.

The protest had inflicted considerable damage on the sugar estates. Tens of thousands of *arrobas* of cane had perished. There had been talk early during the 1917 *zafra* of reaching the 4-million-ton mark, a new Cuban production record. In the end, producers barely reached three million tons. But even the destruction wrought by protesting peasants was not without salutary effects for the sugar producers. Wrote Manuel Rionda to a friend in London:

> I was not one-half as anxious during the disturbed conditions in Cuba as you may think. After all, as there was no loss of life, what difference does it make whether we have a few thousand dollars more or less. . . . The rebellion has put a setback on the development of the Island and, perhaps, after all that is the best thing, because we were going rather too fast in the production of Cuba which was exceeding the supply of laborers with the consequent continued advance in wages and, furthermore, as the production of beets is increasing in this country, if Cuba had reached close to 4,000,000 tons, there would have been an enormous surplus after the war which would have had to seek foreign markets.[118]

8 Epilogue

The rural exodus constitutes a silent but clearly perceptible criticism of the position of an entire working class. In addition to the fact that they are very badly off economically, they have resigned themselves to a life with no hope of real improvement, since they can hardly keep from feeling enslaved and are frequently deprived of their basic right to organize in defense of their interests.
—Ferdinand Tönnies, *Desarrollo de la cuestión social,* 1927

Oriente was transformed, irrevocably. Sugar in the east was no longer as it had been traditionally, one agricultural form out of many. It had become the principal one. Eastern Cuba had finally overtaken the west. By 1929, an estimated 5.8 million acres of land were under sugar cultivation—approximately 64 percent of the entire province.[1] In a larger sense, the process that began in the western provinces a century earlier was complete. For generations an independent system of subsistence agriculture flourished on the edges of a capitalist economy. Sometimes it was a tense coexistence, sometimes a conflicting one. But by the 1880s in the west and the 1910s in the east, market conditions had made this arrangement untenable. The land had become too valuable and labor too expensive to permit the local agricultural economy to continue. Sugar could admit no other purpose. It appropriated land, it consolidated land, it monopolized land. It reduced wages and depressed living standards. These developments converged in a fateful combination. Everywhere sugar expanded, it displaced and dispossessed farmers and peasants. Everywhere it degraded and despoiled. The sugar system transformed the character of the class structure by transforming the context of class relations. The expansion of the sugar latifundia and the increasing emphasis on production for the export market combined to reduce the land available for production of local use. A class of independent farmers and peasants was uprooted from the land and converted to wage labor. Wrote Fernando Ortiz:

> The small Cuban landowner, independent and prosperous, the backbone of a strong rural middle class, is gradually disappearing. The farmer is becoming a member of the proletariat, just another laborer, without roots in the soil, shifted from one district to another. The whole life of the *central* is permeated by the provisional quality of dependence, which is a characteristic of colonial populations whose members have lost their stake in their country.[2]

Not all farmers and peasants accepted their plunge into indigence compliantly. Many migrated, while others resisted and eventually rebelled. The forms of resistance were not everywhere the same. In the west, during the last decades of the nineteenth century, rural unrest found expression in the outbreak of widespread banditry, eventually fusing with the anticolonial rebellion of 1895–1898.

Banditry resumed after 1898 and persisted into the early years of the republic. Much of this was due to generalized conditions of distress and destitution after the war. But if banditry after 1898 was the only result of postwar dislocation, it should have affected all regions of the island in the same fashion. It did not; banditry in the republic during the early twentieth century occurred largely in the eastern half of the island. It never assumed the scope and strength of earlier outlawry in the west, although the sources were similar. Instead, rural unrest in the east was expressed in collective and spontaneous outbursts of rural violence. The effects were comparable. But the response was different in the east, and during the early years of the republic it was comparatively limited.

After 1912 sporadic peasant protest in Oriente assumed the form of jacqueries because of changing conditions in rural Cuba. Certainly the expansion of the sugar system had displaced the rural population in both the east and west. However, in the nineteenth century the opportunity for migration cushioned the full effects of rural disarray. Land was available in the east, the last frontier for Cubans in search of a new beginning. For decades Oriente had served as a place of last resort as generations of peasants sought to elude the advance of the market economy. They pushed into unsettled and unknown expanses, seeking to return as much as possible to old ways. Oriente could absorb the landless, the homeless, the jobless.

But inexorably the market economy followed them into Oriente. Sugar appropriated the last expanses of available land. It was not scattered bands of outlaws attacking persons of property and privilege that gave principal expression to rural unrest in the east. It was the mass of the peasantry. After the early 1900s, migration no longer offered a remedy to impoverishment. There was no more land, no more Orientes. The result was the explosions of 1912 and 1917, enormously destructive outbursts of rage. Peasants struck out spontaneously but not randomly at the sources of their oppression: the cane fields, the mills, the mines, the railroads, the records offices.

Because so much of the property was foreign, moreover, and much of it North American, rural protest inevitably brought Cubans into conflict with the United States. The uprisings in 1912 and 1917 resulted in U.S. armed interventions. Foreign property protected its presence with foreign troops.

Economic and social subjugation of the peasants to the regimen of the sugar latifundia was only one aspect of the new order. The arrival of corporate estate was accompanied, in increasing numbers, by the repressive apparatus of the state. An expanded network of rural guard posts descended on the eastern province to provide added protection for the sugar estates.[3] Abusive, arbitrary, and high-handed, the rural guards would come to terrorize the next generation of farmers and peasants.[4]

II   Not all lands were appropriated, not all peasants were expelled. Enclave communities persisted in the east. Peasant production did not cease. Population pressures and the continuing subdivision of plots meant that the actual number of peasant producers actually increased, but necessarily on an increasingly precarious basis.

Vast numbers of displaced farmers joined the swelling ranks of the rural proletariat as part-time itinerant workers on the large estates, part-time indigent cultivators on marginal land. They occupied the worst of both worlds: low-paid laborers, low-producing farmers.[5]

Orientales never reconciled themselves to the new order of their world. Social conflict continued through the next several decades. Peasant lands were subject to continual seizures, and peasant evictions continued. There was no respite. The populat lexicon gave new meaning to *geófagos:* land devourers, property owners who seized the land at every opportunity. Tens of thousands retreated into the impenetrable folds of the mountain ranges that rimmed eastern Oriente.[6] Thousands of others moved into untended tracts of land, and within several decades the problem of squatters *(precaristas)* assumed frightful proportions. An estimated 14,000 squatters occupied almost 9 percent of the total farms of the republic, almost 3 percent of the total farm area. An estimated 84 percent of the total number of squatters were located in Oriente. One-fifth of the farms in Oriente were occupied by *precaristas.*[7] Evictions continued, and were frequently accompanied by violence. These conditions set the stage for continuing conflict between *precaristas* on the one hand and landowners and the armed forces on the other.[8]

These conditions persisted for decades, even through the 1950s. When Fidel Castro and the other survivors of the "Granma" expedition arrived in the Sierra Maestra in 1956, they stepped into a tradition of rebellion, however vague and ill-defined. They came upon armed struggle, they did not introduce it. Hugh Thomas wrote, "In the Sierra Maestra . . . there was a state of half civil war long before Castro set up camp there in 1956, between landlord's agents and *precaristas.*"[9] The *fidelistas* discovered communities of outcasts, peasants surviving at precarious levels of subsistence, by whatever means necessary.[10] Almost half of the population of the Sierra Maestra lived as squatters. They continued to exist at the margins of criminality, as outlaws and bandits, in the inhospitable mountains. These communities remained in more or less a permanent state of rebellion.

They were also among the earliest recruits in the emerging rebel army. Hugh Thomas described Crescencio Pérez, one of the first peasants to join Castro, as "a bandit more than a radical, a common criminal."[11] Crescencio Pérez immediately offered the service of 100 peasants.[12] For many peasants the decision to support the armed struggle in the 1950s was very much an extension of earlier struggles. Carlos Franqui wrote of these years:

> The Sierra was an extremely inhospitable zone, impenetrable, rebellious, populated with miserable persecuted families, who grew and developed like one big family; the Sierra Maestra—the site of the slaves' struggle in the Wars of Independence, of anti-imperialist uprisings, and of struggles against peasant evictions and abuses of land grabbers and the rural guard —was in physical and human terms, suited for guerrilla warfare, and the incorporation of the ancient and prestigious Cresencio opened all doors.[13]

As the armed struggle of the late 1950s spread across the Oriente mountain ranges, the expanding guerrilla columns discovered peasant fugitives at almost every site of new operations. These were mostly *escopeteros*, poorly armed peasants who were outlaws and bandits, many of whom were integrated directly into the rebel army. When Raúl Castro established the Second Front "Frank País," in early 1958, in the areas of Guantánamo, Alto Songo, San Luis, Baracoa, Sagua, and Mayarí, he encountered hundreds of *escopeteros* operating in the region. Select individuals of these groups were incorporated into the Second Front column. By the end of 1958, the Second Front had recruited a total of 1,000 *escopeteros* into the guerrilla army.[14] Peasants soon assumed command positions in the guerrilla columns, including Crescencio Pérez, Victor Mora, and Guillermo García. An estimated 7,000 guerrillas were engaged in military operations in late 1958. "This total,"

Neill Macaulay concluded, "is evidence of an extensive 26 of July guerrilla organization and indicated a significant involvement of rural people in the Fidelista revolutionary movement."[15] By the end of the revolutionary war, perhaps as much as fully half of the rebel army was made up of squatters and field hands from the coffee and sugar estates around the Sierra Maestra.[16]

Certainly not all outlaws of the region welcomed the newcomers, who, after all, aspired to impose on the region a new moral order. During the early weeks and months, clashes between guerrillas and bandits occurred with recurring regularity, as the guerrilla command sought to establish its authority over the province. The guerrillas pursued cattle rustlers, highwaymen, and robbers, a new generation of *plateados*, who preyed often as much upon the peasants as the property owners.[17] Rural outlaws were thus at once the first adversaries as well as the earliest allies of the rebel army.

Throughout the insurgency, guerrilla bands received the sympathy and support of local peasant communities. "Support from the peasants is almost absolute," Castro wrote in July 1957, and again a month later: "Among the people—the peasants—our control is absolute, our support unconditional and unanimous. I cannot remember having had so very many courageous collaborators. The entire Sierra is up in arms."[18] The tradition of rural unrest had transformed itself into an enduring enmity against the sugar latifundia, the foreigners that owned them, and the rural guards that protected them. Nowhere else on the island was land as impassioned an issue and as powerful a longing as it was among the displaced and dispossessed *montuno* families of eastern Cuba. The first territory occupied by the rebel army, Ernesto Che Guevara later recalled, was

> inhabited by a class of peasants different in its social and cultural roots from those that inhabit the regions of extensive, semi-mechanized Cuban agriculture. In fact, the Sierra Maestra, locale of the first revolutionary column, is a place that serves as a refuge to all

the peasants who struggle daily against the landlord. They go there as squatters on the land belonging to the state or some rapacious landlord, searching for a new piece of land that will yield them some small wealth. They struggled continuously against the exactions of the soldiers, always allied with the land-owning power. . . . The soldiers who made up our first guerrilla army of rural people came from that part of this social class which was most aggressive in demonstrating its love for the land and its possession.[19]

Developments in Cuba tend to support the conventional wisdom that peasants by themselves are unable to accomplish revolution.[20] Certainly that is one inference to draw from the events of 1895–1898, and again from 1956–1958. But just as persuasively, developments in Cuba suggest that revolution would have been impossible without peasant participation. Their grievances served as one of the principal sources of social unrest, the basis of their decisive participation in revolutionary upheavals. Certainly the peasantry had the capability to take the initiative, and it did. But in every instance, either with Spain in the late nineteenth century or the United States in the early twentieth, peasants found themselves facing alone the vast power of foreign armed forces. Ultimately the grievances of peasants became the grievances of all Cubans, if in slightly modified form. This provided the common ground for collective action.

Notes

1 The Passing of the Old

1 José R. Alvarez Díaz et al., *A Study on Cuba* (Coral Gables, Fla.: University of Miami Press, 1965), pp. 91–92; Ramiro Guerra y Sánchez, *Sugar and Society in the Caribbean: An Economic History of Cuban Agriculture* (New Haven, Conn.: Yale University Press, 1964), p. 63; Ramiro Guerra y Sánchez et al., *Historia de la nación cubana* (Havana: Editorial Historia de la Nación Cubana, S.A., 1952), 7:153; H. E. Friedlaender, *Historia económica de Cuba* (Havana: Jesús Montero, 1944), p. 432; Francisco López Segrera, *Cuba: capitalismo dependiente y subdesarrollo (1510–1959)* (Havana: Editorial de Ciencias Sociales, 1982), pp. 124–26.

2 Susan Schroeder, *Cuba: A Handbook of Historical Statistics* (Boston: G. K. Hall, 1982), p. 261. Manuel Moreno Fraginals uses slightly different figures, but records similar fluctuations (*El ingenio. Complejo económico social cubano del azúcar* [Havana: Editorial de Ciencias Sociales, 1978], 3:37).

3 Alvarez Díaz et al., *A Study on Cuba*, p. 93.

4 José del Castillo, "The Formation of the Dominican Sugar Industry: From Competition to Monopoly, from National Semiproletariat to Foreign Proletariat," in *Between Slavery and Free Labor: The Spanish-Speaking Caribbean in the Nineteenth Century*, ed. Manuel Moreno Fraginals, Frank Moya Pons, and Stanley L. Engerman (Baltimore: Johns Hopkins University Press, 1985), pp. 215–34; H. Hoetink, *El pueblo dominicano, 1850–1900: Apuntes para su sociología histórica* (Stantiago de los Caballeros: Universidad Católica y Mestre, 1971), p. 22.

5 Manuel Moreno Fraginals, "Plantations in the Caribbean: Cuba, Puerto Rico, and the Dominican Republic in the Nineteenth Century," in *Between Slavery and Free Labor*, ed. Moreno Fraginals, Moya Pons, and Engerman, p. 9.

6 For an excellent treatment of the transformation from slavery to wage labor, see Rebecca J. Scott, *Slave Emancipation in Cuba: The Transition to Free Labor, 1860 – 1899* (Princeton, N.J.: Princeton University Press, 1985).

7 Adam Badeau, "Report on the Present Condition of Cuba," February 7, 1884, Despatches from United States Consuls in Havana, 1783–1906, General Records of the Department of State, RG 59, National **199**

Archives, Washington, D.C. (hereinafter cited as Despatches/ Havana).

8 Vickers to Assistant Secretary of State Davis, October 24, 1883, Despatches from U.S. Consuls in Matanzas, 1820–1899, General Records of the Department of State, RG 59, National Archives, Washington, D.C. (hereinafter cited as Despatches/Matanzas).

9 Pierce to Assistant Secretary of State Davis, August 10, 1883, Despatches from U.S. Consuls in Cienfuegos, 1876–1906, General Records of the Department of State, RG 59, National Archives, Washington, D.C. (hereinafter cited as Despatches/Cienfuegos).

10 Ramiro Guerra y Sánchez, *Por las veredas del pasado, 1880–1902* (Havana: Editorial Lex, 1957), p. 22.

11 Badeau to Secretary of State, March 6, 1884, Despatches/Havana; see also Guerra y Sánchez, *Por las veredas del pasado, 1880–1902*, p. 22.

12 Gaston Descamps, *La crisis azucarera y la Isla de Cuba* (Havana: La Propaganda Literaria, 1885), p. 143.

13 Badeau, "Report on the Present Condition of Cuba," February 7, 1884, Despatches/Havana.

14 Fe Iglesias, "Azúcar y crédito durante la segunda mitad del siglo XIX en Cuba," *Santiago* 52 (December 1983), 141.

15 *El País*, November 26, 1889; see also Hernán Venegas Delgado, "Apuntes sobre la decadencia trinitaria en el siglo XIX," *Islas* 46 (September–December 1973), 159–251.

16 *New York Times*, July 17, 1884.

17 *Diario de Matanzas*, January 18, 1885.

18 Vickers to Davis, July 2, 1884, Despatches/Matanzas.

19 Vickers to Davis, August 27, 1884, Despatches/Matanzas. For a compilation of economic woes in Cuba during these years, see Círculo de Hacendados, *Informe de Círculo de Hacendados de la Isla de Cuba sobre las reformas económicas, administrativas y demanda de la situación de la agricultura* (Havana: Imprenta "La Correspondencia de Cuba," 1887).

20 Maturin M. Ballou, *Due South, or Cuba Past and Present* (Boston: Houghton, Mifflin, 1886), pp. 39, 43, 45, 49, 51–52, 168.

21 In Oscar Pino Santos, "Raíces económicas del 24 de febrero," *Carteles* 37 (February 26, 1956), 77.

22 Crowe to Foreign Office, October 18, 1888, FO 277, no. 57, Embassy and Consular Archives, Cuba, 1870 onwards, Public Record Office, Kew, London, England (hereinafter cited as PRO).

23 Williams to Hunter, November 1, 1884, Despatches/Havana.

24 See Williams to Porter, January 12, 1887, Despatches/Havana; and Francisco Moreno, *Cuba y su gente (apuntes para la historia)* (Madrid: Establecimiento Tipográfico de Enrique Teodora, 1887), pp. 158–59.

25 Vickers to Davis, August 27, 1884, Despatches/Matanzas.

26 *La Lucha*, March 18, 1889.

27 Ballou, *Due South, or Cuba Past and Present*, p. 133.

28 Massimo Livi-Bacci, "Fertility and Population Growth in Spain in

the Eighteenth and Nineteenth Centuries," *Daedalus* 97 (Spring 1968), p. 525.

29   Crowe to Foreign Office, October 18, 1888, FO 277, no. 57, Embassy and Consular Archives, Cuba, 1870 onwards, PRO.

30   Rafael María Merchán, *Cuba, justificación de sus guerras de independencia,* 2d ed. (Havana: Imprenta Nacional de Cuba, 1961), p. 38; Duvon C. Corbitt, "Immigration in Cuba," *Hispanic American Historical Review* 2 (May 1942), 302–04; Centro de Estudios Demográficos, *La población de Cuba* (Havana: Editorial de Ciencias Sociales, 1976), pp. 70–72.

31   See *Diario de la Marina,* August 16, 1892; *El Pais,* August 24, 1892.

32   Eusebio Hernández y Pérez, *El período revolucionario de 1879 a 1895* (Havana: Cultural, S.A., 1914), p. 57.

33   Fernando Portuondo del Prado, *Historia de Cuba,* 6th ed. (Havana: Instituto Cubano del Libro, 1965), p. 434. See also José Rivero Muñiz, "Los cubanos en Tampa," *Revista Bimestre Cubana* 74 (Primer Semestre, 1958), 5–140; José Luciano Franco, "Panamá: refugio de la rebeldía cubana en el siglo XIX," *Casa de las Américas* 15 (July–August 1974), 16–26.

34   Guerra y Sánchez, *Historia de la nación cubana,* 4:199. For a general discussion of sugar production, see Julio E. Le Riverend Brusone, "Sobre la industria azucarera cubana durante el siglo XIX," *El Trimestre Económico* 11 (April–June 1944), 52–70.

35   Fe Iglesias, "The Development of Capitalism in Cuban Sugar Production, 1860–1900," in *Between Slavery and Free Labor,* ed. Moreno Fraginals, Moya Pons, and Engerman, pp. 70–71.

36   Fe Iglesias, "Algunos aspectos de la distribución de la tierra en 1899," *Santiago* 40 (December 1980), 152–54; Félix Goizueta-Mimó, "Effects of Sugar Monoculture Upon Colonial Cuba," Ph.D. diss., University of Pennsylvania, 1971, pp. 91–98.

37   Patria Cok Márquez, "La introducción de los ferrocarriles portátiles en la industria azucarera, 1870–1880," *Santiago* 41 (March 1981), 138–147; Lowry Nelson, *Rural Cuba* (Minneapolis: University of Minnesota Press, 1950), p. 93.

38   The sugar latifundia expanded its boundaries at the expense of all other agricultural units, sugar and nonsugar alike, throughout the western regions. In the region of Remedios in Las Villas province, the new regimen of land concentration proceeded swiftly to establish the preeminence of the sugar latifundia. The *centrales* "Narciso," "Adela," "San Agustín," and "Zaza" absorbed older and less efficient estates, including "Soberano," "Oceano," "Encarnación," "Aurora," "Urbaza," and "Luisiana." In the rich zones of Matanzas-Cárdenas-Colón, sugar estates expanded at a frenetic pace. The sugar revolution of the 1880s also transformed the region around Sagua la Grande. Technological improvements and cultivation of new land increased the production of Sagua's six major *centrales* by 50 percent. Nowhere, however, did land concentration occur as suddenly or as spectacularly as in the Cienfuegos region. Between 1884 and 1891,

some thirteen new *centrales* were organized. These new mills, destined to dominate Cuban sugar production for the next quarter century, included "Constancia," "Soledad," "San Lino," "Lequeito," "Caracas," "Hormiguero," "Parque Alto," and "Cieneguita." See Guerra y Sánchez, *Historia de la nación cubana* 7:192–94; Friedlaender, *Historia económica de Cuba*, pp. 436–38; Hernán Venegas Delgado, "Acerca del proceso de concentración de la industria azucarera en la región remediana a fines del siglo XIX," *Islas* 60 (September–December 1982), 73–80.

39 Moreno Fraginals, "Plantations in the Caribbean," p. 4.

40 For an excellent case study of the demise of coffee farmers in one Havana *municipio*, see Ramiro Guerra y Sánchez, *Mudos testigos. Crónicas del ex cafetal Jesús Nazareño* (Havana: Editorial de Ciencias Sociales, 1974), pp. 107–42.

41 For a general discussion of this phenomenon, see Alain de Janvry and Carlos Garramon, "The Dynamics of Rural Poverty in Latin America," *Journal of Peasant Studies* 4 (April 1977), 206–16.

42 Julio E. LeRiverend Brusone, *La Habana (Biografía de una provincia)* (Havana: Imprenta "El Siglo XX," 1960), pp. 242–43.

43 José Ramón González Pérez, *Santa Ana Cidra. Apuntes para la historia de una comunidad* (Havana: Departamento de Orientación Revolucionaria del Comité Central del PCC, 1975), pp. 38–39; see also Iglesias, "Algunos aspectos de la distribución de la tierra en 1899," p. 158.

44 Venegas Delgado, "Acerca del proceso de concentración de la industria azucarera," pp. 69–73.

45 Rebecca J. Scott, "Class Relations in Sugar and Political Mobilization in Cuba," 1868–1899," *Cuban Studies/Estudios Cubanos* 15 (Winter 1985), 21; LeRiverend Brusone, *La Habana*, pp. 243, 350. These developments in late nineteenth-century Cuba were similar to and simultaneous with events occurring elsewhere in the world. "In disparate parts of the world ruled by different states and empires," wrote Joel S. Migdal, "small freeholding peasants almost simultaneously faced catastrophic changes in the rules of land tenure in their societies. It is most striking that these land tenure changes came in a number of countries almost at the same moment in history. . . . Wherever enacted . . . one prime purpose of such laws was to facilitate changes in agricultural production that would increase yields and that would lead to the planting of crops suitable for export. Simultaneous changes in land tenure in seemingly unrelated parts of the globe came in large part because of increased demand in Europe and the United States for cotton, sugar, coffee, jute, indigo, and a number of other select crops. . . . New production techniques for specific crops that were developed at this time also increased the pressure for consolidating land so as to gain greater economies of scale. . . . Whatever the precise purposes and rationalizations for changes in land tenure, they precipitated eruptive, universal dislocations whenever enacted. They signaled changes in agricultural production and class relations that entered so deeply into the fabric

of societies that their effects are often still discernible today" ("Capitalist Penetration in the Nineteenth Century: Creating Conditions for New Patterns of Social Control," in *Power and Protest in the Countryside*, ed. Robert P. Weller and Scott E. Guggenheim [Durham, N.C.: Duke University Press, 1982], pp. 60–61).

46 Guerra y Sánchez, *Sugar and Society in the Caribbean*, pp. 85–93.

47 Cuba, Bureau of the Census, *Census of the Republic of Cuba, 1919* (Havana: Maza, Arroyo y Caso, 1919), p. 258. Mortality figures this high had not been registered in Europe since the end of the seventeenth century. See Fernand Braudel, *Capitalism and Material Life, 1400 – 1800* (New York: Harper and Row, 1973), pp. 37–38; and E. A. Wrigley, *Population and History* (New York: McGraw-Hill, 1969), pp. 62–63.

48 Crowe to Foreign Office, October 18, 1888, FO 277, no. 57, Embassy and Consular Archives, Cuba, 1870 onwards, PRO; Crowe to Foreign Office, August 1, 1890, FO 277, no. 57, Embassy and Consular Archives, Cuba, 1870 onwards, PRO.

49 Raimundo Cabrera, *Cuba and the Cubans* (Philadelphia: The Levytype Company, 1896), p. 141. Benjamín de Cespedes, *La prostitución en la ciudad de La Habana* (Havana: Establecimiento Tipografico O'Reilly, 1888); Memoria de la Comisión de Higiene Especial de la Isla de Cuba, *La prostitución en Cuba y especialmente en La Habana* (Havana: Imprenta P. Fernández y Cía., 1902), pp. 15–18; Ignacio D. Ituarte, *Crímenes y criminales de La Habana* (Havana: n.p., 1893); Francisco Figueras, *Cuba y su evolución colonial* (Havana: Imprenta Avisador Comercial, 1907), pp. 284–85, 296–97.

50 Crowe to Foreign Office, August 1, 1890, FO 277, no. 57, Embassy and Consular Archives, Cuba, 1870 onwards, PRO.

51 Moreno, *Cuba y su gente*, pp. 179–80.

52 Cabrera, *Cuba and the Cubans*, p. 236.

53 *New York Times*, March 12, 1893.

54 Crowe to Foreign Office, October 18, 1888, FO 277, no. 57, Embassy and Consular Archives, Cuba, 1870 onwards, PRO.

55 Ballou, *Due South, or Cuba Past and Present*, p. 49.

56 *New York Times*, December 19, 1890.

57 Williams to Rives, November 24, 1888, Despatches/Havana.

58 John Anthony Froude, *The English in the West Indies* (London: Longmans, Green, 1888), pp. 301–06.

59 Richard Davey, *Cuba, Past and Present* (New York: Charles Scribner's Sons, 1898), p. 137.

60 "Memoria sobre la represión del bandolerismo y destino de los vagos," December 16, 1879, Fondo Gobierno General, legajo 584, no. 28,863, Archivo Nacional de Cuba, Havana, Cuba (hereinafter cited as ANC). The relationship between the abolition of slavery and vagrancy is explored in Scott, *Slave Emancipation in Cuba*, pp. 218–26.

61 Calleja, Santa Clara, to Governor General, January 27, 1881, Fondo Gobierno General, legajo 584, no. 28,863, ANC.

62 *Diario de la Marina*, November 24, 1888.

63   Antonio Pérez, Secretario, Audiencia de La Habana, to Jefe, Sección de Administración, January 9, 1888, Fondo de Asuntos Políticos, legajo 81, no. 23, ANC. See also Gobierno de la Isla de Cuba, "Circular: a los Gobernadores Civiles de las Provincias de esta Isla," January 19, 1888, Fondo de Asuntos Políticos, legajo 81, no. 23, ANC.

64   Manuel Salamanca, "Circular," May 12, 1889, Fondo Gobierno General, legajo 584, no. 28,863, ANC.

65   Williams to Rives, January 28, 1888, Despatches/Havana; see also Williams to Rives, February 3, 1888, Despatches/Havana.

66   Portuondo del Prado, Historia de Cuba, p. 502.

67   "Expediente promovido sobre las proporciones que van tomando el bandolerismo de Puerto Príncipe," March 31, 1887, Fondo de Asuntos Políticos, legajo 81, no. 15, ANC; "Expediente promovido para reunir los estados de hechos criminales cometidos por partidos de bandoleros en las seis provincias de la Isla," n.d., Fondo de Asuntos Políticos, legajo 82, no. 1, ANC; see also "Deposition of Constantino March," Hormiguero Central Company v. the United States, entry 352, case no. 293, Records of the Boundary and Claims Commissions and Arbitrations, RG 76, National Archives, Washington, D.C.

68   Antonio C. N. Gallenga, The Pearl of the Antilles (London: Chapman and Hall, 1873), p. 53.

69   U.S. War Department, Informe sobre el censo de Cuba, 1899 (Washington, D.C.: GPO, 1899), pp. 554–72; Robet B. Hoernal, "Sugar and Social Change in Oriente, Cuba, 1898–1946," Journal of Latin American Studies 8 (November 1976), 221–26; see also Iglesias, "Algunos aspectos de la distribución de la tierra en 1899," p. 126.

70   Vickers to Davis, August 27, 1884, Despatches/Matanzas.

71   See Francisco López Leiva, El bandolerismo en Cuba (Contribución al estudio de esta plaga social) (Havana: Imprenta "El Siglo XX," 1930), pp. 7–22; Maria Poumier-Taquechel, Contribution à l'étude du banditisme social à Cuba. L'histoire et le mythe de Manuel García, "Rey de los Campos de Cuba" (1851–1895) (Paris: Editions L'Harmattan, 1986), pp. 43–53; Figueras, Cuba y su evolución colonial, pp. 293–97.

72   Tesifonte Gallego, La insurrección cubana (Madrid: Imprenta Central de los Ferrocarriles, 1897), pp. 198–200; Alvaro de la Iglesia y Santos, Manuel García (El Rey de los Campos de Cuba): su vida y sus hechos (Havana: La Comercial, 1895), pp. 18, 34–37; López Leiva, El bandolerismo en Cuba, p. 24.

73   Eric J. Hobsbawm, Bandits (New York: Delacorte Press, 1969), p. 18.

74   Eric Hobsbawm, Primitive Rebels (New York: W. W. Norton, 1965), p. 3; cf. Anton Blok, "The Peasant and the Brigand: Social Banditry Reconsidered," Comparative Studies in Society and History 14 (September 1972), 494–503; Pat O'Malley, "Social Bandits, Modern Capitalism and the Traditional Peasantry: A Critique of Hobsbawm," Journal of Peasant Studies 6 (July 1979), 489–501.

75   Eric J. Hobsbawm, "Social Banditry," in Rural Protest: Peasant Movement and Social Change, ed. Henry A. Landsberger (London: Macmillan, 1973), p. 143.

76   Aníbal Quijano Obregón, "Contemporary Peasant Movements," in *Elites in Latin America*, ed. Seymour Martin Lipset and Aldo Solari (New York: Oxford University Press, 1967), pp. 305–06.

77   See Ballou, *Due South, or Cuba Past and Present*, p. 97.

78   For brief biographical sketches of some of the more prominent bandits, see Eduardo Varela Zequeira and Arturo Mora y Varona, *Los bandidos de Cuba*, 2d ed. (Havana: Establecimiento Tipográfico de "La Lucha," 1891), pp. 25–63; Iglesia y Santos, *Manuel García*, pp. 34–37. One of the most complete and scholarly biographies of Manuel García is found in Poumier-Taquechel, *Contribution à l'étude du banditisme social à Cuba*, pp. 84–139.

79   Julio Angel Carreras, "Los bandoleros de la tregua in Santa Clara," *Islas* 51 (May–August 1978), 132.

80   "Expediente sobre datos de bandolerismo en Matanzas," 1888, Fondo Asuntos Políticos, legajo 82, no. 5, ANC; Antonio Pirala, *España y la regencia: anales de diez y seis años (1885–1902)* (Madrid: Librería de Victoriano Suárez, 1904–1907), 2:250–53.

81   "Expediente promovido para reunir datos de bandolerismo de la provincia de La Habana," January 3, 1888, Fondo Asuntos Políticos, legajo 81, no. 21, ANC.

82   "Expediente promovido para reunir datos sobre el bandolerismo de la provincia de Santa Clara," January 9, 1888, Fondo Asuntos Políticos, legajo 80, no. 21, ANC.

83   "Expediente promovido para reunir los estados de hechos criminales cometidos por partidas de bandoleros en las seis provincias de la Isla," n.d., Fondo de Asuntos Políticos, legajo 82, no. 1, ANC.

84   See "Expediente promovido con motivo del secuestro del Exmo. Sor. D. Antonio Galíndez de Aldama," 1888, Fondo de Asuntos Políticos, legajo 82, no. 4, ANC; "Telegrama sobre el secuestro del hacendado Antonio Fernández de Castro, por la partida de Manuel García," September 22, 1894, Fondo de Asuntos Políticos, legajo 84, no. 7, ANC; see also Iglesia y Santos, *Manuel García*, pp. 107–09.

85   For a detailed account of one such attack against the town of Nueva Paz in Havana province, see *Diario de la Marina*, November 14, 1889.

86   Camilo G. Polavieja, *Relación documentada de mi política en Cuba* (Madrid: Imprenta de Emilio Minuesa, 1898), p. 212. Governor General Polavieja claimed that most of these fires were accidental, and undoubtedly many were. However, during the 1892 *zafra*, a North American correspondent in Cuba reported: "Without doubt . . . outlaws have been the cause of the frequent fires among the cane fields which are daily reported" (*New York Times*, April 4, 1892).

87   See Iglesia y Santos, *Manuel García*, p. 55.

88   Edwin F. Atkins, *Sixty Years in Cuba* (Cambridge, Mass.: Riverside Press, 1926), pp. 150–51; see also Carreras, "Los bandoleros de la tregua en Santa Clara," p. 140.

89   *Diario de la Marina*, August 9, 1890; "Expediente promovido para reunir los datos relativos a hechos bandálicos entre los cuales figuran el incendio del paradero del ferrocarril de Quivicán, por la partida de bandidos capitaneados por Manuel García," 1890, Fondo de Asuntos

Políticos, legajo 82, no. 24, ANC; "Expediente promovido por con-
secuencia de oficio de la Empresa Ferrocarriles Unidos de La Habana,
dando cuenta de que en el kilómetro 64, de los bandidos de la partida
de Manuel García, levantaron un carril, descarrilando un tren de carga
e hicieron fuegos al maquinista y conductor," 1890, Fondo de Asuntos
Políticos, legajo 82, no. 25, ANC; see also Rosalie Schwartz, "Bandits
and Rebels in Cuban Independence: Predators, Patriots, and Pariahs,"
Bibliotheca Americana 1 (November 1982), 92.

90 Ballou, *Due South, or Cuba Past and Present,* pp. 63–64.

91 Gollan to Foreign Office, March 31, 1893, FO 277, no. 57, Embassy
and Consular Archives, Cuba, 1870 onwards, PRO.

92 Vickers to Davis, August 27, 1884, Despatches/Matanzas.

93 Crowe to Foreign Office, August 1, 1890, FO 277, no. 57, Embassy and
Consular Archives, Cuba, 1870 onwards, PRO.

94 Gallego, *La insurrección cubana,* p. 247; Eugenio Antonio Flores, *La
guerra de Cuba (Apuntes para la historia)* (Madrid: Tipografía de los
Hijos de M. G. Hernández, 1895), p. 505.

95 Williams to Porter, March 26, 1887, Despatches/Havana.

96 *La Lucha,* September 24, 1894, in Poumier-Taquechel, *Contribution
à l'étude du banditisme social à Cuba,* pp. 120–21.

97 *Diario de la Marina,* March 24, 1887.

98 Governor-General Camilo G. Polavieja was concerned with ending
banditry as much as to restore creditability to colonial government as
to restore stability to rural Cuba. Throughout his administration he
feared that the persistence of outlawry would undermine Spanish
authority on the island *(Relación documentada de mi política en
Cuba,* pp. 85, 195–97).

99 See Merchán, *Cuba;* Cabrera, *Cuba and the Cubans.*

100 López Leiva, *El bandolerismo en Cuba,* p. 29.

101 Crowe to Foreign Office, October 18, 1888, FO 277, no. 57, Embassy
and Consular Archives, Cuba, 1870 onwards, PRO.

102 Vickers to Davis, July 2, 1884, Despatches/Matanzas.

103 *El Popular,* February 11, 1887.

104 In *El Popular,* June 7, 1887.

105 Williams to Porter, May 18, 1887, Despatches/Havana; for a discus-
sion of annexationist sentiment during these years, see José Ignacio
Rodríguez, *Estudio histórico sobre el origen, desenvolvimiento y
manifestaciones prácticas de la anexión de la Isla de Cuba a los
Estados Unidos de América* (Havana: Imprenta "La Propaganda
Literaria," 1900), pp. 243–86; for the views of one planter concern-
ing banditry, see Gabriel Millett, *Mi última temporada en Cuba*
(Madrid: Est. Tip. "Sucesores y Revadeyra," 1894), pp. 69–70.

106 *Diario de la Marina,* December 24, 1884.

107 "Expediente promovido para crear en esta Isla, el Cuerpo de Guar-
dias Rurales," 1889–1890, Fondo de Asuntos Políticos, legajo 82, no.
19, ANC.

108 Gobierno General de la Isla de Cuba, "Decreto," August 8, 1889,
Fondo Gobierno General, legajo 584, no. 28863, ANC.

109 Enrique Edo, *Memoria histórica de Cienfuegos y su jurisdicción*, 3d ed. (Havana: Ucar, García y Cía., 1943), pp. 654–55.

110 *La Lucha*, April 17, 1889; Crowe to Foreign Office, September 5, 1890, FO 277, no. 57, Embassy and Consular Archives, Cuba, 1870 onwards, PRO; Figueras, *Cuba y su evolución colonial*, pp. 289–90.

111 Sabas Marín, "Bando," July 3, 1888, Fondo Gobierno General, legajo 584, no. 28863, ANC.

112 "Expediente promovido para reunir las disposiciones que se dicten sobre bandolerismo durante el mando del Excmo. Sor. Gobernador General D. Camilo Polavieja," 1890, Fondo de Asuntos Políticos, legajo 32, no. 26, ANC; see also Polavieja, *Relación documentada de mi política en Cuba*, pp. 199–200; López Leiva, *El bandolerismo en Cuba*, pp. 22–25; Poumier-Taquechel, *Contribution à l'étude du banditisme social à Cuba*, pp. 73–82.

113 See "Relación nominal de bandidos muertos por la fuerza pública desde 1ro julio de 1887 a 28 marzo de 1888," March 28, 1888, Fondo de Asuntos Políticos, legajo 81, no. 18, ANC.

114 See Iglesia y Santos, *Manuel García*, p. 170; Polavieja, *Relación documentada de mi política en Cuba*, pp. 211–12; Poumier-Taquechel, *Contribution à l'étude du banditisme social à Cuba*, pp. 116–17; Flores, *La guerra de Cuba*, p. 475. The publicity value of public executions was underscored by the following press despatch: "Deep alarm reigns all over the country in consequence of the daily increase of all sorts of crimes, the perpetrators being encouraged in their actions by the complete immunity they enjoy. In spite of daily assassinations, the public never learns whether the assassins are punished, and an execution has not taken place since the days when political prisoners were occasionally garroted" (*New York Times*, July 12, 1883). The bandits captured and subsequently executed by Spanish authorities between 1889 and 1891 included Victoriano Machín, Cristobal Fernández Delgado, Eusebio Moreno y Suárez, Joaquín Alemán, Federico Acosta, José Manuel Martín Pérez, Dionisio Guzmán Pérez, Manuel and José de León Ortiz, Nicanor Duarte Ramos, Venancio, José, and Carmelo Díaz Ramos, Felipe González López, Francisco Paz, Pedro Boitel, Pedro Macías Ortall, José Estrauman Daria, Valentín González López, Guillermo Pérez Cruz, José Sánchez Ortega, Pablo Cantero, and Teodoro Galano.

115 Polavieja, *Relación documentada de mi política en Cuba*, p. 205.

116 Colonel Guillermo R. Fort, Chief of Operations, Guardia Civil, Madruga, "Relación," December 19, 1894, Fondo Gobierno General, legajo 584, no. 28863, ANC.

117 Esteban Montejo, *Autobiography of a Runaway Slave*, ed. Miguel Barnet, trans. Jocasta Innes (London: Bodley Head, 1968), p. 113; see also Eduardo Zamacois, *La alegría de andar* (Madrid: Renacimiento, 1920), pp. 153–54; García to Lachambre, n.d., in Varela Zequeira and Mora y Varona, *Los bandidos de Cuba*, p. 212; Rafael Gutiérrez Fernández, *Los heroes del 24 de febrero* (Havana: Casa Editorial Carasa y Cía., 1932), pp. 123–24.

118   This practice was one of the ways Brazilian bandits garnered support
      from the peasantry; see Linda Lewis, "The Oligarchical Limitations
      of Social Banditry in Brazil: The Case of the 'Good' Thief Antonio
      Silvino," *Past and Present* 82 (February 1979), 137–38; Peter
      Singlemann, "Political Structure and Social Banditry in Northeast
      Brazil," *Journal of Latin American Studies* 7 (1975), 62–64.

119   Montejo, *Autobiography of a Runaway Slave*, p. 119. The account is
      corroborated in a oral history narrative of Lorenzo Yanes, a farmer in
      Melena del Sur, who at the age of ninety-two recounted several
      instances of peasant support of Manuel García (Lorenzo Yanes and
      René Batista Moreno, "Retratos de una vida hazañera," *Bohemia* 63
      [January 22, 1971], 98–99); see also López Leiva, *El bandolerismo en
      Cuba*, pp. 27–29.

120   Colonel Guillermo R. Fort, Chief of Operations, Guardia Civil,
      Madruga, "Relación," December 19, 1894, Fondo Gobierno General,
      legajo 584, no. 28863, ANC. Another intelligence report of compar-
      able detail is available for the *municipio* of Quivicán in central
      Havana province; see Lieutenant Justo Pardo González, Operations,
      Guardia Civil, Quivicán, "Relación," December 18, 1894, Fondo
      Gobierno General, legajo 584, no. 28863, ANC; see also Varela
      Zequeira and Mora y Varona, *Los bandidos de Cuba*, p. 44.

121   Polavieja, *Relación documentada de mi política en Cuba*, p. 211.

122   Ibid., p. 88; throughout his memoir, Polavieja complains of peasant
      support of bandits and how this collaboration made the Spanish task
      all but impossible (pp. 87, 195, 213).

123   Luis Estévez y Romero, *Desde el Zanjón hasta Baire*, 2d ed.
      (Havana: Editorial de Ciencias Sociales, 1974), 1:311; Portuondo del
      Prado, *Historia de Cuba*, p. 502; Gutiérrez Fernández, *Los heroes
      del 24 de febrero*, p. 131.

124   Merchán, *Cuba*, p. 88.

125   Varela Zequeira and Mora y Varona, *Los bandidos de Cuba*, p. 79.

126   Luis Alonso Martín, "Circular from the Civil Governor of Havana
      Concerning the Suppression of Highway Robbery," November 14,
      1887, in Cabrera, *Cuba and the Cubans*, pp. 305–06.

127   *Voz de Cuba*, April 8, 1888.

128   Sabas Marín, "Circular," *Diario de la Marina*, April 19, 1888; see
      also *La Lucha*, April 17, 1888; Sabas Marín, "Bando," July 3, 1888,
      Fonda Gobierno General, legajo 584, no. 28863, ANC.

129   *Gaceta de La Habana*, April 3, 1889.

130   Ehringer to Porter, December 29, 1886, Despatches/Cienfuegos.

131   Governor Polavieja wrote of one incident in which a peasant couple
      dutifully reported a visit by Manuel García to the authorities, and
      were subsequently killed. The best that Polavieja could do was to
      secure public charity for the orphaned children. On the body of the
      dead man, Garcia had left the following note: "Hernández had been
      my friend since boyhood. I killed him because he tried to deliver me
      to the Guards. I have never before killed a woman, but I killed his

wife because she induced him to betray me. I hurt only those who hurt me" (*Relación documentada de mi política en Cuba*, pp. 206–07; *New York Times*, October 6, 1891).

The Promise of the New

1 See Matías Duque, *Nuestra patria* (Havana: Imprenta Montalvo, Cárdenas y Cía., 1923), p. 143; Kenneth F. Kiple, *Blacks in Colonial Cuba, 1774–1899* (Gainesville: University Presses of Florida, 1976), p. 81; Rafael Fermoselle, *Política y color en Cuba* (Montevideo: Ediciones Geminis, 1974), p. 26; Donna M. Wolf, "The Cuban 'Gente de Color' and the Independence Movement, 1879–1895," *Revista/ Review Interamericana* 5 (Fall 1975), 403–21; Thomas T. Orum, "The Politics of Color: The Racial Dimension of Cuban Politics During the Early Republican Years, 1900–1912," Ph.D. diss., New York University, 1975, pp. 31–49.

2 *Historia de Manuel García, Rey de los Campos de Cuba (Desde la cuna hasta el sepulcro), por uno que lo sabe todo* (Havana: Imprenta y Librería "La Moderna Poesía," 1898), 1:65–80; Rafael Gutiérrez Fernández, *Los heroes del 24 de febrero* (Havana: Carasa y Cía., 1932), pp. 121–43; Eduardo Varela Zequeira and Arturo Mora y Varona, *Los bandidos de Cuba*, 2d ed. (Havana: Establecimiento Tipográfico de "La Lucha," 1891), p. 86; Jorge Petinaud and Raúl Rodríguez, "Manuel García no fué un bandido," *Granma*, December 1, 1985, p. 8.

3 See Octavio Ramón Costa y Blanco, *Juan Gualberto Gómez: una vida sin sombra* (Havana: Imprenta "El Siglo XX," 1950), pp. 118–19; Emilio Reverter Delmas, *Cuba española. Reseña histórica de la insurrección cubana en 1895* (Barcelona: Centro Editorial de Alberto Martín, 1897–1898), 1:3; Eduardo Anillo Rodríguez, *Cuatro siglos de vida* (Havana: Imprenta "Avisador Comercial," 1915), p. 82; Gutiérrez Fernández, *Los heroes del 24 de febrero*, pp. 144–56; Petinaud and Rodríguez, "Manuel García no fué un bandido," p. 8.

4 Alvaro de la Iglesia y Santos, *Manuel García (El Rey de los Campos de Cuba). Su vida y sus hechos* (Havana: La Comercial, 1895), p. 200.

5 See Francisco J. Ponte Domínguez, *Matanzas (Biografía de una provincia)* (Havana: Imprenta "El Siglo XX," 1959), p. 240; Oswaldo Morales Patiño, *El capitán chino. Teniente coronel Quirino Zamora: Historia de un mambí en la provincia de La Habana* (Havana: Municipio de La Habana, 1953), p. 131; Miguel Angel Varona Guerrero, *La guerra de independencia de Cuba, 1895–1898* (Havana: Editorial Lex, 1946), 2:836; Juan Bautista Casas y González, *La guerra separatista de Cuba* (Madrid: Tipográfico de San Francisco de Sales, 1896), pp. 116–19. In his account of the war years, Esteban Montejo alludes to a number of different commanders under whom he served, characterizing them variously as former "bandits," "lawless men,"

and "highwaymen." *(The Autobiography of a Runaway Slave,* ed. Miguel Barnet, trans. Jocasta Innes [London: Bodley Head, 1968], pp. 182–208).

6   See "Deposition of José Alvarez Morales," Constancia Sugar Company *v.* the United States, entry 352, claim no. 196, Records of Boundary and Claims Commission and Arbitration, RG 76, National Archives, Washington, D.C. (hereinafter cited as BCCA/RG 76). José Alvarez Morales was a rural worker who joined the "Matagás"-Matos unit upon the outbreak of the war. See also Grover Flint, *Marching with Gómez* (Boston: Lamson, Wolffe, 1898), pp. 49–50; Manuel Martínez-Moles, *Epítome de la historia de Sancti-Spíritus desde el descubrimiento de sus costas (1494) hasta nuestros días (1934)* (Havana: Imprenta "El Siglo XX," 1936), pp. 168–69; Gutiérrez Fernández, *Los heroes del 24 de febrero,* p. 156.

7   For accounts of the invasion, see José S. Llorens y Maceo, *Con Maceo en la invasión* (Havana: n.p., 1928); Juan J. E. Casasús, *La invasión. Sus antecedentes, sus factores, su finalidad. Estudio crítico-militar* (Havana: Imprenta Habana, 1950); Fernando Gómez, *La insurrección por dentro. Apuntes para la historia* (Havana: M. Ruiz y Cia., 1897), p. 210; Benigno Souza y Rodríguez, *Biografía de un regimiento mambí: El regimiento "Calixto García"* (Havana: Imprenta "El Siglo XX," 1939), pp. 113–33.

8   José Miró Argenter, *Crónicas de la guerra* (Havana: Instituto del Libro, 1970), 1:227–36. See also José Luciano Franco, *Antonio Maceo. Apuntes para una historia de su vida* (Havana: Editorial de Ciencias Sociales, 1975), 2:240–66; Ramiro Guerra y Sánchez, *Por las veredas del pasado, 1880–1902* (Havana: Editorial Lex, 1957), pp. 37, 39; Gonzalo de Quesada and Henry Davenport Northrop, *Cuba's Great Struggle for Freedom* (New York: n.p., 1898), p. 67.

9   Maceo to Director, *Washington Star,* January 27, 1896, in Antonio Maceo, *Antonio Maceo. Ideología política. Cartas y otros documentos,* ed. Sociedad Cubana de Estudios Históricas e Internacionales (Havana: Cárdenas y Cía., 1950–1952), 2:196; see also Maceo to Estrada Palma, February 27, 1896, in Antonio Maceo, *Antonio Maceo: documentos para su vida,* ed. Julian Martínez Castells (Havana: Archivo Nacional de Cuba, 1945), p. 136. This increment is corroborated by Major Anastasio Ramírez García, who later recalled that the *Ejército Invasora* departed from Santa Clara with 3,000 officers and men arrived to Pinar del Río with 10,000 ("Deposition of Anastasio Ramírez García," Hormiguero Central Company *v.* the United States, entry 352, claim no. 293, BCCA/RG 76).

10   Benigno Souza y Rodríguez, *Ensayo histórico sobre la invasión* (Havana: Imprenta del Ejercito, 1948), p. 187; Llorens y Maceo, *Con Maceo en la invasión,* pp. 73–74, 82; Antero Regalado, *Las luchas campesinas en Cuba* (Havana: Editorial Orbe, 1979), p. 49.

11   Miró Argenter, *Cronicas de la guerra* 1:263; see also Guerra y Sanchez, *Por las veredas del pasado, 1880–1902,* pp. 50–51; Julián Sán-

chez, *Julián Sánchez cuenta su vida,* ed. Erasmo Dumpierre (Havana: Instituto Cubano del Libro, 1970), pp. 27, 37.

12　Headquarters of the Army of Liberation, "Proclamation," July 4, 1896, in *Correspondencia diplomática de la delegación cubana en Nueva York durante la guerra de 1895 a 1898,* ed. Joaquín Llaverías y Martínez (Havana: Imprenta del Archivo Nacional, 1943–1946), 5:176–77.

13　Supplies were often difficult to come by, and sometimes they did not come at all. "Until now I have received no resources, absolutely none," Antonio Maceo complained to General Máximo Gómez in June 1896; "I am making the war with supplies I have on different occasions taken from the enemy." This complaint was repeated six months later by Maceo's successor in Pinar del Río, General Juan Rius Rivera. "An army of 50,000 could be placed in Havana province before the winter is over if we had but the arms and ammunition," Rius Rivera lamented. "We cannot fight alone with our hands, not even with machetes, against an enemy that is fully equipped." See Maceo to Gómez, June 27, 1896, in Leonardo Griñán Peralta, *Antonio Maceo, análisis caracterológico* (Havana: Editorial Trópico, 1936), p. 191; Maceo to Estrada Palma, February 27, 1896, in *Antonio Maceo: documentos para su vida,* pp. 133–34; and *New York World,* January 18, 1897. For other accounts of Cuban shortages during the western campaign, see Llorens y Maceo, *Con Maceo en la invasión,* pp. 92, 122–23; Eduardo Rosell, "Diario de operaciones del comandante Eduardo Rosell, Jefe de Estado Mayor del brigadier Pedro Betancourt," in Carlos M. Trelles y Govín, *Matanzas en la independencia de Cuba* (Havana: Imprenta "Avisador Comercial," 1928), pp. 171–72; Manuel Piedra Martel, *Memorias de un mambí* (Havana: Instituto del Libro, 1968), pp. 101–03; Nestor Carbonell y Rivero, *Resumen de una vida heroica* (Havana: Imprenta "El Siglo XX," 1945), pp. 35–36.

14　Fermín Valdés Domínguez, *Diario de soldado* (Havana: Universidad de La Habana, 1972–1974), 1:197.

15　Máximo Gómez, "A los señores hacendados y dueños de fincas ganaderas," July 1, 1895, Fondo Donativos y Remisiones, legajo 257, no. 14, Archivo Nacional de Cuba (hereinafter cited as ANC). Nor was this warning issued lightly. On several occasions, insurgent army units mounted operations against mills that defied the Cuban ban on the *zafra,* attacking the workers in the fields. These attacks had the desired result. Recalled one mill superintendent: "It was cause for the workmen to be afraid of going out in the fields during the war" ("Deposition of Anselmo Rabassa," Constancia Sugar Company v. the United States, entry 352, claim no. 196, BCCA/RG 76).

16　Máximo Gómez, "A los hombres honrados victimas de la tea," November 11, 1895, Fondo Archivo Máximo Gómez, legajo 7, no. 212, ANC.

17　Headquarters of the Army of Liberation, "Proclamation," July 4,

1896, in *Correspondencia diplomática de la delegación cubana en Nueva York durante la guerra de 1895 a 1898*, ed. Llaverías y Martínez, 5:176–77.

18 José Clemente Vivanco, "A propuesto del Sub-Secretario de Relaciones Exteriores, ciudadano Dr. Eusebio Hernández," July 3, 1896, Fondo Archivo Máximo Gómez, legajo 9, no. 11, ANC; Vivanco to Cisneros Betancourt, May 15, 1896, Fondo Archivo Máximo Gómez legajo 9, no. 11, ANC; see also Eusebio Hernández y Pérez, *Dos conferencias históricas* (Havana: Cultural, S.A., n.d.), pp. 72–73, Miguel Angel Carbonell, *Eusebio Hernández* (Havana: Editorial Guáimaro, 1939), 2:37–41.

19 See "Manuscrito del acuerdo del Consejo de Gobierno en sesión 13 de julio de 1896 en relación a la prohibición de la zafra de 1896 a 1897," July 30, 1896, Fondo Donativos y Remisiones, legajo 624, no. 34 ANC; "Documento manuscrito que contiene acuerdo tomado por el Consejo de Gobierno donde quedan prohibidas todas las operaciones de zafra de 1896 a 1897," November 6, 1896, Fondo Donativos y Remisiones, legajo 553, no. 19, ANC. The moratorium was subsequently extended to the 1897–1898 harvest. See República de Cuba, Consejo de Gobierno, "Acuerdo," November 30, 1897, Fondo Donativos y Remisiones, legajo 614, no. 24, ANC; Máximo Gómez, "Orden general del día," January 21, 1897, Fondo Donativos y Remisiones, legajo 547, no. 44, ANC.

20 In Souza y Rodríguez, *Ensayo histórico sobre la invasión*, p. 76.

21 Maceo to Estrada Palma, February 27, 1896, in Maceo, *Antonio Maceo: documentos para su vida*, p. 136.

22 Maceo to Estrada Palma, April 14, 1896, in ibid., p. 137.

23 See Edwin F. Atkins, *Sixty Years in Cuba* (Cambridge, Mass.: Riverside Press, 1926), pp. 181, 190, 227; "Statement of L. F. Hughes, Assistant Manager of Ingenio Soledad," September 18, 1898, in U.S. Treasury Dept., *Report on the Commercial and Industrial Condition of the Island of Cuba* (Washington, D.C.: GPO, 1899), p. 266; "Statement of Mr. Louis Ponvert, planter," September 20, 1898, in ibid., p. 130; Franklin Matthews, *The New-Born Cuba* (New York: Harper & Brothers, 1899), p. 351; Osgood Welsh, "Cuba as Seen From the Inside," *Century Magazine* 56 (August 1898), 590–93. Nor could planters after 1896 reasonably expect relief from Spanish authorities. Recalled one planter: "I had a plantation in Havana Province, we asked [General] Weyler for protection and he told me that the Spanish Army didn't come to Cuba to protect private interests, but only to sustain and defend the Sovereignty of Spain" ("Deposition of Manuel Antonio Recio de Morales," Constancia Sugar Company *v.* the United States, entry 352, claim no. 196, BCCA/RG 76).

24 "Extract From a Letter Received, February 22, 1896, Dated at Havana," Philip Phillips Family Papers, Manuscript Division, Library of Congress, Washington, D.C.

25 "Deposition of General José Lachambre, "Central Teresa *v.* the United States, entry 352, claim no. 97, BCCA/RG 76.

26 "Deposition of Captain Ramón Sánchez Varona," Constancia Sugar Company *v.* the United States, entry 352, claim no. 196, BCCA/RG 76.

27 "Deposition of Major Florentino Yriondo de la Vara," Hormiguero Central Company *v.* the United States, entry 352, claim no. 293, BCCA/RG 76.

28 See Weyler's reconcentration decree for Pinar del Río, October 21, 1896, in Melchor Fernández Almagro, *Historia política de la España contemporánea* (Madrid: Ediciones Pegaso, 1956–1959), 2:306–07; Valeriano Weyler, *Mi mando en Cuba* (Madrid: Imprenta de Felipe González Rojas, 1910–1911), 2:427–28.

29 "Deposition of Laureano Llorente," Mapos Sugar Company *v.* the United States, entry 352, claim no. 121, BCCA/RG 76. See also Martínez-Moles, *Epítome de la historia de Sancti-Spíritus desde el descubrimiento de sus costas (1494) hasta nuestros días (1934)*, pp. 139–41.

30 William J. Calhoun, "Report on Cuba," June 22, 1897, Special Agents, 48, General Records of the Department of State, RG 59, National Archives, Washington, D.C. For other accounts of the Spanish campaign under Weyler, see "Deposition of Esteban Valladares," Constancia Sugar Company *v.* the United States, entry 352, claim no. 196, BCCA/RG 76.

31 Varona Guerrero, *La guerra de independencia de Cuba, 1895–1898*, 2:780.

32 See Raimundo Cabrera, *Episodios de la guerra. Mi vida en la manigua. (Relato del coronel Ricardo Buenamar)*, 3d ed. (Philadelphia: La Compañía Levytype, 1898), pp. 265–70; Horatio S. Rubens, *Liberty, the Story of Cuba* (New York: Warren and Putnam, 1932), pp. 310–18; Emilio Roig de Leuchsenring, *Weyler en Cuba* (Havana: Editorial Páginas, 1947), pp. 90–102; José Antonio Medel, *La guerra hispano-americana y sus resultados*, 2d ed. (Havana: P. Fernández y Cía., 1932), pp. 110–11; Francisco de P. Machado, *¡Piedad! Recuerdos de la reconcentración* (Havana: Imprenta y Papelería de Rambla, Bouza y Cía., 1927), pp. 20–22; Varona Guerrero, *La guerra de independencia de Cuba, 1895–1898*, 2:780; Guerra y Sánchez, *Por las veredas del pasado, 1880–1902*, pp. 95–105; Sánchez, *Julián Sánchez cuenta su vida*, pp. 50–51.

33 "Deposition of Enrique Ubieta," Hormiguero Central Company *v.* the United States, entry 352, case no. 293, BCCA/RG 76. A similar account was given by Marcos García Castro, Mayor of Sancti Spíritus during the war ("Deposition of Marcos García Castro," ibid.).

34 See "Deposition of Tomás Padro Griñán," Richard K. Sheldon, Executor, *v.* the United States, entry 352, claim no. 120, BCCA/RG 76.

35 Rodríguez to Quesada, March 29, 1896, in Gonzalo de Quesada, *Archivo de Gonzalo de Quesada*, ed. Gonzalo de Quesada y Miranda (Havana: Imprenta "El Siglo XX," 1948–1951), 2:188.

36 Maceo to F. Pérez Carbó, November 19, 1896, in *Antonio Maceo.*

Ideología política. Cartas y otros documentos, 2:350–51. Major José
S. Llorens y Maceo agreed: "General Weyler was our best ally from
the opposing camp" *(Con Maceo en la invasión,* p. 109).

37 Valdés Domínguez, *Diario de soldado,* 1:209.

38 Lee to Day, June 12, 1897, Personal Correspondence, General Lee to
Secretary of State, 1897–1898, John Bassett Moore Papers, Manu-
script Division, Library of Congress, Washington, D.C. For other
accounts of the effects of the reconcentration policy, see Valeriano
Weyler, *Mi mando en Cuba,* 1:127–29; Máximo Gómez, "Las tres
faces principales de la guerra de Cuba," in *Papeles dominicanos de
Máximo Gómez,* ed. Emilio Rodríguez Domorizi (Ciudad Trujillo:
Editora Montalvo, 1954), p. 67; Ricardo Burguete, *¡La guerra! Cuba
(Diario de un testigo)* (Barcelona: Casa Editorial Maucci, 1902),
p. 167.

3 Aftermath of War

1 *State,* November 5, 1898.

2 *Washington Evening Star,* September 24, 1898.

3 James H. Wilson, "Special Report of Brigadier General James H.
Wilson, U.S.V., Commanding the Department of Matanzas and
Santa Clara, on the Industrial, Economic, and Social Conditions
Existing in the Department at the Date of American Occupation and
at the Present Time," September 7, 1899, in John R. Brooke, *Civil
Report of Major-General John R. Brooke, U.S. Army, Military Gov-
ernor, Island of Cuba* (Washington, D.C.: GPO, 1900), pp. 334–35.

4 Fitzhugh Lee, "Special Report of Brigadier General Fitzhugh Lee,
U.S.V., Commanding Department of Province of Habana and Pinar
del Río," September 19, 1899, in Brooke, *Civil Report,* p. 342.

5 U.S. War Dept., Office of Director of Census of Cuba, *Informe sobre
el censo de Cuba, 1899* (Washington, D.C.: GPO, 1900), p. 77. Census
officials in 1899 estimated the loss of life at 267,273. More recent
demographic studies suggest the total may have been as high as
387,000. For the census figures, see the English-language edition of
the above: U.S. War Dept., *Report on the Census of Cuba, 1899*
(Washington, D.C.: GPO, 1900), p. 718; see also Juan Pérez de la Riva
and Blanca Morejón Seijas, "Demografía histórica: La población de
Cuba, la guerra de independencia y la inmigración del siglo XX,"
Revista de la Biblioteca Nacional "José Martí" 13 (May–August
1971), pp. 17–27.

6 Ibid., pp. 152–53.

7 Ibid., p. 734; see also Centro de Estudios Demográficos, *La población
de Cuba* (Havana: Editorial de Ciencias de Sociales, 1976), pp. 22–23.

8 U.S. War Dept., *Informe sobre el censo de Cuba, 1899,* pp. 92–93.
The effects of these developments stand in sharp relief in the age
group 10–14 in the 1907 census and the 21–24 group in the 1919
census. The following is the population data for native born:

Males

	1907	1919	% Change
0–5	158,499	179,300	13.1
5–10	103,486	193,589	87.0
10–14	83,817	167,754	100.0
15–17	56,218	75,134	33.6
18–19	40,610	42,415	4.4
20	20,264	12,131	−40.1
21–24	79,257	48,976	−38.2
25–29	76,651	78,208	2.0
30–34	55,448	82,919	50.0
35–44	97,159	123,776	27.3
45–54	66,479	80,154	20.5
55–64	33,836	51,021	50.7

Females

	1907	1919	% Change
0–5	154,387	174,254	12.8
5–10	101,942	188,116	84.5
10–14	80,274	163,513	103.6
15–17	64,824	84,484	30.3
18–19	45,503	43,653	−4.0
20	24,752	15,064	−39.1
21–24	74,407	60,874	−18.1
25–29	75,408	96,601	28.1
30–34	53,303	81,270	52.4
35–44	91,566	117,869	28.7
45–54	61,899	76,799	24.0
55–64	34,799	47,768	37.2

9 Great Britain, Foreign Office, Diplomatic and Consular Reports,
  *Report for the Year 1899 on the Trade and Commerce of the Island of
  Cuba* (London: H.M. Stationery Office, 1900), p. 14.
0 Raymond Leslie Buell et al., *Problems of the New Cuba* (New York:
  Foreign Policy Association, 1935), p. 43; Wilson, "Special Report,"
  pp. 334, 337.
1 Havana declined from 238,000 acres to 105,000, while Matanzas
  dropped from 365,838 to 161,766. The total figures for 1895 are ap-
  proximate, for no information was available for Camagüey province
  (U.S. War Dept., *Informe sobre el censo de Cuba, 1899*, p. 554).
2 José P. Alvarez Díaz, et al., *A Study on Cuba* (Coral Gables, Fla.:
  University of Miami Press, 1965), pp. 96–97; U.S. War Dept., Census,
  Informe sobre el censo de Cuba, 1899, pp. 551, 563–64; Julio E.
  LeRiverend Brusone, *La Habana (Biografía de una provincia)*
  (Havana: Imprenta "El Siglo XX," 1960), pp. 458–59; George Bronson

Rea, "The Destruction of Sugar Estates in Cuba," *Harper's Weekly* 4 (October 16, 1897), 10–34; L. V. de Abad, "The Cuban Problem," *Gunton's Magazine* 21 (December 1901), 515–25; Richard J. Hinton "Cuban Reconstruction," *North American Review* 164 (January 1899), 92–102; Franklin Matthews, "The Reconstruction of Cuba," *Harper's Weekly* 42 (July 14, 1899), 700–01; Jorge Quintana, "Lo que costó a Cuba la guerra de 1895," *Bohemia* 52 (September 11, 1960) 4–6, 107–08.

13 U.S. War Dept., *Informe sobre el censo de Cuba, 1899,* pp. 44–45; see also Felipe Pazos, "La economía cubana en el siglo XIX," *Revista Bimestre Cubana* 47 (January–February 1941), 105–06; Abad, "The Cuban Problem," p. 521.

14 William Ludlow, "Special Report of Brigadier General William Ludlow, U.S.V., Commanding the Department of Habana," September 15, 1899, in Brooke, *Civil Report,* p. 361. See also Maria Poumier, "La vida cotidiana en las ciudades cubanas en 1898," *Universidad de La Habana* 196–97 (February–March 1972), 192.

15 See Manuel Piedra Martel, *Mis primeros treinta años: Memorias* (Havana: Editorial Minerva, 1944), p. 496; Enrique J. Conill, *Enrique J. Conill, soldado de la patria,* ed. Gaspar Carbonell Rivero (Havana: P. Fernández y Cía., 1956), p. 21.

16 Carbonne to de Quesada, October 29, 1898, in *New York Times* November 5, 1898.

17 *New York Times,* September 24, 1898. See also Rodríguez to Masó n.d., in *Actas de las Asambleas de Representantes y del Consejo de Gobierno durante la guerra de independencia,* ed. Joaquín Llaverías y Martínez and Emeterio S. Santovenia (Havana: Imprenta y Papelería de Rambla, Bouza y Cía., 1927–1933), 4:151; Miguel Angel Varona Guererro, *La guerra de independencia de Cuba, 1895–1898* (Havana Editorial Lex, 1946), 3:1704–06; Rodolfo Bergés, *Cuba y Santo Domingo. Apuntes de la guerra de Cuba de mi diario de campaña 1895–96–97–98* (Havana: Imprenta "El Score," 1905), p. 167.

18 Mahoney to Polhamus, n.d., *Daily Picayune* (New Orleans), October 29, 1898.

19 Díaz Silveira to García, August 31, 1898, in Gonzalo de Quesada Documentos históricos (Havana: Editorial de la Universidad de La Habana, 1965), p. 486.

20 See Shafter to Corbin, August 16, 1898, in U.S. Congress, Senate *Report of the Commission Appointed by the President to Investigate the Conduct of the War Department in the War with Spain,* 55th Cong., 2d sess., rept. no. 885, ser. 3867 (Washington, D.C.: GPO 1900), 2:1099; Shafter to Corbin, August 16, 1898, file 110,293, Records of the Adjutant General's Office, 1780s–1917, RG 94, National Archives, Washington, D.C.; Cecil to Adjutant General, Division of Cuba, February 1, 1899, file 2393, MGC/RG 140.

21 Chaffee to Commanding General, Pinar del Río, January 13, 1899, file 4, RG 140; see also Lawton to Cebreco, September 5, 1898, file 186 Department of Santiago de Cuba, AOOC/RG 395.

22 See Chadwick to Chaffee, May 26, 1899, file 2020, MGC/RG 140; see also Sergio Aguirre, "La desaparición del Ejército Libertador," *Cuba Socialista* 3 (December 1963), 51–68.

23 Porter to Corbin, September 29, 1898, file 132052, AGO/RG 94.

24 Logan to Adjutant General, Department of Santa Clara, February 3, 1899, file 294/11, MGC/RG 350.

25 Davis to Chaffee, January 15, 1899, file 297; MGC/RG 140.

26 Logan to Adjutant General, Department of Santa Clara, February 3, 1899, file 294/11, BIA/RG 350 24; for one such payroll listing, see "A List of Municipal Employees Who Have Served in the Cuban Army," April 1899, file 2020, Segregated Correspondence and Related Documents, MGC/RG 140.

27 Leonard Wood, "Dictates Systems of Government Desired by Cubans," January, 1899, File 331/—, BIA/RG 350.

28 Wood to Assistant Secretary of War, May 6, 1899, file 83, Department of Santiago de Cuba, AOOC/RG 395.

29 Carpenter to Adjutant General, Division of Cuba, July 10, 1899, in U.S. War Department, *Annual Reports, 1899*, ser. 3901, p. 316; Colonel L. H. Carpenter in Puerto Príncipe sought to find positions in public administration for Cuban officers, but acknowledged later he could do little for the soldiers. "The Cuban troops disbanding in the province," he reported, "left many unprovided for and without resources, and this situation became at once a serious problem" (Carpenter to Adjutant General, Division of Cuba), July 10, 1899, in ibid., p. 310.

30 Wood to Adjutant General, Havana, Cuba, March 6, 1899, file 1897, MGC/RG 140.

31 Esteban Montejo, *The Autobiography of a Runaway Slave*, ed. Miguel Barnet, trans. Jocasta Innes (London: Bodley Head, 1968), p. 217.

32 Wood to Secretary of War, September 9, 1898, file 139,813, AGO/RG 94; see also Hermann Hagedorn, *Leonard Wood, A Biography* (New York: Harper, 1931), 1:204.

33 Brooke, *Civil Report*, p. 7.

34 Military Order no. 46, April 24, 1899, in ibid., p. 40.

35 Ibid., p. 30.

36 Ibid., pp. 13, 14.

37 Ibid.

38 Porter to Gage, November 15, 1898, in U.S. Treasury Dept., *Report on the Commercial and Industrial Condition of the Island of Cuba*, p. 9.

39 Perfecto Lacosta, "Report of the Department of Agriculture, Commerce, and Industry," March 15, 1900, U.S. War Dept., *Annual Report of 1900*, vol. 1, pt. 2, sec. 4, p. 6. The Foraker Amendment was enacted in 1899 to prohibit the granting of franchises and concessions of any kind in Cuba during the United States occupation (David F. Healy, *The United States in Cuba, 1898–1902* [Madison: University of Wisconsin Press, 1963], pp. 82, 84).

40 Healy, *The United States in Cuba, 1898–1902*, p. 93.

41 Leonard Wood, "Report of Brigadier General Leonard Wood," July 5, 1902, U.S. War Dept., *Civil Report of Brigadier General Leonard Wood, Military Governor of Cuba, for the Period from January 1 to May 20, 1902* (Washington, D.C.: GPO, 1902), 1:13.

42 See, for example, Argüelles to Wood, April 19, 1901, file 1901/109, MGC/RG 140.

43 Cancio to Wood, April 10, 1901, file 1901/109, MGC/RG 140.

44 Lacosta to General, June 12, 1900, file 1900/3259, MGC/RG 140.

45 Perfecto Lacosta, "Report of the Department of Agriculture, Commerce, and Industry," March 19, 1901, in U.S. War Dept., *Annual Report, 1901* (Washington, D.C., 1901), 1:9.

46 In Brooke, *Civil Report*, p. 150.

47 Julio Domínguez, "Informe," November 20, 1900, file 1900/3589, MGC/RG 140.

48 Eugenio J. Gálvez, "Informe," July 31, 1900, file 1900/3589, MGC/RG 140.

49 U.S. War Dept., *Informe sobre el censo de Cuba, 1899*, p. 668.

50 Military Order no. 139, May 27, 1901, file 1901/109, MGC/RG 140.

51 U.S. War Dept., *Informe sobre el censo de Cuba, 1899*, p. 554; Alberto Arredondo, *Cuba: Tierra indefensa* (Havana: Editorial Lex, 1945), p. 156.

52 Cancio to Wood, April 10, 1901, file 1901/109, RG 140.

53 In Brooke, *Civil Report*, p. 155.

54 J. F. Fuente, "Informe," July 20, 1900, file 1900/3589, MGC/RG 140.

55 José Castillo, "Informe," November 26, 1900, file 1900/3589, MGC/RG 140.

56 Ignacio Pizarro, "Informe," July 6, 1900, file 1900/3589, MGC/RG 140; Tomás Aroix Etchandi, "Informe," September 3, 1900, file 1900/3589, MGC/RG 140.

57 H. Morales, "Informe," August 19, 1900, file 1900/3589, MGC/RG 140.

58 Antonio Ferrer, "Informe," November 15, 1900, file 1900/3589, MGC/RG 140.

4 A Promise Lost

1 For a general discussion of rural conditions in postwar Cuba, see Ramón M. Alfonso, *Viviendas del campesino pobre en Cuba* (Havana: Librería e Imprenta "La Moderna Poesia," 1904).

2 Dumas to Director of Census, December 20, 1899, in U.S. War Department, Office of Director of Census, *Informe sobre el censo de Cuba, 1899* (Washington, D.C.: GPO, 1900), p. 648. "The census enumerator in 1899," Victor S. Clark reported during his travel to Cuba in 1902, "found many unauthorized occupiers holding parcels of uncertain extent" ("Labor Conditions in Cuba," *Bulletin of the Department of Labor* 41 (July 1902), 672).

3 I am indebted to Fe Iglesias for this information; see also Centro de

Estudios Demográficos, *La población de Cuba* (Havana: Editorial de Ciencias Sociales, 1976), pp. 126–29, 139–40.

4   Spain, *Censo de la población de España según el empradonamiento hecho en 31 de diciembre de 1887* (Madrid: Junta General de Estadística, 1889); U.S. War Dept., *Informe sobre el censo de Cuba, 1899*, pp. 78–79, 189.

5   Secretario, Gobierno de la Isla de Cuba, "Memoria: censo de la población de la Isla de Cuba, 1887," November 12, 1889, Fondo Miscelánea, legajo 4041, no. CM, Archivo Nacional de Cuba, Havana, Cuba (hereinafter cited as ANC). U.S. Dept., *Informe sobre el censo de Cuba, 1899*, pp. 78–79, 189; Kenneth F. Kiple, *Blacks in Colonial Cuba, 1774–1899* (Gainesville: University Presses of Florida, 1976), pp. 98–99.

6   These include El Caney, El Cristo, El Cobre, Jiguaní, Mayarí, Niquero, and Puerto Padre. See U.S. War Dept., *Informe sobre el censo de Cuba, 1899*, pp. 742, 746.

7   Ibid., p. 734.

8   The east was also substantially above the national figure of 89 percent native-born (ibid., pp. 228–30).

9   Ibid., p. 572.

10 Ramiro Guerra y Sánchez, et al., *Historia de la nación cubana* (Havana: Editorial Historia de la Nación Cubana, S.A., 1952), 4:211.

11 Adolfo Sáenz Yáñez, Secretary of Industries, Commerce, and Public Works, "Answers to the Questions Proposed to this Department by the Honorable John R. Brooke, Military Governor," November 9, 1899, file 1899/2594, Records of the Military Government of Cuba, RG 140, National Archives, Washington, D.C. (hereinafter cited as MGC/RG 140). See also U.S. War Dept., Adjutant General's Office, Military Information Division, *Military Notes on Cuba 1898* (Washington, D.C.: GPO, 1898), pp. 436–38.

12 Rafael Gutiérrez Fernández, *Oriente heroico* (Santiago de Cuba: Tipografía "El Nuevo Mundo," 1915), pp. 103–04; Levi Marrero, *Geografía de Cuba* (Havana: Editorial "Alfa," 1951), pp. 634–36.

13 U.S. War Department, Office of Director of Census, *Informe sobre el censo de Cuba, 1899*, pp. 556, 568–69.

14 For detailed analysis of all the coffee *fincas* and tobacco *vegas* in Oriente in 1905, including the names of proprietors, size of farms, production data, and land values in Cuba, Provincia de Oriente, *Memoria sobre el estado de la provincia y sobre los trabajos realizados por el gobierno y el consejo provinciales durante el año fiscal de 1904 a 1905* (Havana: Librería e Imprenta "La Moderna Poesía," 1906), pp. 209–45, 257–74.

15 Data drawn from U.S. War Dept., *Informe sobre el censo de Cuba, 1899*, pp. 88, 96–97, 127, 132, 142, 204, 212, 340.

16 Ibid., pp. 157–63.

17 Ibid., pp. 555, 566.

18 See Adolfo Sáenz Yáñez, Secretary of Industries, Commerce, and Public Works, "Answers to the Questions Proposed to this Depart-

ment by the Honorable John R. Brooke, Military Governor," November 9, 1899, file 1899/2594, MGC/RG 140; see also Frank Steinhart, "Annual Report: Fiscal Year Ending June, 1903," General Records of the Department of State, RG 59, National Archives, Washington, D.C. (hereinafter cited as DS/RG 59). Leonard Wood, et al., *Opportunities in the Colonies and Cuba* (New York: Lewis, Scribner, 1902), pp. 182–86.

19 Portuondo to Secretary of Agriculture, August 15, 1899, in John R. Brooke, *Civil Report of Major-General John R. Brooke, U.S. Army, Military Governor, Island of Cuba* (Washington, D.C.: GPO, 1900), pp. 313–15; "Table of Public Lands Now Known to Exist on the Island of Cuba," ibid. For a detailed analysis of public lands in Oriente, see Cuba, Provincia de Oriente, *Memoria sobre el estado de la provincia*, pp. 555–58.

20 U.S. War Dept., *Informe sobre el censo de Cuba, 1899*, p. 566.

21 See "Padrón de predios de agricultura y familias que los cultivan en la Prefectura de Melones, distrito de Holguín," May 29, 1896, Fondo Revolución de 1895, legajo 10, no. 2754, ANC; Prefectura de Vicana, Distrito de Manzanillo, "Relación de colonias existentes en esta Prefectura con explicación del estado en que se encuentran," August 24, 1896, Fondo Revolución de 1895, legajo 9, no. 2493, ANC.

22 Major James H. McLeary, Inspector General, "Report of Tour Inspection," December 19, 1898, file 1487, Records of the United States Overseas Operations and Commands, 1898–1942, RG 395, National Archives, Washington, D.C. (hereinafter cited as AOOC/RG 395).

23 Comerciantes y Proprietarios, "Petition to Leonard Wood," January 25, 1900, file 1900/1124, MGC/RG 140.

24 Manuel Hidalgo, "Informe," November 15, 1900, file 1900/3589, MGC/RG 140.

25 See U.S. War Dept., *Informe sobre el censo de Cuba, 1899*, p. 566.

26 Francisco Mastrapa, "Informe," July 18, 1900, file 1900/3589, MGC/RG 140.

27 José Rodríguez, "Informe," November 22, 1900, file 1900/3589, MGC/RG 140.

28 Bartolomé Falcón Paz, "Informe," September 20, 1900, file 1900/3589, MGC/RG 140.

29 D. M. Galeano, "Informe," November 13, 1900, File 1900/3589, MGC/RG 140; see also G. Pelayo Yero Martínez, *Baracoa: cuna de historia y tradición* (Baracoa: Imprenta "La Nueva Democracia," n.d.), pp. 35–36.

30 U.S. War Dept., *Informe sobre el censo de Cuba, 1899*, p. 566.

31 *Cuba Bulletin* 2 (February 1904), 12.

32 *Commercial and Financial World* 9 (April 7, 1906), 10.

33 Pulaski F. Hyatt and John T. Hyatt, *Cuba: Its Resources and Opportunities* (New York: J. S. Ogilvie, 1898), p. 95.

34 See "Developing Oriente," *Cuba Magazine* 1 (September 1909), 4–7; George Reno, "Oriente, the California of Cuba," *The Cuban Review* 25 (August 1927), pp. 14–20; George Fortune, " 'What's Doing' in

Cuba for the Younger American," *Cuba Magazine* 3 (February 1912), 336–40; Thomas J. Vivian and Ruel P. Smith, *Everything About Our New Possessions* (New York: R. F. Fenno and Co., 1899), pp. 112–19.

35 Edward Marshall, "A Talk With General Wood," *Outlook* 68 (July 20, 1901), 670.

36 Leonard Wood, *Report by Brigadier General Leonard Wood on Civic Conditions in the Department of Santiago and Puerto Principe* (Cristo, Cuba: Adjutant General's Office, 1899), p. 9, copy located in file 1899/1594, MGC/RG 140.

37 Ibid., pp. 21–23; Marshall, "A Talk with General Wood," p. 670. For one survey of mines and mineral resources undertaken at the behest of the military government as a means to disseminate public information about investment potential, see Harriet Connor, *Report on the Mineral Resources of Cuba in 1901* (Baltimore: Guggenheimer, Weil, 1903).

38 Marshall, "A Talk with General Wood," p. 670; see also Wood et al., *Opportunities in the Colonies and Cuba*, pp. 125–272.

39 Leonard Wood, "The Need for Reciprocity with Cuba," *Independent* 52 (December 12, 1901), 2929.

40 *The World,* October 8, 1897.

41 *The State,* September 20, 1898.

42 Irene Wright, *Cuba* (New York: Macmillan, 1910).

43 Marshall, "A Talk with General Wood," p. 670.

44 Military Order No. 139, May 27, 1901, File 1901/109, MGC/RC 140.

45 Wood to Root, May 30, 1901, Leonard Wood Papers, Manuscript Division, Library of Congress, Washington, D.C.

46 Wood to Root, May 18, 1901, Wood Papers.

47 In Brooke, *Civil Report,* p. 149.

48 Robert B. Hoernel, "Sugar and Social Change in Oriente, Cuba, 1898–1946," *Journal of Latin American Studies* 8 (November 1976), 226.

49 Civil Order no. 34, February 7, 1902, in Cuba, Military Governor, *Civil Orders and Proclamations of the Department of Cuba, 1899–1902* (Havana, n.d.), 2:n.p. "We have got to do something here in the way of modifying the existing railroad law," Wood wrote to Elihu Root upon proposing new laws. "These modifications really filtered through other channels" (Wood to Root, January 12, 1901, Wood Papers).

50 Wood to Root, January 4, 1902, Wood Papers.

51 See "Rollo de recurso de apelación establecido por Ricardo H. Beathie y otros, en el expediente de expropiación forzosa promovido por The Cuban Eastern Railroad Company de una faja e la 'Estancia MacKinley,' " September 8, 1906, Fondo Audiencia de Santiago de Cuba, legajo 17, no. 10, ANC.

52 Leland H. Jenks, *Our Cuban Colony* (New York: Vanguard Press, 1928), pp. 151–52; Thomas, *Cuba, the Pursuit of Freedom* (New York: Harper and Row, 1971), pp. 464–66; Hoernel, "Sugar and Social Change," pp. 229–30.

53 "Rollo de apelación de los autos sobre expropiación forzosa de una faja, de terreno de la Finca 'El Escorial,' para la construcción de la línea ferrea de The Cuba Company," January 16, 1903, Fondo Audiencia de Santiago de Cuba, legajo 8, no. 8, ANC.

54 *Gaceta de La Habana*, March 5, 1902, pp. 867–78, file 1902/284, MGC/RG 140.

55 For a general discussion, see Grace E. Harrah, "The Hacienda Comunera," *Cuba Review and Bulletin* 4 (August 1906), 9–10; Francisco Pérez de la Riva, *Origen y régimen de la propiedad territorial en Cuba* (Havana: Imprenta "El Siglo XX," 1946), pp. 61–66; Leopoldo Cancio, "Haciendas comuneras," *Cuba y América* 6 (January 1902), 227–36; see also Violeta Serrano, "La hacienda comunera," *Economía y Desarrollo* 39 (January–February 1977), 108–31; Esteban Tranquilino Pichardo y Jiménez, *Agrimensura legal de la isla de Cuba* (Havana: Imprenta y Librería Antigua de Voldepares, 1902), pp. 193–368; Carlos Manuel Céspedes y Quesada, *Haciendas comuneras* (Santiago de Cuba: Imprenta de "El Cubano Libre," 1903), pp. 5–24; for instances of litigation to consolidate *pesos de posesión*, see "Rollo del recurso de apelación por Esteban Molina Cruz en el enjuicio que promovido contra Flores Hernández y otros sobre la finca 'Embarcadero,' en la Hacienda 'Arroyo Blanco' de Gibara," July 15, 1908, Fondo de Audiencia de Santiago de Cuba, legajo 24, no. 15, ANC; "Rollo del recurso de apelación establecido por Joaquín Romeu en el juicio de deslinde de la Hacienda 'Guanaybas,' " February 26, 1915, Fondo Audiencia de Santiago de Cuba, legajo 21, no. 16, ANC.

56 U.S. War Dept., *Informe sobre el censo de Cuba, 1899*, p. 553.

57 Parraga and Méndez Capote to Govín, December 26, 1901, file 4167-1901, MGC/RG 140; see also Grace E. Harrah, "The Hacienda Comunera," *Cuba Review and Bulletin* 4 (July 1906), 10, 12.

58 "Rollo del recurso de apelación establecido por Pedro R. Rodríguez, Síndico de la hacienda 'El Canal' contra el Síndico y representante de la hacienda 'Cabezuela' Sres. José Galvez y Antonio Avila, en el incidente de impugnación al plano de dicha hacienda 'El Canal,' " June 21, 1909, Fondo Audiencia de Santiago de Cuba, legajo 7, no. 20, ANC; see also *Cuba Magazine* 2 (October 1910), 33–35.

59 Lowry Nelson, *Rural Cuba* (Minneapolis: University of Minnesota Press, 1950), pp. 96–97; see also Rogelio de Armas y Herrera, *Estudio sobre deslindes* (Baracoa: Taller Tipográfico "La Crónica," 1913); Antero Regalado, *Las luchas campesinas en Cuba* (Havana: Editorial Orbe, 1979), pp. 47–48, 57. For details of the proceedings of a judicial survey of one *hacienda comunera*, see "Rollo del recurso de apelación, establecido por Federico Sánchez Junco en el incidente de impugnación al plano de deslinde de la Hacienda Comunera 'San José de Potrerillo,' seguido por Librada González," June 22, 1909, Fondo Audiencia de Santiago de Cuba, legajo 5, no. 9, ANC.

60 "Haciendas Comuneras: considerations," file 1901-4167, MGC/RG 140.

61 Cancio, Cruz Pérez, and Giberga to Wood, December 20, 1901, file 1901/4167, MGC/RG 140.
62 See J.M.W. Duvant, "Real Estate Titles in Cuba," *Cuba Review and Bulletin* 4 (June 1906), 13–15.
63 Wood, *Report* [on] . . . *Santiago and Puerto Principe*, p. 21.
64 H. D. Dumont, *Report on Cuba*, 2d ed. (New York: Merchant's Association, 1903), p. 20.
65 Raymond Leslie Buell et al., *Problems of the New Cuba* (New York: Foreign Policy Association, 1935), p. 52.
66 Forbes Lindsay, *Cuba and Her People of To-day* (Boston: L. C. Page, 1911), pp. 122–23.
67 Demetrio Castillo, "Civil Government of the Province of Santiago de Cuba," June 30, 1900, file 1900/3562, MGC/RG 140.
68 José Rodríguez, "Informe," November 22, 1900, file 1900/3589, MGC/RG 140; see also "Expediente formado con relaciones por los Jueces de Primera Instancia del Territorio relativos a los libros del Registro Civil de sus respectivo partidos, que hayan desaparecido con motivo de la guerra," 1906, Fondo Audiencia de Santiago de Cuba, legajo 61, no. 2, ANC.
69 Francisco Mastrapa, "Informe," July 18, 1900, file 1900/3589, MGC/RG 140.
70 Gilson Willets, "Business Opportunities in Our New Colonies," *Leslie's Weekly* 88 (January 5, 1899), 12.
71 See "Rollo del recurso de apelación establecido por la Empresa The Cuban Company, Jaime Almirall Poc y Pablo Reugo Marlote, en los autos de calificación y reporto del juicio de deslinde de la Hacienda 'Tacajao,'" October 28, 1910, Fondo Audiencia de Santiago de Cuba, legajo 9, no. 14, ANC; see also Oscar Pino Santos, "Los mecanismos imperialistas de apropiación de la tierra en Cuba (Caso de la United Fruit Co.)," *Santiago* 23 (September 1976), 181–89; Oscar Zanetti and Alejandro García, *United Fruit Company: Un caso del dominio imperialista en Cuba* (Havana: Editorial de Ciencas Sociales, 1976), pp. 57–59.
72 Zona Fiscal de Manzanillo, "Relación de las fincas que han adquirido en compra los no residentes en la Isla de Cuba desde la fecha de la ocupación americana," March 25, 1902, file LMC 1902/31, MGC/RG 140.
73 See Wright, *Cuba*, pp. 469–70; 481; Luis Fernández Marcané, *La nacionalización de los ingenios cubanos* (Havana: Imprenta "El Siglo XX," 1921), pp. 6–7; Ariel James, *Banes: Imperialismo y nación en una plantación azucarera* (Havana: Editorial de Ciencias Sociales, 1976), pp. 100–37; Zanetti and García, *United Fruit Company*, pp. 57–59, 67, 77–78; Marrero, *Geografía de Cuba*, pp. 634–35. For the use made by United Fruit of Civil Order 62, see "Rollo de apelación del incidente al juicio declarativo de mayor cuantía promovido por Marcelino Garrido y Peña contra la Empresa de Banes-United Fruit, en reclamación de la finca rústica 'El Desingaño,'" February 18, 1903,

Fondo Audiencia de Santiago de Cuba, legajo 8, no. 9, ANC; "Rollo del recurso de apelación establecido por Antonio R. Fernández y otros en el incidente que promovido en el juicio de deslinde de la Hacienda 'El Retrete,'" June 24, 1908, Fondo Audienca de Santiago de Cuba, legajo 24, no. 14, ANC.

74 See "Synopsis of Reports by Different Land Companies Respecting their Properties in Cuba," *Cuban Review* 5 (December 1906), p. 78; for an account of the activities of one land company with dealings in Holguín, see "Rollo del recurso de apelación establecido por Secundo Fariñas en el incidente promovido por la Cuba Land Sindicate, en al juicio de deslinde de la finca 'El Canal,'" May 25, 1908, Fondo Audiencia de Santiago de Cuba, legajo 29, no. 20, ANC.

75 See *Cuba Bulletin* 1 (July 1903), 3; and *Cuba Bulletin* 2 (January 1904), 10.

76 *Cuba Review* 5 (May 1907), 20; *Cuba Review* 6 (July 1908), 12–13; *Cuba Review* 8 (May 1910), 25.

77 See Wright, *Cuba*, pp. 452–57; *Cuba Magazine* 1 (October 1909), 4–7; Jenks, *Our Cuban Colony*, pp. 143–44.

78 Herbert Squiers to John Hay, September 17, 1904, DS/RG 59; for accounts of North American colonists, see James J. Adams, *Pioneering in Cuba* (Concord, N.H.: The Rumford Press, 1901); H. C. Henrickson, "A Journey Through Eastern Cuba," *Cuba Magazine* 1 (April 1910), 8–12.

79 Atherton Brownell, "The Commercial Annexation of Cuba," *Appleton's Magazine* 8 (October 1906), 411; see also James H. Hitchman, "U.S. Control Over Cuban Sugar Production, 1898–1902," *Journal of Inter-American Studies and World Affairs* 12 (January 1970), 96–97; and Frank G. Carpenter, "Cuba in 1905," *Cuba Review* 3 (November 1905), 11.

80 José M. Alvarez Acevedo, *La colonia española en la economía cubana* (Havana: Ucar, García y Cía., 1936), p. 239.

81 Rionda to Czarnikow, MacDougal, and Company, February 20, 1909, Cuban Letters, November 1908–April 1909, Braga Brothers Collection, Latin American Collection, University of Florida Library, Gainesville, Florida.

82 Antonio Calvache, *Historia y desarrollo de la minería en Cuba* (Havana: Editorial Neptuno, 1944), p. 64.

83 See Lisandro Pérez, "Iron Mining and Socio-Demographic Change in Eastern Cuba, 1884–1940," *Journal of Latin American Studies* 14 (November 1982), 390–95; Jenks, *Our Cuban Policy*, pp. 291–92; Cuba, Bureau of the Census, *Census of the Republic of Cuba, 1919* (Havana: Maza, Arroyo y Caso, 1920), p. 76; Cuba, Provincia de Oriente, *Memoria sobre el estado de la provincia y sobre los trabajos realizados por el gobierno y el consejo provinciales durante el año fiscal de 1904 a 1905*, pp. 275–411; for an account of the expansion of the mining companies, see "Rollo del recurso de apelación, establecido por la 'Juraguá Iron Company' en el expediente que tiente promovido sobre expropriación de un faja de terreno de la Finca

'Jutisi,' " September 30, 1910, Fondo Audiencia de Santiago, legajo 11, no. 5, ANC.

84 See "Rollo del recurso de apelación establecido por Fornelio Sierra en el juicio de deslinde de la Hacienda 'Dajal' y 'Limones,' contra el Síndico de la comunidad," November 11, 1908, Fondo Audiencia de Santiago de Cuba, legajo 29, no. 24, ANC; "Rollo del recurso de apelación establecido por United Fruit Company en las diligencias sobre gastos y costos en el deslinde de la Hacienda 'Mulas,' " May 10, 1907, Fondo Audiencia de Santiago de Cuba, legajo no. 6, ANC.

85 Wood to Adjutant General, Division of Cuba, October 31, 1899, file 1899/2594, MGC/RG 140.

86 James H. McLeary, "Report of Tour Inspection," December 19, 1898, file 1487, AOOC/RG 395.

87 Wright, *Cuba*, p. 459.

88 See "Palmarito del Cauto," *Cuba Magazine* 1 (January 1910), 5–7.

89 See "San Pedro de Paso Estancia," *Cuba Magazine* 1 (January 1910), 8–10; For proceedings against squatters, see "Rollo de la causa seguida por el delito de 'Usurpación de Terrenos' de Diego Yedra," April 5, 1902, Fondo Audiencia de Santiago de Cub, legajo 12, no. 7, ANC.

90 See Tomás Simón García, "Notes from Baracoa," *Cuba Review* 4 (November 1906), 13.

5 Deferred Hopes Denied

1 Francisco López Leiva, *El bandolerismo en Cuba (Contribución al estudio de esta plaga social)* (Havana: Imprenta "El Siglo XX," 1930), p. 30; see also Grover Flint, *Marching with Gómez* (Boston: Lamson, Wolffe, 1898), pp. 25–26.

2 Davis to Chafee, January 15, 1899, file 1899/297, Records of the Military Government of Cuba, RG 140, National Archives, Washington, D.C. (hereinafter cited as MGC/RG 140).

3 See petition of Tomás Cardosa, et al., June 15, 1907, Fondo Secretaria de la Presidencia, legajo 63, no. 17, Archivo Nacional de Cuba, Havana, Cuba.

4 See *The State*, September 18, 1898; *New York Journal*, February 28, 1899; "Statement of Commissioner Robert P. Porter, Given Before the United States Commission for the Evacuation of Cuba," September 1898, in U.S. Treasury Dept., *Report on the Commercial and Industrial Condition of Cuba. Appendix* (Washington, D.C.: GPO, 1900), p. 152.

5 *The State*, December 10, 1898.

6 For conditions of banditry in Pinar del Río, see Fitzhugh Lee, "Special Report of Brigadier General Fitzhugh Lee, U.S.V., Commanding Department of Province of Habana and Pinar del Río," September 19, 1899, in John R. Brooke, *Civil Report of Major-General John R. Brooke, U.S. Army, Military Governor, Island of Cuba* (Washington, D.C.: GPO, 1900), p. 343.

7   Navarro to Brooke, September 20, 1899, file 1899/6968, MGC/RG 140.

8   Avalos to Adjutant General, Military Government, November 12, 1901, file 1901/194, MGC/RG 140.

9   *The State,* April 11, 1899.

10   Leonard Wood, "Report of Brigadier General Leonard Wood, United States Volunteers, Commanding Department of Santiago," in U.S. War Dept., *Annual Reports of the War Department: Report of the Major-General Commanding the Army, 1899,* House, 56th Cong., 1st sess., H. doc. no. 2, ser. 3901 (Washington, D.C.: GPO, 1899), p. 302.

11   Leonard Wood, "Civil Report of Major General Leonard Wood, United States Volunteers, Military Governor of Cuba," in U.S. War Dept., *Annual Report of the Military Governor of Cuba on Civil Affairs,* House, 56th Cong., 2d sess., H. doc. no. 2, ser. 4080–87 (Washington, D.C.: GPO, 1901), vol. 1, pt. 1, p. 63.

12   Davis to Chaffee, January 15, 1899, file 1899/297, MGC/RG 140.

14   Decades later, the subject of guerrillas still filled Esteban Montejo with rancor: "The real guerrillas were stupid countrymen. . . . Fire blazed from their eyes, they were men full of poison, rotten to the core. . . . I never met worse people in my life. Even now, all this time later, there are a few of them left on this island. Time has passed but they haven't changed. . . . When I think of those bastards, at a time when people like me were fighting against hunger, struggling through mud and all the foul stink of war, I feel like hanging the lot of them. But the sad thing is they never punished the guerrillas· in Cuba. . . . The guerrillas ought to have been exterminated" *(The Autobiography of a Runaway Slave,* ed. Miguel Barnet, trans. Jocasta Innes (London: Bodley Head, 1968), pp. 208–11.

15   See de Monteaguedo to Wood, March 19, 1901, file 1901/41, MGC/RG 140; Julio Angel Carreras,· "El bandolerismo en la república burguesa," *Santiago* 50 (June 1983), 150.

16   Portuondo to Brooke, January 24, 1899, unnumbered, Letters Received, Segregated Correspondence and Related Documents, MGC/ RG 140.

17   See Ricardo Varona Pupo, *Banes (Crónicas)* (Santiago de Cuba: Imprenta Ros Masó, 1930), pp. 48, 85, 86–87; Windus to District Commander, San Luis, March 29, 1899, file 1606, Records of the U.S. Army Overseas Operations and Commands, 1898–1942, RG 395, National Archives, Washington, D.C. (hereinafter cited as AOOC/RG 395).

18   U.S. War Dept., Office of Director of Census, *Informe sobre el censo de Cuba, 1899* (Washington, D.C.: GPO, 1900), pp. 198–200, 566.

19   See Fowler to Assistant Adjutant General, Santiago de Cuba, June 18, 20, 21, 1899, file 1589, AOOC/RG 395; Lieutenant Colonel Juan Vaillant, "Reseña para la hoja de servicios de teniente coronel Juan Vaillant, Jefe de la Provincia de Santiago de Cuba," and Lieutenant Colonel Juan Vaillant, Jefe Guardia Rural, Provincia de Santiago de Cuba, "Novedades ocurridos en esta provincia en los años 1899 a 1900 con motivo del bandolerismo," February 11, 1902, file 1902/1201, MGC/RG 140.

20 See Luis Gastón, "Report of Associate Justice Gastón Concerning his Visit to the Court of 'Instrucción' of Holguín," October 19, 1899, John R. Brooke Papers, Historical Society of Pennsylvania, Philadelphia.

21 The *State*, January 10, 1899.

22 L. H. Carpenter, "Report of L. H. Carpenter, Commanding Department of Puerto Príncipe," July 10, 1899, in U.S. War Dept., *Annual Report of the War Department, 1899*, House, 56th Cong., 1st sess., House doc. no. 2, ser. 3899–3904 (Washington, D.C.: GPO, 1899), vol. 1, pt. 1, p. 331.

23 Paxton to Adjutant General, Santiago de Cuba, September 12, 1899, file 1589, AOOC/RG 395; see also the *State*, April 11, 1899.

24 Bates to Adjutant General, Division of Cuba, January 28, 1899, file 196, AOOC/RG 395.

25 James D. Richardson, ed., *A Compilation of the Messages and Papers of the Presidents, 1789–1902* (Washington, D.C.: Library of Congress, 1896–1902), 10:63–64.

26 Brooke, *Civil Report*, p. 7.

27 See *Diario de la Marina*, August 22, 1901; Carreras, "El bandolerismo en la república burguesa," pp. 148–49. Nothing was as central to North American hopes for control of Cuba than the goodwill and allegiance of the local elites, precisely those classes that had earlier supported Spain. "Our supporters are the producers and the merchants," Leonard Wood insisted. "Our best friends are the country people, the planters and the commercial classes." He feared that the United States could "have a great deal of disgust and discontentment unless we show these people that it means something for them to be under the protection of the United States." It was no easy task "to instill wild enthusiasm into the people over the advantages of American protection," said Wood; without meeting basic needs. "We do not want to get the *real Cuban people*, I mean the producers and merchants, against us" (Wood to Platt, January 12, 1901, and December 19, 1900, Leonard Wood Papers, Library of Congress, Manuscript Division, Washington, D.C.).

28 Bates to Adjutant General, Division of Cuba, January 28, 1899, file 196, Santa Clara, AOOC/RG 395.

29 *Washington Evening Star*, January 25, 1899. At a McKinley cabinet meeting, Secretary of War Russell A. Alger made a strong case for a constabulary as a source of employment: "Honorable and profitable employment would be given to a considerable proportion of the Cuban soldiers, who might otherwise in the absence of individual employment, drift into evil courses or become a dissatisfied and dangerous element in the community" (*Washington Evening Star*, November 1, 1898).

30 Logan to Adjutant General, Department of Santa Clara, February 3, 1899, file 294/11, Records of the Bureau of Insular Affairs, RG 350, National Archives, Washington, D.C.

31 Wood to McKinley, October 27, 1899, Wood Papers; see also Wood to Adjutant General, Washington, D.C., November 11, 1899, file 2594,

MGC/RG 140; Frank Steinhart, "Memorandum," December 28, 1928, Correspondence, 1928–1931, Hermann Hagedorn Papers, Library of Congress, Manuscript Division, Washington, D.C.

32 Adams to Cameron, February 26, 1899, in *Letters of Henry Adams*, ed. Worthington Chauncy Ford (Boston: Houghton Mifflin, 1930–1938), 2:20.

33 Foraker to Wilson, May 22, 1899, James Harrison Wilson Papers, Library of Congress, Manuscript Division, Washington, D.C.

34 Lee to Foraker, November 29, 1899, in Joseph Benson Foraker, *Notes of a Busy Life*, 3d ed. (Cincinnati: Steward and Kidd Company, 1917), 2:48.

35 In John G. Holme, *The Life of Leonard Wood* (New York: Doubleday, Page, 1920), pp. 77–78.

36 See Wood to Roosevelt, August 18, 1899, Theodore Roosevelt Papers, Library of Congress, Manuscript Division, Washington, D.C. "There was no news in Cubans killing Cubans," wrote Wood's biographer (Hermann Hagedorn, *Leonard Wood, A Biography* [New York: Harper, 1931] 1:214).

37 Moore to Adjutant General, June 28, 1899, file 1806, AOOC/RG 395.

38 See Navarro to Brooke, September 8, 1899, file 1899/6968, MGC/RG 140.

39 See Harvard to Wood, September 21, 1899, Wood Papers.

40 Paxton to Adjutant General, Santiago de Cuba, September 12, 1899, file 1589, AOOC/RG 395.

41 Harvard to Wood, September 21, 1899, Wood Papers.

42 Ibid.

44 Vaillant, "Reseña."

45 Slocum to General, July 2, 1901, MGC/RG 140; for complete enlistment requirements, see Cuba, Camagüey, *Reglamento para el gobierno interior del Cuerpo de la Guardia Rural* (Camagüey): n.p., 1899).

46 Scott to Hoppin, December 6, 1900, file 1900/5165, MGC/RG 140.

47 See Usabiega to Wood, May 26, 1901, file 194, MGC/RG 140; Domínguez to Wood, May 16, 1901, file 1901/194, MGC/RG 140; Garcia, Llana and Company to Wood, January 18, 1901, file 1901/138, MGC/RG 140.

48 See Peña to Hatfield, February 3, 1901, file 1901/879, MGC/RG 140; Craig to Wood, February 2, 1901, file 1901/879, MGC/RG 140; W. I. Consuegra, Acting Chief, Rural Guard, "Monthly Report for November, 1900," file 1900/6105, MGC/RG 140; de Jesús Monteagudo to Fitzhugh Lee, October 31, 1900, file 1900/138, MGC/RG 140.

49 See Cuba, Guardia Rural, *Memoria explicativa de los trabajos realizados por el cuerpo durante el año fiscal 1906* (Havana: n.p., 1906), pp. 89–95.

50 See Tubal Pérez, "Why the Attack on Moncada? Nieves Cordero Tells His Story and that of 'The Cape,'" *Granma*, February 11, 1973, p. 9.

51 Wood to Wood, October 11, 1898, Wood Papers.

52 *Washington Evening Star*, June 20, 1899; See also Hagedorn, *Leonard Wood*, 1:256; E. G. Rathbone, "Memoranda for Senator Hanna," n.d., Roswell R. Hoes Papers, Manuscript Division, Library of Congress, Washington, D.C.; López Leiva, *El bandolerismo en Cuba*, p. 30.

53 Moore to Cavanaugh, June 30, 1899, file 1806, AOOC/RG 395.

54 Harvard to Wood, September 21, 1899, Wood Papers.

55 *The State*, January 10, 1899.

56 Wood, "Report" (1899), vol. 1, pt. 1, p. 302.

57 See Moore to Adjutant General, June 28, 1899, file 1806, AOOC/RG 395.

58 Fowley to Assistant Adjutant General, June 21, 1899, file 1487, AOOC/RG 395. The inability to execute captured bandits often embarrassed commanders. Reported one rural guard officer in 1907: "I am still pushing the pursuit of the Mayari gang. We have now captured six and killed one. I am sorry to report the capture of so many, but they were encountered under such circumstances that we would not kill them without raising a row. Hope to have better luck with some of the four leaders who are still out" (in Wittemyer to Foltz, October 22, 1907, file 146/20, Records of the Provisional Government of Cuba, RG 199, National Archives, Washington, D.C.).

59 See Moore to Adjutant General, Santiago de Cuba, July 11, 1899, file 1806, AOOC/RG 395.

60 Evans to Adjutant General, Department of Cuba, September 16, 1901, file 1901/194, MGC/RG 140.

61 Rivero to Chief Justice of Audiencia, July 10, 1901, in "Report of the Chief Justice of the Audiencia of Santiago de Cuba," November, 1901, file 1901/4852, MGC/RG 140. This sentiment was also expressed by municipal officials. The mayor of Calabazar, in Santa Clara province, complained, "The people here hold the opinion that the rural police body is anti-democratic for its not depending directly on the municipal authorities" (Leopoldo Ramos, "Informe," August 30, 1900, file 1900/3589, MGC/RG 140).

62 See Juan A. Calderón, "El terror en Gibara y Holguín," *La Discusión*, July 20, 1899.

63 Wilson to Grant, September 14, 1899, Letterbook, Wilson Papers.

64 Brooke to Adjutant General, November 14, 1899, Brooke Papers.

6 Resisting the End

1 See Cuba, Provincia de Oriente, *Memoria sobre el estado de la provincia y sobre los trabajos realizados por el gobierno y el consejo provinciales durante el año fiscal de 1904 a 1905* (Havana: Librería e Imprenta "La Moderna Poesía," 1906), p. 497.

2 Mason to Leech, April 27, 1912, FO 277, no. 183, Embassy and Consular Archives, Cuba, 1870 onwards, Public Records Office, Kew, London, England (hereinafter cited as PRO).

3 See W. Mason, "Report on 'San Pedro de Paso de la Estancia,' " FO

277, no. 183, Embassy and Consular Archives, Cuba, 1870 onwards, PRO.

4 U.S. War Dept., Office of Director of Census, *Informe sobre el censo de Cuba, 1899* (Washington, D.C.: GPO, 1900), p. 212; Cuba, Under the Provisional Government of the United States, *Censo de la República de Cuba, 1907* (Washington, D.C.: GPO, 1908), p. 215.

5 The town of Palenque in Alto Songo traced its origins to settlements of runaway slaves. See Ricardo V. Rousett, *Historial de Cuba* (Havana: Librería "Cervantes" de Ricarco Veloso, 1918), 3:124. For a general discussion of fugitive slave settlements in Oriente province, see José Luciano Franco, *Los palenques de los negros cimarrones* (Havana: Colección Historia, 1973), pp. 102–16; Fernando Ortiz, *Hampa afro-cubana: los negros esclavos* (Havana: Revista Bimestre Cubana, 1916), pp. 391–423.

6 B. E. Fernow, "The High Sierra Maestra," *Bulletin of the American Geographical Society* 39 (1907), 257.

7 Juan Lorente, "Informe," January 8, 1900, file 1900/3589, Records of the Military Government of Cuba, RG 140, National Archives, Washington, D.C. (hereinafter cited as MGC/RG 140).

8 Data derived from U.S. War Dept., *Informe sobre el censo de Cuba, 1899* p. 566; Félix R. Garayta, "Descripción de las tierras de Cuba: provincia de Oriente," unpublished manuscript, Biblioteca del Archivo Nacional, Havana, Cuba, 1930, 1:33–35, 186–209, 272–320, 503–28.

9 U.S. War Dept., *Informe sobre el censo de Cuba, 1899* p. 520; Cuba, *Censo de la República de Cuba, 1907* p. 584.

10 Rousset, *Historial de Cuba,* 3:118.

11 U.S. War Dept., *Informe sobre el censo de Cuba, 1899,* pp. 736–37, 742. How much of this recorded decline is attributable to the failure to register new births during the wars is impossible to ascertain. It must be assumed that it was a factor.

12 Ibid.

13 Ibid., p. 215.

14 Oriente was followed by Camagüey at 10.93 per thousand, Pinar del Río 12.27, Santa Clara 14.81, Matanzas 16.59, and Havana, 18.18. (Cuba, Bureau of the Census, *Census of the Republic of Cuba, 1919* [Havana: Maza, Arroyo y Caso, 1920], p. 254).

15 Cuba, *Censo de la República de Cuba, 1907* p. 376.

16 Ibid, p. 199.

17 See Irene A. Wright, "The Guantánamo Valley," *Cuba Magazine* 2 (March 1911), 15–22; *Times of Cuba,* June 1917, pp. 76, 78; John Moody, *Moody's Analysis of Investments: Public Utilities and Industrials, 1917* (New York: Moody's Investment Service, 1917), pp. 997, 1174.

18 U.S. War Dept., *Informe sobre el censo de Cuba, 1899,* p. 566; Cuba, Provincia de Oriente, *Memoria sobre el estado de la provincia y sobre los trabajos realizados por el gobierno y el consejo provinciales durante el año fiscal de 1904 a 1905,* p. 167.

19 Data derived from U.S. War Dept., *Informe sobre el censo de Cuba, 1899*, p. 566; "Expediente relativo a los estados que dispone el Articulo 310 de la Ley Hipotecaria y que elevan los Registradores de la Propriedad en abril de cada año y que han de ser elevados a la sección de los registros y del notario, según dispone el Articulo 310 de dicha ley," 1911, Fondo Audiencia de Santiago de Cuba, legajo 3, no. 17, Archivo Nacional de Cuba, Havana, Cuba (hereinafter cited as ANC).

20 See Brooks to Villalón, November 5, 1906, Fondo Secretaria de la Presidencia, legajo 115, no. 101, ANC; McCoy to Villalón, November 9, 1906, ibid.

21 See República de Cuba, Secretaria de Hacienda, Sección de Estadística, *Inmigración y movimiento de pasajeros en el año 1912* (Havana: Imprenta y Papelería "La Propagandista," 1912), pp. 10, 12, 19.

22 See Cuba, *Censo de la República de Cuba, 1907*, pp. 322, 512. These percentages are approximate, and probably err on the conservative side. They were derived by eliminating from the total *municipio* population all inhabitants under 18 years of age, as well as all women over 17, the majority of whom as housewives were classified as "without gainful occupation." To the balance was added the total number of unemployed, and the total was subtracted from the entire *muncipio* population, yielding the number of unemployed males over 17.

23 See U.S. War Dept., *Informe sobre el censo de Cuba, 1899*, p. 447; Cuba, *Censo de la República de Cuba, 1907*, p. 524.

24 Great Britain, Foreign Office, Diplomatic and Consular Reports, Annual Series, *Cuba 1911* (London: H.M. Stationery Office, 1912), p. 8.

25 Francisco Pérez de la Riva, *El café. Historia de su cultivo y explotación en Cuba* (Havana: Jesús Montero, 1944), pp. 214–15.

26 For a discussion of the importance of male support of the rural household, see Stephen Gudeman, *The Demise of a Rural Economy: From Subsistence to Capitalism in a Latin American Village* (London: Routledge and Kegan Paul, 1978), pp. 41–42.

27 Division of Latin American Affairs, "Confidential Memorandum," 837.00/478, June 1911, DS/RG 59.

28 Jackson to Secretary of State, April 26, 1910, 837.00.377, DS/RG 59.

29 Arthur A. Schomburg, "General Evaristo Estenoz," *Crisis* 4 (July 1912), 143–44.

30 Cuba, *Censo de la República de Cuba, 1907*, pp. 545–56; see also Alberto Arredondo, *El negro en Cuba. Ensayo* (Havana: Editorial "Alfa," 1939), pp. 60–61.

31 *La Lucha*, June 9, 1910.

32 For an account of these developments, see Thomas T. Orum, "The Politics of Color: The Racial Dimension of Cuban Politics During the Early Republican Years, 1900–1912," Ph.D. diss., New York University, 1975, pp. 158–212; Martha Verónica Alvarez Mola and Pedro Martínez Pirez, "Algo acerca del problema negro en Cuba hasta 1912," *Universidad de La Habana* 179 (May–June 1977), 79–93.

33 Orum, "The Politics of Color," pp. 153, 155; Cuba, *Censo de la República de Cuba, 1907* pp. 316–17.
34 Holaday to Jackson, May 2, 1910, 837.00/380, DS/RG 59.
35 Jackson to Secretary of State, April 26, 1910, 837.00/377, DS/RG 59.
36 See *La Lucha* for May 1912.
37 *La Lucha,* May 28, 1912.
38 "Expediente referente a los alzamientos de negros, dirigido por el Partido Independiente de Color, encabezados por Evaristo Estenoz y Pedro Ivonet," April–June 1912, Fondo Secretaria de la Presidencia, legajo 110, no. 2, ANC.
39 Beaupré to Secretary of State, May 24, 1912, 837.99/637, DS/RG 59.
40 Beaupré to Secretary of State, June 4, 1912, 837.00/713, DS/RG 59. Fifty years later, it still baffled observers. Wrote Hugh Thomas of the end of the 1912 uprising: "The movement fell away, almost as mysteriously as it had begun" *(Cuba: the Pursuit of Freedom* [New York: Harper and Row, 1971], p. 523).
41 Davis to Law, June 25, 1912, 837.00/884, DS/RG 59.
42 Holaday to U.S. Legation, Havana, May 25, 1912, 837.00/622, DS/RG 59.
43 More typically, Henry A. Landsberger suggests, jacqueries are "peasant uprisings in which the prime motive is reputed to be to gain immediate relief from pent-up frustrations through the destruction of property and the commission of violence against persons" ("Peasant Unrest: Themes and Variations," in *Rural Protest: Peasant Movements and Social Change* ed. Landsberger [New York: Harper and Row, 1973], p. 21. Chalmers Johnson characterized a jacquerie as a "simple rebellion," motivated by the "belief that the system had been betrayed by its elite; violence was invoked to purge the system of its violators, and, so to speak, to set it back on the tracks" *(Revolutionary Change,* 2d ed. [Stanford, Calif.: Stanford University Press, 1982], pp. 123–24); see also Ekkart Zimmerman, *Political Violence, Crises, and Revolutions: Theories and Research* (Boston: G. K. Hall, 1983), pp. 339, 374, 546; Robert Forster and Jack P. Greene, eds., *Preconditions of Revolution in Early Modern Europe* (Baltimore: Johns Hopkins Press, 1970), pp. 2, 56. Developments in Oriente in 1912 conform also to the theoretical propositions linking rebellion with deprivation. "Men . . . are angered over the loss of what they once had or thought they could have," Ted Robert Gurr writes. "Men who are frustrated have an innate disposition to do violence to its source in proportion to the intensity of their frustration." And bearing directly on events in 1912: "Aggressive responses tend to occur only when they are evoked by an external cue, that is, when the angered person sees an attackable object or person that he associates with the source of frustration. . . . An angered person is not likely to strike out at any object in his environment, but only at the targets he thinks are responsible" *(Why Men Rebel* [Princeton, N.J.: Princeton University Press, 1970], pp. 34, 37, 46).
44 Holaday to Beaupré, June 13, 1912, 837.99/763, DS/RG 59.
45 Goodrich to Holaday, October 10, 1913, file 1913/350, Miscellaneous

Correspondence, Santiago de Cuba, Records of the Foreign Service Post of the Department of State, RG 85, National Archives, Washington, D.C. (hereinafter cited as FSP/RG 84). For accounts of the assault against property, see Peterson to Lewis, June 14, 1912, 837.00.834, DS/RG 59; Beaupré to Secretary of State, May 27, 1912, 837.00/623, and May 30, 1912, 837.00/642, DS/RG 59.

46 *La Lucha,* May 25, 1912, June 10, 1912.
47 *La Lucha,* May 22, 30, 1912, June 4, 1912.
48 Forbes Lindsay, *Cuba and Her People of To-Day* (Boston: L. C. Page, 1911), p. 111.
49 For accounts of these attacks, see *La Lucha,* May 22, 27, 28, 1912; *Diario de la Marina,* May 27, 1912, June 1, 8, 1912. See also Orum, "The Politics of Color," pp. 221–57; Beaupré to Secretary of State, May 27, 1912, 837.00/623, DS/RG 59; *La Lucha,* May 24, 1912, June 3, 4, 1912.
50 *Diario de la Marina,* May 22, 28, 1912; *La Lucha,* May 23, 29, 1912; see also José A. García y Castañeda, *La municipalidad holguinera. (Comentario histórico). 1898–1953* (Holguín: Imprenta Hermanos Legra, 1955), p. 37.
51 Commanding Officer, "U.S.S. Petrel," to Secretary of the Navy, Division of Operations, July 17, 1912, 837.00/908, DS/RG 59.
52 Karmany to Commander, Fourth Division, June 10, 1912, 837.00/799, DS/RG 59.
53 *La Lucha,* June 27, 1912.
54 *La Lucha,* May 28, 1912.
55 See *La Lucha,* June 11, 1912.
56 Beaupré to Secretary of State, June 4, 1912, 837.00/713, DS/RG 59.
57 *La Lucha,* June 11, 1912.
58 *Diario de la Marina,* June 8, 1912.
59 Brooks to Leech, July 9, 1912, FO 288, no. 183, Embassy and Consular Archives, Cuba, 1870 onwards, PRO.
60 Ham to Holaday, June 25, 1912, 837.00/877, DS/RG 59.
61 Goodrich to Lewis, July 20, 1912, 837.00/911, DS/RG 59.
62 Bayliss to Beaupré, June 15, 1912, 837.00/827, DS/RG 59.
63 Brooks to Leech, July 9, 1912, FO 277, no. 183, Embassy and Consular Archives, Cuba, 1870 onwards, PRO.
64 Commanding Officer, "U.S.S. Petrel," to Secretary of the Navy, Division of Operations, July 17, 1912, 837.00/908, DS/RG 59.
65 For estimates of the number of Cubans of color killed, see Juan Jerez Villarreal, *Oriente (Biografía de una provincia)* (Havana: Imprenta "El Siglo XX," 1960), p. 307. Some estimates were as high as 35,000. See Marianne Masferrer and Carmelo Mesa-Lago, "The Gradual Integration of the Black in Cuba: Under the Colony, the Republic, and the Revolution," in *Slavery and Race Relations in Latin America,* ed. Robert Brent Toplin (Westport, Conn.: Greenwood Press, 1974), p. 360.
66 See Carvalho to Manduley, May 27, 1912, Fondo Secretaria de la Presidencia, legajo 110, no. 2, ANC.
67 Captain Frank Parker, "Final Report as Instructed to Rural Guard of

Cuba, 1909–1919," February 4, 1919, file no. 5586-19, Records of the War Department General and Special Staffs, RG 165, National Archives, Washington, D.C.

7 Farewell to Hope

1 Susan Schroeder, *Cuba: A Handbook of Historical Statistics* (Boston: G. K. Hall, 1982), p. 261.

2 José R. Alvarez Díaz et al., *A Study on Cuba* (Coral Gables: University of Miami Press, 1965), p. 235.

3 Rionda to Czarnikow-Rionda, March 15, 1911, Cuban Matters Letter Book, September 1909–March 1912, RG II, Braga Brothers Collection, University of Florida Library, Gainesville, Florida.

4 See Ariel James, *Banes: Imperialismo y nación en una plantación azucarera* (Havana: Editorial de Ciencias Sociales, 1976), pp. 25–26, 142–43.

5 John Moody, *Moody's Analysis of Investments. Pt. 2: Public Utilities and Industrials: 1917* (New York: Moody's Investment Service, 1917), pp. 997, 1174, 1224–25, 1280, 1622, 2029, 2038; Raúl Maestri, *El latifundismo en la economía cubana* (Havana: Editorial "Hermes," 1929), pp. 54–55; *Tunas de ayer y de hoy* (Victoria de las Tunas: "Razón," 1951), pp. 143, 145; see also Robert W. Dunn, *American Foreign Investments* (New York: Viking Press, 1926), pp. 112–22. The rapid expansion of North American–owned sugar estates between 1914 and 1916 alarmed many Cubans. As early as 1915, a number of congressmen advocated legislation designed to restrict foreign ownership of land in Cuba. See Wilfredo Fernández, *Problemas cubanos. Vendiendo la tierra se vende la República* (Havana: 1916); Luis Fernández Marcané, *La nacionalización de los ingenios cubanos* (Havana: Imprenta "El Siglo XX," 1921); León Primelles, *Crónica cubana, 1915–1918* (Havana: Editorial Lex, 1955), pp. 64–65, 183–84.

6 U.S. War Dept., Office of Director of Census, *Informe sobre el censo de Cuba, 1899* (Washington, D.C.: GPO, 1900), p. 571; Levi Marrero, *Geografía de Cuba* (Havana: Editorial "Alfa," 1951), p. 682. U.S. War Dept., *Informe sobre el censo de Cuba, 1899* p. 554.

7 See Alvarez Díaz et al., *A Study on Cuba*, p. 237; "Ingenios que han fabricado azúcar en la zafra de 1900 and 1901," file 1902/1074, Records of the Military Government of Cuba, RG 140, National Archives, Washington, D.C. (hereinafter cited as MGC/RG 140); *Times of Cuba*, June 1917, pp. 72–78; Henry H. Morgan, "Sugar Cane Situation in the Provinces of Oriente and Camagüey, Cuba," June 21, 1917, 837.61351/17, General Records of the Department of State, RG 59, National Archives, Washington, D.C. (hereinafter cited as DS/RG 59).

8 Cuba, Bureau of the Census, *Census of the Republic of Cuba, 1919* (Havana: Maza, Arroyo y Caso, 1920), pp. 69–71.

9 Irene Wright, *Cuba* (New York: Macmillan, 1910), p. 481. See also *Cuba Review* 5 (March 1907), 7.

10   Teresa Casuso, *Cuba and Castro*, trans. Elmer Grossberg (New York: Random House, 1961), p. 9. "If things go on like this," *El Mundo* editorialized in April 1916, "We will be planting cane in the patios of our homes" (Primelles, *Crónica cubana, 1915–1918*, p. 182).

11   Félix R. Garayta, "Descripción de las tierras de Cuba: Provincia de Oriente," unpublished manuscript, biblioteca del Archivo Nacional de Cuba, Havana, Cuba, 1930, 1:55–84, 168–85; *Facts About Sugar* 3 (August 19, 1916), 101; Carlos Martí, *Films cubanos. Oriente y Occidente* (Barcelona: Sociedad de Publicaciones, 1915), p. 250.

12   "Coffee Planters in Cuba," *Cuba Review* 13 (December 1914), 12; Great Britain, Department of Overseas Trade, *Report on the Economic Conditions in Cuba* (London: H.M. Stationery Office, 1923), p. 19.

13   Cuba, *Census of the Republic of Cuba, 1919*, pp. 57–58.

14   Ibid., p. 950; see also Martí, *Films cubanos*, p. 45.

15   Data drawn from U.S. War Dept., *Informe sobre el censo de Cuba, 1899*, p. 566; "Expediente relativo a los estados que dispone el Articulo 310 de la Ley Hipotecaria y que elevan los Registradores de la Propriedad en abril de cada año y que han de ser elevados a la sección de los Registros y del Notario, según dispone el Articulo 310 de dicha ley," 1911, Fondo Audiencia de Santiago de Cuba, legajo 3, no. 17, Archivo Nacional de Cuba (hereinafer cited as ANC).

16   Juan Jerez Villarreal, *Oriente (Biografía de una provincia)* (Havana: Imprenta "El Siglo XX," 1960), p. 307; Antonio Núñez Jiménez, *Geografía de Cuba*, 2d ed. (Havana: Editorial Lex, 1959), pp. 253–55.

17   Cuba, Provincia de Oriente, *Memoria sobre el estado de la provincia y sobre los trabajos realizados por el gobierno y el consejo provinciales durante el año fiscal de 1904 a 1905*, (Havana: Librería e Imprenta "La Moderna Poesía," 1906), pp. 427–44.

18   Grace E. Harrah, "The Present Status of Properties in Land in Eastern Cuba," *Cuba Review and Bulletin* 5 (June 1907), 13; see also José A. García y Castañeda, *La municipalidad holguinera. (Comentario histórico) 1898–1955* (Holguín: Imprenta Hermanos Legra, 1955), pp. 102–03.

19   Enrique Lavedán, "Los ladrones de tierras en Oriente," *Gráfico* 3 (February 7, 1914), 10.

20   José Yglesias, *In the Fist of the Revolution* (New York: Pantheon, 1968), pp. 41–42.

21   Bertot to Holaday, January 11, 1915, file 1915/800, Santiago de Cuba, Records of the Foreign Service Posts of the Department of State, RG 84, National Archives, Washington, D.C. (hereinafter cited as FSP/RG 84).

22   Van Horne to de Quesada, July 16, 1901, in Gonzalo de Quesada, *Archivo de Gonzalo de Quesada*, ed. Gonzalo de Quesada y Miranda (Havana: Imprenta "Siglo XX," 1948–1951), 2:329.

23   Cuba, Under the Provisional Government of the United States, *Censo de la Republica de Cuba, 1907* (Washington, D.C.: GPO, 1908), p. 577.

24 Cuba, *Census of the Republic of Cuba, 1919,* p. 749.

25 *Cuba Review* 10 (December 1911), 14.

26 The Spanish-American Iron Company, Cuban Steel Ore Company, and the Juraguá Iron Company to Whiteside, January 15, 1901, file 1901/372, MGC/RG 140.

27 See Marrero, *Geografía de Cuba,* p. 632; Oscar Zanetti and Alejandro García, *United Fruit Company: Un caso del dominio imperialista en Cuba* (Havana: Editorial de Ciencias Sociales, 1976), pp. 210–12.

28 *Facts about Sugar* 3 (October 7, 1916), 217.

29 L. V. de Abad, "Problemas fundamentales," *Diario de la Marina,* June 1, 1912, p. 7.

30 *Facts About Sugar* 3 (September 30, 1916), 198.

31 *Facts About Sugar* 4 (October 27, 1917), 329.

32 Willett and Gray, *Weekly Statistical Sugar Trade Journal* 40 (July 13, 1916), 278.

33 Rionda to Ganzoni, May 14, 1918, Confidential Letter Books, 1908–1942, RG II, ser. 4, Braga Brothers Collection.

34 *La Lucha,* March 3, 1912; Juan Pérez de la Riva, "Cuba y la migración antillana, 1900–1931," in de la Riva et al., *La república neocolonial: anuario de estudios cubanos* (Havana: Editorial de Ciencias Sociales, 1975–1978), 2:25–26.

35 Data compiled from Cuba, Secretaria de Hacienda, Sección de Estadistica, *Inmigración y movimientos de pasajeros en el año . . . 1912–1919* (Havana: Imprenta y Papelería "La Propagandista," 1913–1920); see also Leslie Buell et al., *Problems of the New Cuba* (New York: Foreign Policy Association, 1935), pp. 214–15.

36 Holaday to Gibson, August 17, 1912, 837.00/920, DS/RG 59.

37 *La Lucha,* May 14, 1912.

38 See *La Lucha,* April 2, 1916; *Havana Post,* April 1, 1916; see also Primelles, *Crónica cubana, 1915–1918,* p. 72; Mats Lundahl, "A Note on Haitian Migration to Cuba, 1890–1934," *Cuban Studies/Estudios Cubanos* 12 (July 1982), 21–36; Evelio Tellería Toca, "Más de un cuarto de millón de braceros importados," *Granma,* April 14, 1970, p. 2; "El jamaiquino y el haitiano," *La Lucha,* October 19, 1919, p. 12; Juan Pérez de la Riva, "La inmigración antillana en Cuba durante el primer tercio del siglo XX," *Revista de la Biblioteca Nacional 'José Martí'* 18 (May–August 1975), 74–88; Franklin W. Knight, "Jamaican Migrants and the Cuban Sugar Industry, 1900–1934," in *Between Slavery and Free Labor: The Spanish-Speaking Caribbean in the Nineteenth Century,* ed. Manuel Moreno Fraginals, Frank Moya Pons, and Stanley L. Engerman (Baltimore: Johns Hopkins University Press, 1985), pp. 94–114.

39 Wright, *Cuba,* p. 502.

40 Cuba, *Census of the Republic of Cuba, 1919,* p. 392.

41 Ibid., pp. 540–42.

42 Ibid. These developments bode ill; one demographer posits: "The higher the proportion of youthful population, and the greater the unemployment, the greater are the possibilities of dissatisfaction,

instabilities, and violence" (Nazli Choucri, *Population Dynamics and International Violence* [Boston: D.C. Heath, 1974], p. 72).

43 See Cuba, *Censo de la República de Cuba, 1907*, pp. 523, 570; *Census of the Republic of Cuba, 1919*, pp. 646, 732. A particular increase was made in women between the ages of 25 and 44, who in 1919 represented 55 percent of the total female agricultural labor force, up from 41 percent in 1907. The number of females between the ages of 10 and 24 engaged in agriculture declined from 39 percent in 1907 to 26 percent in 1919.

44 This theme is most compellingly developed in Carmen Diana Deere and Magdalene León de Leal, "Peasant Production, Proleterianization, and the Sexual Division of Labor in the Andes," in *Women and Development*, ed. Lourdes Beneria (New York: Praeger, 1982), pp. 65–93.

45 Cuba, *Census of the Republic of Cuba, 1919*, pp. 234–35.

46 Cuba, *Censo de la República de Cuba, 1907*, p. 577; *Census of the Republic of Cuba, 1919*, pp. 748–50.

47 Cuba, *Census of the Republic of Cuba, 1919*, p. 323.

48 See García y Castañeda, *La municipalidad holguinera*, p. 44.

49 The percentage for males is based on the work age population 15–64 years of age. The percentage for the male population of color in 1919 is skewed, due to the inclusion of West Indian workers. The censuses did not distinguish native from foreign population of color (Cuba, *Censo de la República de Cuba, 1907*, pp. 524–25; *Census of the Republic of Cuba, 1919*, pp. 547–648; see also Alvarez Díaz, et al., *A Study on Cuba*, p. 207).

50 Goodrich to Holaday, December 20, 1914, file 1915/900, Santiago de Cuba, FSP/RG 84.

51 Cuba, *Censo de la República de Cuba, 1907*, pp. 431–33; *Census of the Republic of Cuba, 1919*, pp. 540–42.

52 See U.S. War Dept., *Informe sobre el censo de Cuba, 1899* pp. 366; Cuba, *Censo de la República de Cuba, 1907*, pp. 267–70; *Census of the Republic of Cuba, 1919*, pp. 364–67, 567.

53 Cuba, *Census of the Republic of Cuba, 1919*, pp. 462–85. The percentage of the population under 5 years of age in other provinces was as follows:

	Total No.	Native White	Colored
Pinar del Río	14.8%	15.3%	13.6%
Havana	12.0	12.8	10.9
Matanzas	14.0	15.1	12.2
Santa Clara	14.8	15.5	13.2
Camagüey	15.8	16.3	14.1

54 Oscar Lewis, Ruth M. Levine, and Susan M. Rigdon, *Neighbors: Living the Revolution. An Oral History of Contemporary Cuba* (Urbana: University of Illinois Press, 1978), p. 258.

55 Cuba, *Censo de la República de Cuba, 1907*, pp. 401–03; *Census of the Republic of Cuba, 1919*, pp. 306–08.

56 For proceedings against squatters, see "Causa seguida por el delito de 'Usurpación de Terrenos,' contra Ramon Duranona y José Risalia Núñez," November 15, 1915, Fondo Audiencia de Santiago de Cuba, legajo 1, no. 11, ANC; "Causa seguida por el delito de 'Estafa' contra Juan de la Rosa Teruel," November 15, 1916, Fondo Audiencia de Santiago de Cuba, legajo 45, no. 3, ANC; "Rollo del la causa seguida por el delito de 'Usurpación de Terrenos,' contra Pedro Paisán y Juliana Bosch," March 6, 1915, Fondo Audiencia Santiago de Cuba, legajo 2, no. 13, ANC.

57 Lowry Nelson, *Rural Cuba* (Minneapolis: University of Minnesota Press, 1950), p. 97.

58 Robert B. Hoernel, "Sugar and Social Change in Oriente, Cuba, 1898–1946," *Journal of Latin American Studies* 8 (November 1976), 235.

59 Martí, *Films cubanos*, pp. 75–76.

60 In Morgan to Hoover, August 4, 1917, 837.50/13, DS/RG 59.

61 Cuba, *Census of the Republic of Cuba, 1919*, p. 234; see also Henry M. Wolcott, "Cuba," *Cuba Review* 14 (August 1916), 27–73.

62 P. Merrill Griffith, "Santiago," *Cuba Review* 14 (November 1916), 13.

63 *New York Times*, December 23, 1917; See also Luis Marino Pérez, "La actual situación económica de Cuba," *Reforma Social* 6 (March 1916), 521–31.

64 *La Lucha*, July 20, 1913. Court proceedings involving violent crime in Oriente increased noticeably between 1912 and 1918. See Fondo Audiencia de Santiago de Cuba, ANC, during these years.

65 During the 1906 Liberal revolution, an estimated 10,000 Cubans took to the field, and long after Liberals and Moderates had reached a reconciliation, many supporters of the original Liberal movement remained in the field, officially classified as bandits and criminals (see Alejandro Rodríguez, "Report of Commanding General, Armed Forces of Cuba," Appendix H, in Charles E. Magoon, *Report of Provisional Administration: From October 13th, 1906, to December 1st, 1907* [Havana, 1908], pp. 506–07).

66 See Primelles, *Crónica cubana, 1915–1918*, pp. 110–11; Julio Angel Carreras, "El bandolerismo en la república burguesa," *Santiago* 50 (June 1983), 145–59.

67 See the *Havana Post*, January 31, 1914; February 13, 1914; March 19, 1914; *La Lucha*, March 13, 1913.

68 Rionda to Rionda, February 9, 1910, Travelling Letter Books, RG II, ser. 3, Braga Brothers Collection. "These frequent fires," one correspondent reported, "are causing a great deal of alarm among the growers. The rural guard stationed around these townships wherein cane is grown have been ordered to form into patrolling gangs in order to look after the interests of the colonists" (*Havana Post*, January 7, 1914). See also "Rollo de la causa seguida sobre 'Incendio en campos de caña,' de la colonia Palmarito, de los Hermanos Francisco y Ramón Rodes," March 30, 1908, Fondo Audiencia de Santiago de Cuba, legajo 5, no. 12, ANC.

69 Solis was especially successful in both kidnaping and extortion, collecting an estimated $40,000 between 1908 and 1911. *(Cuba Review* 10 [December 1911], 13).

70 Holaday to Gonzales, January 18, 1915, file 1915/800, Santiago de Cuba, FSP/RG 84; see news accounts reported in *La Lucha, Diario de la Marina,* and the *Havana Post* for the years 1910–1915; see also Captain John Furlong, "Memo for the Chief of Staff," September 30, 1907, 146/17, Records of the Provisional Government of Cuba, RG 199, National Archives, Washington, D.C.

71 Rionda to Czarnikow-Records, January 5, 1911, Travelling Letter Books, RG II, ser. 3, Braga Brothers Collection.

72 *Havana Post,* March 25, 1913.

73 Guillermo Rubiera, "Mario García Menocal y Deop," in Vicente Báez, ed., *La enciclopedia de Cuba* (Madrid 1975), 9:137; *Havana Post,* July 16, 1914.

74 *Havana Post,* October 30, 1916. For a general discussion of crime and criminality in Cuba during these years, see Jorge Ibarra, *Un análisis psicosocial del cubano: 1898–1925* (Havana: Editorial de Ciencias Sociales, 1985), pp. 235–64.

75 See "Rollo del recurso de apelación establecido por Salvador Estévez Vallano, contra Ramón Argüelles, Síndico en el juicio de deslinde de la Hacienda 'Arroyo Blanco de Gibara,'" March 19, 1909, Fondo Audiencia de Santiago de Cuba, legajo 7, no. 4, ANC; "Rollo del recurso de apelación establecido por Fornelio Sierra en el juicio de deslinde de la hacienda 'Dajao y Limones,' contra el síndico de la comunidad, November 11, 1908, Fondo Audiencia de Santiago, legajo 29, no. 24, ANC; see also *La Lucha,* March 20, 1912; Zanetti and García, *United Fruit Company,* pp. 60–62; Leyda Oquendo, "Despojo y rebeldía del campesino cubano," *Bohemia* 69 (January 7, 1977), 85–89.

76 See "Rollo del recurso de apelación establecido por Pedro de la Vega en el incidente de oposición al deslinde de la finca 'Hato del Medio,' de los señores Manuel L. Arango y otros," September 25, 1906, Fondo Audiencia de Santiago de Cuba, legajo 17, no. 6, ANC.

77 *La Lucha,* June 9, 1913.

78 See *Diario de la Marina,* October 11, 1914, *La Lucha,* October 11, 1914; *Havana Post,* October 12, 1914.

79 James, *Banes,* pp. 144–45.

80 *La Lucha,* January 12, 1916.

81 *La Lucha,* April 16, 1916.

82 *La Lucha,* July 2, 1917; see also Martí, *Films cubanos,* pp. 186–88.

83 See Confluente Sugar Company, "General Report," 1916–1917, Fondo Donativos y Remisiones, legajo 403, no. 25, ANC; see also Primelles, *Crónica cubana, 1915–1918,* pp. 64, 365.

84 For the United Fruit–Banes connection, see Ricardo Varona Pupo, *Banes (Crónicas)* (Santiago de Cuba: Imprenta Ros Masó, 1930), pp. 188–94; see also Martí, *Films cubanos,* p. 29; Zanetti and García, *United Fruit Company,* p. 56.

85 For accounts of the electoral dispute, see Matías Duque, *Ocios del presidio, 1917* (Havana: Imprenta "Avisador Comercial," 1917), pp. 23–25.

86 Bernardo Merino and F. de Ibarzabal, *La revolución de febrero. Datos para la historia*, 2d ed. (Havana: Librería "Cervantes" de Ricardo Velaso, 1918), pp. 101–03.

87 Luis Loret de Mola, "Sobre la guerra civil de 1917: Memorandum," *Boletín del Archivo Nacional* 60 (January–December, 1961), 179–81; see Herminio Portell Vilá, "La Chambelona en Camagüey," *Bohemia* 52 (May 8, 1960), 12–13, 119; "La Chambelona en Occidente," *Bohemia* 52 (May 22, 1960), 36–37, 82; "La Chambelona en Oriente," *Bohemia* 52 (April 24, 1960), 12–13, 124; "La Chambelona en Las Villas" *Bohemia* 52 (May 15, 1960), 36–37, 98; P. Merrill Griffith, "City Taken by Military Forces," February 12, 1917, file 1917/800, Miscellaneous Correspondence, Santiago de Cuba, FSP/RG 84.

88 Waldemar León, "Caicaje: batalla final de una revuelta," *Bohemia* 59 (June 30, 1967), 100–02.

89 Portell Vilá, "La Chambelona en Occidente," p. 82; Miguel de Marcos Suárez, *Carlos Mendieta* (Havana: n.p., 1923), p. 117.

90 In Gonzales to Lansing, February 28, 1917, 837.00/1155, DS/NA RG 59.

91 Statement of N. Arthur Helmar, Division of Latin American Affairs, "Memorandum," March 28, 1917, 837.00/1315, DS/RG 59.

92 Ulzurrán to Rionda, March 20, 1917, Correspondence Files, Incoming, RG II, ser. 1, Braga Brothers Collection.

93 H. M. Wolcott, "Political Conditions in Oriente Province," May 22, 1917, file 1917/800, Miscellaneous Correspondence, Santiago de Cuba, FSP/RG 84.

94 Rionda to Jaretzki, March 17, 1917, Correspondence File, ser. 1, RG II, Braga Brothers Collection.

95 Lindelie to Gronna, March 16, 1917, 837.00/1308, DS/RG 59; Lindelie described the insurgent chieftains in mid-March as "neighbors and friends of ours." "The great difficulty in which I find myself," another estate manager wrote, "is that there is no one single Chief or head with whom I can treat, there being present in our neighborhood seven men ranking as Captains, Colonels and General, constantly giving unintelligible orders and counter orders and always finding a group ready to obey" (Diary of John R. Bullard, Jobabo, Cuba, March 8, 1917, 837.00/1472, DS/RG 59).

96 It was this consideration that led Manuel Rionda to predict confidently in early February 1917 that the political dispute would be settled quickly, and peacefully: "I do not fear any complications. This however is due more to the fact that all Cuban leaders of both parties are men of wealth, largely interested in sugar plantations and consequently likely to be heavy losers in case of disturbances" (Rionda to Jaretski, February 9, 1917, Travelling Letter Books, 1908–1926, RG II, ser. 3, Braga Brothers Collection).

97 Littleton to Polk, March 17, 1917, file 228, drawer 77, Frank L. Polk

Papers, Sterling Memorial Library, Yale University; *New York Times*, March 15, 1917.

98   Littleton to Polk, May 7, 1917, 837.00/1358, DS/RG 59.
99   Griffith to Secretary of State, May 15, 1917, 837.00/1361, DS/RG 59; Schmutz to Secretary of State, February 26, 1917, 837.00/1165, DS/RG 59; Primelles, *Crónica cubana, 1915–1918*, p. 324.
100 Griffith to Secretary of State, April 12, 1917, file 1917/800, Santiago de Cuba, FSP/RG 84; see also Merino and Ibarzabal, *La revolución de febrero*, pp. 220–48.
101 Fletcher to Lansing, March 19, 1917, 837.000/1248, DS/RG 59.
102 Wolcott to Secretary of State, May 1, 1917, 837.00/1375, DS/RG 59.
103 Naval Station, Guantánamo Bay, to Naval Operations, May 1, 1917, 837.00/1329, DS/RG 59.
104 Loló de la Torriente, *Mi casa en la tierra* (Havana: Imprenta Ucar, García, S.A., 1956), pp. 89–93; Rionda to Ganzoni, April 4, 1917, Confidential Letter Books, 1908–1942, RG II, ser. 4, Braga Brothers Collection; Henry H. Morgan, "Sugar Cane Situation in the Provinces of Oriente and Camagüey, Cuba," June 21, 1917, 837.61351/17, DS/RG 59; Statement of N. Arthur Helmar, Division of Latin American Affairs, "Memorandum," March 28, 1917, 837.00/1315, DS/RG 59.
105 Cuba, *Census of the Republic of Cuba, 1919*, p. 933.
106 Kobler, et al., to United States Consul, Santiago de Cuba, "Petition," April 20, 1917, file 1917/800, Miscellaneous Correspondence, Santiago de Cuba, FSP/RG 84.
107 Wolcott to Secretary of State, May 22, 1917, file 1917/800, Santiago de Cuba, FSP/RG 84.
108 Morgan to Secretary of State, May 30, 1917, 837.61351/12, DS/RG 59.
109 See Confidential War Diary, U.S. Naval Station, Guantánamo, Cuba, April 7, 1917 to April 30, 1917, Naval Records Collection of the Office of Naval Records and Library, RG 45, National Archives, Washington, D.C. (hereinafer cited as ONRL/RG 45). Commanding Officer, "U.S.S. Paducah," to Senior Officer, April 15, 1917, Subject File, 1911–1927, ONRL/RG 45.
110 Morgan to Secretary of State, June 16, 1917, 837.61351/17, DS/RG 59.
111 Henry H. Morgan, "Situation in Oriente Province, Cuba, and the Necessity for Sending One Regiment of U.S. Troops to that Part of the Island," June 28, 1917, 837.00/1394, DS/RG 59.
112 *New York Times*, II, June 3, 1917.
113 United States Vice-Consul, Antilla, "Post-Revolution Conditions in Oriente Province, Cuba," July 31, 1917, 837.00/1408, DS/RG 59.
114 Rionda to MacDougal, September 25, 1917, Confidential Letter Books, 1908–1942, RG II, ser. 4, Braga Brothers Collection.
115 Shaw to Major General Commandant, "Report of Operations," November 3, 1917, 837.00/1398, DS/RG 59.
116 See Francisco López Leiva, *El bandolerismo en Cuba (Contribucón al estudio de esta plaga social)* (Havana: Imprenta "El Siglo XX," 1930), pp. 20–36.

117 These accounts are found in *La Lucha*, December 28, 1917, January 11, 1920, December 25, 1918; *Diario de la Marina*, January 11, 1920.

118 Rionda to Ganzoni, May 11, 1917, Confidential Letter Books, 1908–1942, RG II, ser. 4, Braga Brothers Collection; see also Oscar Zanetti, "Actitudes e intereses en torno a la inmigración antillana en Cuba," unpublished manuscript, Department of History, University of Havana, p. 4; copy in author's possession.

8 Epilogue

1 Robert B. Hoernel, "Sugar and Social Change in Oriente, Cuba, 1898–1946," *Journal of Latin American Studies* 8 (November 1976), 239.

2 Fernando Ortiz, *Cuban Counterpoint: Tobacco and Sugar*, trans. Harriet de Onis (New York: Random House, 1970), p. 53.

3 See Cuba, Congreso, Cámara de Representantes, Octavo Período Congresional, *Memoria de los trabajos realizados durante las cuatro legislaturas ordinarias y las dos extraordinarias del octavo período congresional, comprendido del dos de abril de mil novecientos diez y siete y siete de abril de mil novecientos diez y nueve* (Havana, 1919), p. 816; José Gonzalez Valdés, "La Guardia Rural," *Boletín del Ejercito* 4 (February 1919), p. 783–85; Oscar Pérez Vega, "El frente interior y la Guardia Rural," *Boletín del Ejército* 6 (May–June 1955), 83–91.

4 Louis A. Pérez, Jr., *Army Politics in Cuba, 1898–1958* (Pittsburgh, Pa.: University of Pittsburgh Press, 1976), pp. 83–91.

5 Vladimir Akulai and Domingo Rodríguez Fragaso, "La situación socio-económica del campesinado cubano antes de la revolución," *Islas* 54 (May–August 1976), 64–65.

6 For an excellent study of one Sierra community with antecedents in the displacements and dispossessions in the early twentieth century, see Juan Pérez de la Riva, "Estudio demográfico del Alto Naguas," in *El Barracón y otros ensayos* (Havana: Editorial de Ciencias Sociales, 1975), pp. 317–37.

7 Francis Adams Truslow et al., *Report on Cuba* (Baltimore: International Bank for Reconstruction and Development, 1951), pp. 90–91; Dudley Seers et al., *Cuba, the Economic and Social Revolution* (Chapel Hill: University of North Carolina Press, 1964), p. 79; Hoernel, "Sugar and Social Change," p. 247.

8 For accounts of these incidents, see Antero Regalado Falcón, *Las luchas campesinas in Cuba* (Havana: Editorial Orbe, 1979), pp. 69–77; Santiago Cardosa Arias, "Ventas de Casanova: lucharon por su tierra," *Cuba* 2 (March 1963), 30–38; J. Mayo, "Dos décadas de luchas contra el latifundismo," *Bohemia* 77 (May 26, 1978), 84–89; Leyda Oquendo, "Despojo y rebeldía del campesino cubano," *Bohemia* 49 (February 25, 1977), 84–89; Pedro Luis Padrón, "Desalojos campesinos," *Verde Olivo* 15 (February 25, 1973), 26–28.

9   Hugh Thomas, *Cuba, the Pursuit of Freedom* (New York: Harper and
    Row, 1969), p. 1108.

10 See Antonio Núñez Jiménez, *Cuba, con la mochila al hombro*
    (Havana: Ediciones Unión/Reportajes, 1963), p. 120.

11 Thomas, *Cuba*, p. 901. For a social profile of some of the early peasant
    recruits, see Luis Rolando Cabrera, "Baldomero, el montuno que
    salvó a seis expedicionarios del 'Granma,' " *Bohemia* 51 (March 22,
    1959), 46–47, 128; Vicente Cubillas, " 'Yo fuí el primer guía de Fidel al
    llegar el Granma,' " *Revolución*, December 2, 1959, p. 8; Juan
    Hidalgo, "Guillermo García: el primer campesino que se unió a Fidel
    en la Sierra Maestra," *Hoy* 2 (June 21, 1963), 6; Regino Martín,
    "Charla con el comandante Crescencio Pérez: un heroe de leyenda,"
    Carteles, 40 (February 8, 1959), 38–40, 82.

12 Bert Useem, "Peasant Involvement in the Cuban Revolution," *Jour-*
    nal of Peasant Studies 5 (October, 1977), 106; Thomas, *Cuba*, p. 902.
    The Sierra Maestra, asserted Guillermo Cabrera Infante, "was largely
    inhabited by . . . outlaws like Crecencio Pérez, who was the first to
    give effective help to Castro in the Sierra and who has been sanctified
    by the revolution, though he was actually a brigand who had spent
    years hiding from justice in the mountains and lived as a smuggler"
    (in Rita Guibert, *Seven Voices: Seven Latin American Writers Talk*
    to Rita Guibert [New York: Vintage, 1973], p. 365).

13 Carlos Franqui, *Diary of the Cuban Revolution* (New York: Viking,
    1980), p. 530.

14 See Raúl Castro, "Diario de campaña: alzamientos en masa en la
    región oriental," *Revolución*, January 29, 1959, p. 2; Euclides Vaz-
    quez Candela, "El Segundo Frente Oriental 'Frank País:' pequeña
    República insurgente," *Revolución*, March 11, 1963, p. 8; Franqui,
    Diary of the Cuban Revolution, p. 510.

15 Neill Macaulay, "The Cuban Rebel Army: A Numerical Survey,"
    Hispanic American Historical Review 58 (May, 1978), 288–91.

16 Thomas, *Cuba*, p. 1043. For several general discussions of the peasant
    participation in the Cuban revolution, see Víctor Alba, "Cuba: A
    Peasant Revolution," *World Today* 15 (May 1959), 183–95; Gil Carl
    Alroy, "The Meaning of 'Peasant Revolution,': the Cuban Case,"
    International Review of History and Political Science 2 (December
    1965), 87–96, and "The Peasantry in the Cuban Revolution," *Review*
    of Politics 29 (January 1967), 87–99.

17 See Raúl Castro, "Diario de campaña: lucha implacable contra el
    bandolerismo," *Revolución*, January 28, 1959, p. 2; Roger González
    Guerrero, "Por la ruta de la columna num. 6," *Verde Olivo* 7 (Sep-
    tember 18, 1966), 66; Raúl Castro, "De la Sierra Maestra al Segundo
    Frente Oriental 'Frank País,' " *Verde Olivo* 5 (March 8, 1964), 6, 54;
    and (March 15, 1964), 23–24.

18 Franqui, *Diary of the Cuban Revolution*, pp. 193–224. See also An-
    tonio Enrique Lussón, "El paso de la columna 9 al Segundo Frente
    Oriental," *Verde Olivo* 5 (March 8, 1964), 9; González Guerrero, "Por
    la ruta," pp. 66–69.

19 Ernesto Che Guevera, "Cuba: Excepción histórica o vanguardia en la lucha anticolonialista?" in *Obra revolucionaria*, ed. Roberto Fernández Retamar, 2d ed. (Mexico City: Ediciones ERA, 1968), pp. 517–18.
20 See Barrington Moore, Jr., *Social Origins of Dictatorship and Democracy* (Boston: Beacon Press, 1966), pp. 453–83.

Bibliography

Archival Sources

U.S. National Archives

General Records of the Department of State. Record Group 59.
Records of the Adjutant General's Office, 1780s–1917. Record Group 94.
Records of the Boundary and Claims Commission and Arbitrations. Record Group 76.
Records of the Bureau of Insular Affairs. Record Group 350.
Records of the Military Government of Cuba. Record Group 140.
Records of the Post Office Department, Record Group 28.
Records of the Provisional Government of Cuba. Record Group 199.
Records of the United States Army Overseas Operations and Commands, 1898–1942. Record Group 395.
Records of the War Department General and Special Staffs. Record Group 165.
Naval Records Collection of the Office of Naval Records and Library. Record Group 45.

Cuban National Archives

Fondo Archivo Máximo Gómez.
Fondo Asuntos Políticos.
Fondo Audiencia Santiago de Cuba.
Fondo Donativos y Remisiones.
Fondo Gobierno General.
Fondo Miscelánea.
Fondo Revolución de 1895.
Fondo Secretaria de la Presidencia.

British Public Record Office

Embassy and Consular Archives, Cuba, 1870 onwards, FO 277.
Cuba. Letter Books 1877 to 1881. FO 277.
Cuba. Registers of Correspondence, 1842 to 1913. FO 278.
Santiago de Cuba. Miscellaneous Out-Letter Books, 1832–1905. FO 453.

Manuscript Collections

Braga Brothers Collection. Latin American Library, University of Florida.
John R. Brooke Papers. Historical Society of Pennsylvania, Philadelphia.

Hermann Hagedorn Papers. Manuscript Division, U.S. Library of Congress.

Roswell R. Hoes Papers. Manuscript Division, U.S. Library of Congress.

John Bassett Moore Papers. Manuscript Division, U.S. Library of Congress.

Philip Phillips Family Papers. Manuscript Division, U.S. Library of Congress.

Frank L. Polk Papers. Sterling Memorial Library, Yale University.

José Ignacio Rodríguez Papers. Manuscript Division, U.S. Library of Congress.

Theodore Roosevelt Papers. Manuscript Division, U.S. Library of Congress.

James Harrison Wilson Papers. Manuscript Division, U.S. Library of Congress.

Leonard Wood Papers. Manuscript Division, U.S. Library of Congress.

Theses and Unpublished Manuscripts

Garayta, Félix R. "Descripción de las tierras de Cuba: Provincia de Oriente. 2 vols. Biblioteca del Archivo Nacional de Cuba, Havana, 1930.

Goizueto-Mimó, Félix. "Effects of Sugar Monoculture Upon Colonial Cuba." Ph.D. diss., University of Pennsylvania, 1971.

Orum, Thomas T. "The Politics of Color: The Racial Dimension of Cuban Politics During the Early Republican Years, 1900–1912." Ph.D. diss., New York University, 1975.

Zanetti, Oscar. "Actitudes e intereses en torno a la inmigración antillana en Cuba." Manuscript, Department of History, University of Havana, n.d.

Documents

Brooke, John R. *Civil Report of Major-General John R. Brooke, U.S. Army, Military Governor, Island of Cuba.* Washington, D.C.: GPO, 1900.

Cuba. Bureau of the Census. *Census of the Republic of Cuba, 1919.* Havana: Maza, Arroyo y Caso, 1920.

———. Camagüey. *Reglamento para el gobierno interior del Cuerpo de la Guardia Rural.* Camagüey: n.p., 1899.

———. Guardia Rural. *Memoria explicativa de los trabajos realizados por el cuerpo durante el año fiscal 1906.* Havana: n.p., 1906.

———. Memoria de la Comisión de Higiene Especial de la Isla de Cuba. *La prostitución en Cuba y especialmente en La Habana.* Havana: Imprenta P. Fernández y Cía., 1902.

———. Provincia de Oriente. *Memoria sobre el estado de la provincia y sobre los trabajos realizados por el gobierno y el consejo provinciales durante el año fiscal de 1904 a 1905.* Havana: Librería e Imprenta "La Moderna Poesía," 1906.

—————. Provincia de Oriente. *Memoria sobre el estado de la provincia y sobre los trabajos realizados durante el año fiscal 1905 a 1906.* Havana: Imprenta y Almacen de Papel "La Exposición," 1907.

—————. Provincia de Oriente. *Memoria sobre el estado de la provincia y sobre los trabajos realizados durante el año fiscal 1906 a 1907.* Santiago de Cuba: Imprenta de "El Cubano Libre," 1907.

—————. Secretaria de Hacienda. Sección de Estadística. *Inmigración y movimiento de pasajeros en el año . . . 1912–1918.* Havana: Imprenta "La Propagandista," 1913–1919.

—————. Under the Provisional Government of United States. *Censo de la Republica de Cuba, 1907.* Washington, D.C.: GPO, 1908.

Great Britain. Department of Overseas Trade. *Report on Economic Conditions in Cuba.* London: H.M. Stationary Office, 1923.

—————. Foreign Office. Annual Diplomatic and Consular Reports. *Report for the Year 1899 on the Trade and Commerce of the Island of Cuba.* London: H.M. Stationery Office, 1900.

—————. *Cuba 1907.* London: H.M. Stationery Office, 1909.

—————. *Cuba 1911.* London: H.M. Stationery Office, 1912.

Magoon, Charles E. *Report of Provisional Administration: From October 13th, 1906, to December 1st, 1907.* Havana: n.p., 1908.

Pepper, Charles M. *Report on Trade Conditions in Cuba.* 59th Cong., 1st sess., S. Doc. 439. Washington, D.C.: GPO, 1906.

Spain. *Censo de la población de España según el empradonamiento hecho en 31 de diciembre de 1887.* Madrid: Junta General de Estadística, 1889.

U.S. Congress. Senate. *Report of the Commission Appointed by the President to Investigate the Conduct of the War Department with Spain,* 8 vols. 56th Cong., 1st sess., ser. 3859–3866. Washington, D.C.: GPO, 1900.

U.S. Treasury Department. *Report on the Commercial and Industrial Condition of Cuba. Appendix.* Washington, D.C.: GPO, 1899.

U.S. War Department. *Annual Reports of the War Department: Report of the Major-General Commanding the Army: 1899.* 56th Congress, 1st session, H. Doc. 2, ser. 3901. Washington, D.C.: GPO, 1899.

—————. *Military Notes on Cuba 1909.* Washington, D.C.: GPO, 1909.

—————. Office of Director of Census. *Informe sobre el censo de Cuba, 1899.* Washington, D.C.: GPO, 1900.

—————. Adjutant General's Office. Military Information Division. *Military Notes on Cuba, 1898.* Washington, D.C.: GPO, 1898.

Wood, Leonard. *Report by Brigadier General Leonard Wood on Civic Conditions in the Department of Santiago and Puerto Principe.* Cristo, Cuba: Adjutant General's Office, 1899.

Newspapers

Boletín Comercial
Daily Picayune
Diario de la Marina

Diario de Matanzas
La Discusión
Gaceta de La Habana
Havana Post
La Lucha
New York Times
El País
El Popular
The State
The Times of Cuba
Voz de Cuba
Washington Evening Star
The World

Memoirs, Autobiographies, and Reminiscences

Adams, James M. *Pioneering in Cuba*. Concord, N.H.: Rumford Press, 1901.

Anillo Rodríguez, Eduardo. *Cuatro siglos de vida*. Havana: Imprenta "Avisador Comercial," 1919.

Atkins, Edwin F. *Sixty Years in Cuba*. Cambridge, Mass.: Riverside Press, 1926.

Ballou, Maturin M. *Due South, or Cuba Past and Present*. New York: Houghton, Mifflin, 1885.

Berchon, Charles. *A través de Cuba*. Sceaux: Imprenta de Charaire, 1910.

Bergés, Rodolfo. *Cuba y Santo Domingo. Apuntes de la guerra de Cuba de mi diario de campaña: 1895–96–97–98*. Havana: Imprenta "El Score," 1905.

Burguete, Ricardo. *¡La guerra! (Diario de un testigo)*. Barcelona: Casa Editorial Maucci, 1902.

Cabrera, Raimundo. *Episiodios de la guerra. Mi vida en la manigua. (Relato del coronel Ricardo Buenamar)*. 3d ed. Philadelphia: La Compañía Levytype, 1898.

———. *Mis malos tiempos*. Havana: Imprenta "El Siglo XX," 1920.

Casuso, Teresa. *Cuba and Castro*. Trans. Elmer Grossberg. New York: Random House, 1961.

Conill, Enrique J. *Enrique J. Conill, soldado de la patria*. Ed. Gaspar Carbonell Rivero. Havana: P. Fernández y Cía., 1956.

Davey, Richard. *Cuba Past and Present*. New York: Charles Scribner's Sons, 1898.

Duque, Matías. *Ocios del presidio, 1917*. Havana: Imprenta Avisador Comercial, 1917.

Ferrer, Horacio. *Con el rifle al hombro*. Havana: Imprenta "El Siglo XX," 1950.

Flint, Grover. *Marching with Gómez*. Boston: Lamson, Wolffe and Company, 1898.

Foraker, Joseph Benson. *Notes of a Busy Life*. 2 vols. 3d ed. Cincinnati: Steward and Kidd, 1917.

Froude, James Anthony. *The English in the West Indies.* New York: Charles Scribner's Sons, 1888.

Gallenga, Antonio C. N. *The Pearl of the Antilles.* London: Chapman and Hall, 1873.

Guerra y Sánchez, Ramiro. *Por las veredas del pasado, 1880–1902.* Havana: Editorial Lex, 1957.

Llorens y Maceo, José S. *Con Maceo en la invasión.* Havana: n.p., 1928.

Machado, Francisco de P. *¡Piedad! Recuerdos de la reconcentración.* Havana: Imprenta y Papelería de Rambla, Bouza y Ca., 1927.

Menéndez Roque, Vicente. *Otros días.* Havana: n.p., 1962.

Millet, Gabriel. *Mi última temporada en Cuba.* Madrid: Est. Tip. "Sucesores y Revadeyra," 1894.

Miró Argenter, José. *Crónicas de la guerra.* 3 vols. Havana: Instituto del Libro, 1970.

Montejo, Esteban. *The Autobiography of a Runaway Slave.* Trans. Jocasta Innes. Ed. Miguel Barnet. London: Bodley Head, 1968.

Piedra Martel, Manuel. *Memorias de un mambí.* Havana: Instituto Cubano del Libro, 1968.

Polavieja, Camilo G. *Relación documentada de mi política en Cuba.* Madrid: Imprenta de Emilio Minuesa, 1898.

Sánchez, Julián. *Julián Sánchez cuenta su vida.* Ed. Erasmo Dumpierre. Havana: Instituto Cubano del Libro, 1970.

Solano Alvarez, Luis. *Mi actuación militar. Apuntes para la historia de la revolución de febrero de 1917.* Havana: Imprenta "El Siglo XX," 1920.

Torriente, Loló de la. *Mi casa en la tierra.* Havana: Imprenta Ucar, García, S.A., 1956.

Valdés Domínguez, Fermín. *Diario de soldado.* 4 vols. Havana: Universidad de La Habana, 1972–1974.

Weyler, Valeriano. *Mi mando en Cuba.* 5 vols. Madrid: Imprenta de Felipe González Rojas, 1910–1911.

Books

Albanes Martínez, Juan. *Historia breve de la ciudad de Holguín.* Holguín: Editorial Eco, 1947.

Alfonso, Ramón M. *Viviendas del campesino pobre en Cuba.* Havana: Librería e Imprenta "La Moderna Poesía," 1904.

Alvarez Díaz, José R., et al. *A Study on Cuba.* Coral Gables, Fla.: University of Miami Press, 1965.

Armas y Herrera, Rogelio. *Estudio sobre deslindes.* Baracoa: Taller Tipográfico "La Crónica," 1913.

Arrendondo, Alberto. *Cuba: Tierra indefensa.* Havana: Editorial Lex, 1945.

———. *El negro en Cuba. Ensayo.* Havana: Editorial "Alfa," 1939.

Báez, Vicente. ed. *La enciclopedia de Cuba.* 9 vols. Madrid, 1975.

Boti, Regino E. *Guantánamo.* Guantánamo: Imprenta de "El Resumen," 1912.

Boyce, William D. *United States Colonies and Dependencies.* Chicago: Rand McNally, 1914.

Braudel, Fernand. *Capitalism and Material Life, 1400–1800.* New York: Harper and Row, 1973.

Brown, Harriet Connor. *Report on the Mineral Resources of Cuba in 1901.* Baltimore: Guggenheimer, Weil, 1903.

Buell, Raymond Leslie, et al. *Problems of the New Cuba.* New York: Foreign Policy Association, 1935.

Buttari, Gaunard, J. *Boceto crítico histórico.* Havana: Editorial Lex, 1954.

Cabrera, Raimundo. *Cuba and the Cubans.* Trans. Laura Guiteras. Philadelphia: Levytype, 1896.

Calvache, Antonio. *Historia y desarrollo de la minería en Cuba.* Havana: Editorial Neptuno, 1944.

Carbonell, Miguel Angel. *Eusebio Hernández.* 2 vols. Havana: Editorial Guáimaro, 1939.

Carbonell y Rivero, Nestor. *Resumen de una vida heroica.* Havana: Imprenta "El Siglo XX," 1945.

Casas y González, Juan Bautista. *La guerra separatista de Cuba.* Madrid: Tipográfico de San Francisco de Sales, 1896.

Casasús, Juan J. E. *La Invasón. Sus antecedentes, sus factores, su finalidad. Estudio crítico-militar.* Havana: Imprenta Habana, 1950.

Castro, José Ignacio. *Baracoa, apuntes para su historia.* Havana: Editorial Arte y Literatura, 1977.

Centro de Estudios Demográficos. *La población de Cuba.* Havana: Editorial de Ciencias Sociales, 1976.

Céspedes, Benjamín de. *La prostitución en la ciudad de La Habana.* Havana: Establecimiento Tipográfico O'Reilly, 1888.

Céspedes de Quesada, Carlos Manuel de. *Haciendas comuneras.* Santiago de Cuba: Imprenta de "El Cubano Libre," 1903.

Círculo de Hacendados. *Informe del Cículo de Hacendados de la Isla de Cuba sobre las reformes económicas, administrativas y demanda de la situación de la agricultura.* Havana: Imprenta "La Corresponden-cia de Cuba," 1887.

Clark, William J. *Commercial Cuba.* New York: Charles Scribner's Sons, 1898.

Connor, Harriet. *Report on the Mineral Resources of Cuba in 1901.* Baltimore: Guggenheimer, Weil, 1903.

Costa y Blanco, Octavio Ramón. *Juan Gualberto Gómez: una vida sin sombra.* Havana: Imprenta "El Siglo XX," 1950.

Cuevas, Ernesto de la. *Narraciones históricas de Baracoa.* 3 vols. Baracoa: Taller Tipográfico "La Crónica," 1920.

DeLisser, Herbert G. *In Jamaica and Cuba.* Kingston: Gleaner, 1910.

Descamps, Gastón. *La crisis azucarera y la Isla de Cuba.* Havana: La Propaganda Literaria, 1885.

Dumont, H. D. *Report on Cuba.* 2d ed. New York: Merchant's Associa-tion, 1903.

Dunn, Robert W. *American Foreign Investments.* New York: Viking, 1926.

Duque, Matías. *Nuestra patria*. Havana: Imprenta Montalvo, Cárdenas y Cía., 1923.

Edo, Enrique. *Memoria histórica de Cienfuegos y su jurisdicción*. 3d ed. Havana: Ucar, García y Cía., 1943.

Estévez Romero, Luis. *Desde el Zanjón hasta Baire*. 2d ed. 2 vols. Havana: Editorial de Cienca Sociales, 1974.

Fermoselle, Rafael. *Política y color en Cuba*. Montevideo: Ediciones Geminis, 1974.

Fernández, Wilfredo. *Problemas cubanos. Vendiendo la tierra se vende la República*. Havana: 1916.

Fernández Almagro, Melchor. *Historia política de la España contemporánea*. 2 vols. Madrid: Ediciones Pegaso, 1956–1959.

Fernández Marcané, Luis. *Defensa de la propiedad privada*. Havana: Editorial Lex, 1947.

———. *La nacionalización de los ingenios cubanos*. Havana: Imprenta "El Siglo XX," 1921.

Figueras, Francisco. *Cuba y su evolución colonial*. Havana: Imprenta Avisador Comercial, 1907.

Fina García, Francisco. *Historia de Santiago de las Vegas*. Santiago de las Vegas: Editorial "Antena," 1954.

Flores, Eugenio Antonio. *La guerra de Cuba (Apuntes para la historia)*. Madrid: Tiopgrafía de los Hijos de M. G. Hernández, 1895.

Ford, Worthington Chauncy, ed. *Letters of Henry Adams*. 2 vols. Boston: Houghton Mifflin, 1930–1938.

Franco, José Luciano. *Antonio Maceo. Apuntes para una historia de su vida*. 3 vols. Havana: Editorial de Ciencias Sociales, 1975.

———. *Los palenques de los negros cimarrones*. Havana: Edición Historia, 1973.

Franqui, Carlos. *Diary of the Cuban Revolution*. New York: Viking, 1980.

Friedlaender, H. E. *Historia económica de Cuba*. Havana: Jesús Montero, 1944.

Gallego, Tesifonte. *La insurrección cubana*. Madrid: Imprenta Central de los Ferrocarriles, 1897.

García y Castañeda, José A. *La municipalidad holguinera. (Comentario histórico.) 1898–1953*. Holguín: Imprenta Hermanos Legra, 1955.

Gómez, Fernando. *La insurrección por dentro. Apuntes para la historia*. Havana: M. Ruiz y Ca., 1897.

Gómez de Cárdenas, Rolando. *Retazos de historia y otros artículos*. Banes: n.p., 1956.

Gómez y Báez, Máximo. *Papeles dominicanos de Máximo Gómez*. Ed. Emilio Rodríguez Demorizi. Ciudad Trujillo: Editora Montalvo, 1954.

González Pérez, José Ramón. *Santa Ana Cidra. Apuntes para la historia de una comunidad*. Havana: Departamento de Orientación Revolucionaria del Comité Central del PCC, 1975.

Griñán Peralta, Leonardo. *Antonio Maceo, análisis caracterológico*. Havana: Editorial Trópico, 1936.

Guerra y Sánchez, Ramiro, et al. *Historia de la nación cubana.* 10 vols.
Havana: Editorial Historia de la Nación Cubana, S.A., 1952.
———. *La industria azucarera de Cuba.* Havana: Cultural, S.A., 1940.
———. *Mudos testigos. Crónica del ex-cafetal Jesús Nazareña.* Havana:
Editorial de Ciencias Sociales, 1974.
———. *Sugar and Society in the Caribbean: An Economic History of
Cuban Agriculture.* New Haven, Conn.: Yale University Press, 1964.
Guevara, Ernesto Che. *Obra revolucionaria.* Ed. Roberto Fernández Re-
tamar. 2d ed. Mexico City: Ediciones ERA, S.A., 1968.
Gutiérrez Fernández, Rafael. *Los heroes del 24 de febrero.* Havana: Casa
Editorial Carasa y Cía., 1932.
———. *Oriente heroico.* Santiago de Cuba: Tipografía "El Nuevo
Mundo," 1915.
Hagedorn, Hermann. *Leonard Wood, A Biography.* 2 vols. New York:
Harper and Brothers, 1931.
Healy, David F. *The United States in Cuba, 1898–1902.* Madison: Uni-
versity of Wisconsin Press, 1963.
Hernández y Pérez, Eusebio. *Dos conferencias históricas.* Havana: Cul-
tural, S.A., n.d.
———. *El período revolucionario de 1879 a 1895.* Havana: Imprenta "El
Siglo XX," 1914.
*Historia de Manuel García, Rey de los Campos de Cuba (desde la cuna
hasta el sepulcro) por uno que lo sabe todo.* 2 vols. Havana: Imprenta
y Librería "La Moderna Poesía," 1898.
Hobsbawm, Eric J. *Bandits.* New York: Delacorte Press, 1969.
———. *Primitive Rebels.* New York: W. W. Norton, 1965.
Hoetink, H. *El pueblo dominicano, 1850–1900: Apuntes para su
sociología histórica.* Santiago de los Caballeros: Universidad
Católica y Mestre, 1971.
Holme, John G. *The Life of Leonard Wood.* New York: Doubleday, Page,
1920.
Ibarra, Jorge. *Un análisis psicosocial del cubano: 1898–1915.* Havana:
Editorial de Ciencias Sociales, 1985.
Hyatt, Pulaski F., and John T. Hyatt. *Cuba: Its Resources and Oppor-
tunities.* New York: J. S. Ogilvie, 1898.
Iglesia y Santos, Alvaro de la. *Manuel García (El Rey de los Campos de
Cuba). Su vida y sus hechos.* Havana: La Comercial, 1895.
Infiesta, Ramón. *Máximo Gómez.* Havana: Imprenta "El Siglo XX," 1937.
Ituarte, Ignacio D. *Crimenes y criminales en La Habana.* Havana: n.p.,
1893.
James, Ariel. *Banes: Imperialismo y nación en una plantación azucarera.*
Havana: Editorial de Ciencias Sociales, 1976.
Jenks, Leland H. *Our Cuban Colony.* New York: Vanguard Press, 1928.
Jerez Villarreal, Juan. *Oriente (Biografía de una provincia).* Havana: Im-
prenta "El Siglo XX," 1960.
Kiple, Kenneth F. *Blacks in Colonial Cuba, 1774–1889.* Gainesville:
University Presses of Florida, 1976.

Kirk, John M. *José Martí: Mentor of the Cuban Nation.* Gainesville: University Presses of Florida, 1983.

Lacalle y Zauquest, Enrique Orlando. *Cuatro siglos de historia de Bayamo.* Bayamo: Monumento Nacional, 1947.

Landsberger, Henry A., ed. *Rural Protest: Peasant Movements and Social Change.* New York: Harper and Row, 1973.

Lavié Vera, Nemesio. *Bayate.* Manzanillo: Editorial "El Art," 1951.

LeRiverend Brusone, Julio E. *La Habana (Biografía de una provincia).* Havana: Imprenta "El Siglo XX," 1960.

Lewis, Oscar, Ruth M. Lewis, and Susan M. Rigdon. *Neighbors: Living the Revolution. An Oral History of Contemporary Cuba.* Urbana: University of Illinois, 1978.

Lindsay, Forbes. *Cuba and Her People To-Day.* Boston: L. C. Page, 1911.

Llaverías y Martínez, Joaquín, ed. *Correspondencia de la delegación cubana en Nueva York durante la guerra de 1895 a 1898.* 5 vols. Havana: Imprenta del Archivo Nacional, 1943–1946.

―――― and Emeterio S. Santovenia, eds. *Actas de las Asambleas de Representantes y del Consejo de Gobierno durante la guerra de independencia.* 6 vols. Havana: Imprenta y Papelería de Rambla, Bouza y Cía., 1927–1933.

López Leiva, Francisco. *El bandolerismo en Cuba (Contribución al estudio de esta plaga social).* Havana: Imprenta "El Siglo XX," 1930.

López Segrera, Francisco. *Cuba: capitalismo dependiente y subdesarrollo (1510–1959).* Havana: Editorial de Ciencias Sociales, 1982.

Maceo, Antonio. *Antonio Maceo. Documentos para su vida.* Ed. Julián Martínez Castells. Havana: Imprenta del Archivo Nacional de Cuba, 1945.

――――. *Antonio Maceo. Ideología política. Cartas y otros documentos.* Ed. Sociedad Cubana de Estudios Históricos e Internacionales, 2 vols. Havana: Cárdenas y Cía., 1950–1952.

Maestri, Raúl. *El latifundismo en la economía cubana.* Havana: Editorial "Hermes," 1929.

Marcos Suárez, Miguel de. *Carlos Mendieta.* Havana: n.p., 1923.

Marrero, Levi. *Geografía de Cuba.* Havana: Editorial "Alfa," 1951.

Martí, Carlos. *Films cubanos. Oriente y Occidente.* Barcelona: Sociedad General de Publicaciones, 1915.

――――. *El país de la riqueza.* Madrid: Renacimiento, 1918.

Martínez-Alier, Juan. *Haciendas, Plantations and Collective Farms: Agrarian Class Societies—Cuba and Peru.* London: Frank Cass, 1977.

Martínez-Escobar, Manuel. *Historia de Remedios.* Havana: Jesús Montero, 1944.

Martínez-Moles, Manuel. *Epítome de la historia de Sancti-Spíritus desde el descubrimiento de sus costas (1494) hasta nuestros días (1934).* Havana: Imprenta "El Siglo XX," 1936.

Matthews, Franklin. *The New-Born Cuba.* New York: Harper, 1899.

Medel, José Antonio. *La guerra hispano-americana y sus resultados.* 2nd ed. Havana: Imprenta P. Fernández y Cía., 1932.

Merchán, Rafael María. *Cuba, justificación de sus guerras de independencia.* 2d ed. Havana: Imprenta Nacional de Cuba, 1961.

Merino, Bernardo, and F. de Ibarzabal Merino. *La revolución de febrero. Datos para la historia.* 2d ed. Havana: Librería "Cervantes" de Ricardo Veloso, 1918.

Moody, John. *Moody's Analysis of Investments. Public Utilities and Industrials, 1917.* New York: Moody's Investment Service, 1917.

Moore, Barrington, Jr. *Social Origins of Dictatorship and Democracy.* Boston: Beacon Press, 1966.

Morales Patiño, Oswaldo. *El capitán Chino. Teniente Coronel Quirino Zamora: Historia de un mambí en la provincia de La Habana.* Havana: Municipio de La Habana, 1953.

Moreno, Antonio L. *Nueva cartilla geográfico de la Isla de Cuba.* Matanzas: Casa Editorial de Sedano y Hernández, 1883.

Moreno, Francisco. *Cuba y su gente (Apuntes para la historia).* Madrid: Establecimiento Tipográfico de Enrique Teodora, 1887.

Moreno Fraginals, Manuel. *El ingenio. Complejo económico social cubano del azúcar.* 3 vols. Havana: Editorial de Ciencias Sociales, 1978.

Munson Steamship Line. *Eastern Cuba.* New York: Munson Steamship Line, 1919.

Mustelier, Gustavo Enrique. *La extinción del negro. Apuntes político-sociales.* Havana: Imprenta de Rambla, Bauza y Cía., 1912.

Nelson, Lowry. *Rural Cuba.* Minneapolis: University of Minnesota Press, 1950.

Núñez Jiménez, Antonio. *Cuba, con la mochila al hombro.* Havana: Editorial Unión/Reportajes, 1963.

———. *Geografía de Cuba.* 2d ed. Havana: Editorial Lex, 1959.

———. *Mayarí.* Havana: Sociedad Espeleologica de Cuba, 1948.

Ortiz, Fernando. *Cuba Counterpoint: Tobacco and Sugar.* Trans. Harriet de Onis. New York: Random House, 1970.

———. *Hampa afro-cubana: los negros esclavos.* Havana: Revista Bimestre Cubana, 1916.

Pelayo Yero Martínez, *Baracoa: cuna de historia y tradición.* Baracoa: Imprenta La Nueva Deomcracia, n.d.

Pérez, Louis A., Jr. *Army Politics in Cuba, 1898–1958.* Pittsburgh, Pa.: University of Pittsburgh Press, 1976.

Pérez de la Riva, Francisco. *El café. Historia de su cultivo y explotación en Cuba.* Havana: Jesús Montero, 1944.

———. *Origen y régimen de la propriedad territorial en Cuba.* Havana: Imprenta "El Siglo XX," 1946.

Pérez de la Riva, Juan, et al. *La república neocolonial.* 2 vols. Havana: Editorial de Ciencias Sociales, 1975–1978.

Pichardo y Jiménez, Esteban Tranquilino. *Agrimensura legal de la isla de Cuba.* 2d ed. Havana: Imprenta y Librería Antigua de Valdepares, 1902.

Pirala, Antonio. *España y la Regencia: Anales de diez y seis años (1885–1902).* 3 vols. Madrid: Librería de Victoriano Suárez, 1904–1907.

Ponte Domínguez, Francisco J. *Matazanas (Biografía de una provincia)*. Havana: Imprenta "El Siglo XX," 1959.

Portuondo del Prado, Fernando. *Historia de Cuba*. 6th ed. Havana: Instituto Cubano del Libro, 1965.

Poumier-Taquechel, Maria. *Contribution à l'étude du banditisme social à Cuba. L'historie et le mythe de Manuel García, "Rey de los Campos de Cuba" (1851–1895)*. Paris: Editions L'Harmattan, 1986.

Primelles, León. *Crónica cubana, 1915–1918*. Havana: Editorial Lex, 1955.

Quesada, Gonzalo de. *Archivo de Gonzalo de Quesada*. Ed. Gonzalo de Quesada y Miranda. 2 vols. Havana: Imprenta "El Siglo XX," 1948–1951.

————. *Documentos históricos*. Havana: Editorial de la Universidad de La Habana, 1965.

Quesada, Gonzalo de, and Henry Davenport Northrop. *Cuba's Great Struggle for Freedom*. New York: n.p., 1898.

Ravelo, Juan María. *Páginas de ayer (Narraciones de Santiago de Cuba)*. Manzanillo: Editorial "El Arte," 1943.

Regalado Falcón, Antero. *Las luchas campesinas en Cuba*. Havana: Editorial Orbe, 1979.

Reverter Delmas, Emilio. *Cuba española. Reseña histórica de la insurrección cubana in 1895*. 6 vols. Barcelona: Centro Editorial de Alberto Martín, 1897–1899.

Richardson, James D. ed. *A Compilation of the Messages and Papers of the Presidents, 1789–1902*. 10 vols. Washington, D.C.: Library of Congress, 1896–1902.

Risquet, Juan F. *La cuestión político-social en la isla de Cuba*. Havana: Tipografía "América," 1900.

Rodríguez, José Ignacio. *Estudio histórico sobre el origen, desenvolvimiento y manifestaciones prácticas de la idea de la anexión de la isla de Cuba a los Estados Unidos de América*. Havana: Imprenta La Propaganda Literaria, 1900.

Roig de Leuchsenring, Emilio. *Weyler en Cuba*. (Havana: Editorial Páginas, 1947.

Rousset, Ricardo V. *Historial de Cuba*. 3 vols. Havana: Librería "Cervantes" de Ricardo Veloso, 1918.

Schroeder, Susan. *Cuba: A Handbook of Historical Statistics*. Boston: G. K. Hall, 1982.

Scott, Rebecca J. *Slave Emancipation in Cuba: The Transformation to Free Labor, 1860–1899*. Princeton, N.J.: Princeton University Press, 1985.

Seers, Dudley, et al. *Cuba, the Economic and Social Revolution*. Chapel Hill: University of North Carolina Press, 1964.

Seigle y Llata, Oscar. *El contrato de arrendamiento de finca rústica, el latifundio y la legislación azucarera*. Havana: Editorial Lex, 1953.

Souza y Rodríguez, Benigno. *Biografía de un regimiento mambí: El regimiento 'Calixto García.' Discursos*. Havana: Imprenta "El Siglo XX," 1939.

————. *Ensayo histórico sobre la invasión.* Havana: Imprenta del Ejército, 1948.

Thomas, Hugh. *Cuba, the Pursuit of Freedom.* New York: Harper and Row, 1971.

Tönnies, Ferdinand. *Desarrollo de la cuestión social.* 2d ed. Barcelona: Editorial Labor, 1933.

Trujillo y Monagas, José. *Los criminales de Cuba y José Trujillo.* Barcelona: Establecimiento Tipográfico de Fidel Giró, 1882.

Truslow, Francis Adams, et al. *Report on Cuba.* Baltimore: International Bank for Reconstruction and Development, 1951.

Tunas de ayer y de hoy. Victoria de las Tunas: "Razón," 1951.

Usategui y Lezama, Angel. *El colono cubano.* Havana: Jesús Montero, 1938.

Valdés de la Paz, Osvaldo. *"Arroyito:" el bandolero sentimental.* Havana: Talleres Tipográficos de "El Magazine de la Raza," 1922.

Vázquez, Ricardo. *Triunvirato: historia de un rincón azucarero de Cuba.* Havana: Comisión de Orientación Revolucionaria del Comité Central del PCC, 1971.

Varela Zequeira, Eduardo, and Arturo Mora y Varona. *Los bandidos en Cuba.* 2d ed. Havana: Establecimiento Tipográfico de "La Lucha," 1891.

Varona Guerrero, Miguel Angel. *La guerra de independencia de Cuba, 1895–1898.* 3 vols. Havana: Editorial Lex, 1946.

Varona Pupo, Ricardo. *Banes (Crónicas).* Santiago de Cuba: Imprenta Ros Masó, 1930.

Vivian, Thomas J., and Ruel P. Smith. *Everything About Our New Possessions.* New York: R. F. Fenno, 1899.

Wallerstein, Immanuel. *The Modern World System. Capitalist Agriculture and the Origins of the European World-Economy in the Sixteenth Century.* New York: Academic Press, 1974.

Wood, Leonard, et al. *Opportunities in the Colonies and Cuba.* New York: Lewis, Scribner, 1902.

Wright, Irene A. *Cuba.* New York: Macmillan, 1910.

Wrigley, E. A. *Population and History.* New York: McGraw-Hill, 1969.

Yglesias, José. *In the Fist of the Revolution. Life in a Cuban Country Town.* New York: Pantheon, 1968.

Zamacois, Eduardo. *La alegría de andar.* Madrid: Renacimiento, 1920.

Zanetti, Oscar, and Alejandro García. *United Fruit Company: Un caso del dominio imperialista en Cuba.* Havana: Editorial de Ciencias Sociales, 1976.

Articles

Abad, L. V. "The Cuban Problem." *Gunton's Magazine* 21 (December 1901), 515–25.

Aguirre, Sergio. "La desaparición del Ejército Libertador." *Cuba Socialista* 3 (December 1963), 51–68.

Akulai, Vladimir, and Domingo Rodríguez Fragaso. "La situación socio-económica del campesinado cubano antes de la revolución." *Islas* 54 (May–August 1976), 55–80.

Alba, Víctor. "Cuba: A Peasant Revolution." *World Today* 15 (May 1959), 183–95.

Alroy, Gil Carl. "The Meaning of 'Peasant Revolution': The Cuban Case." *International Review of History and Political Science* 2 (December 1965), 87–96.

———. "The Peasantry in the Cuban Revolution." *Review of Politics* 29 (January 1967), 87–99.

Alvarez Mola, Martha Verónica, and Pedro Martínez Pirez, "Algo acerca del problema negro en Cuba hasta 1912." *Universidad de La Habana*, no. 179 (May–June 1966), 79–93.

Batchelder, Robert B. "The Evolution of Cuba Land Tenure and its Relation to Certain Agro-Economic Problems." *Southwestern Social Science Quarterly* 33 (December 1952), 238–46.

Blok, Anton. "The Peasant and the Brigand: Social Banditry Reconsidered." *Comparative Studies in Society and History* 14 (September 1972), 494–503.

Booy, Theodoor de. "The Town of Baracoa and the Eastern Part of Cuba." *Pan American Bulletin* 45 (November 1917), 627–39.

Brownell, Atherton. "The Commercial Annexation of Cuba." *Appleton's Magazine* 8 (October 1906), 406–11.

Cabrera, Luis Rolando. "Baldomero, el montuno que salvó a seis expedicionarios del 'Granma.' " *Bohemia* 51 (March 22, 1959), 46–47, 128.

Cancio, Leopoldo. "Hacienda comunera." *Cuba y América* 6 (January 1902), 227–36.

Cardosa Arias, Santiago. "Ventas de Casanova: lucharon por su tierra." *Cuba* 2 (March 1963), 30–38.

Carpenter, Frank G. "Cuba in 1905." *Cuba Review* 3 (November 1905), p. 11.

Carreras, Julio Angel. "El bandolerismo en la república burguesa." *Santiago* 50 (June 1983), 145–61.

———. "Los bandoleros de la tregua en Santa Clara." *Islas* 51 (May–August 1978), 127–46.

Castillo, José del. "The Formation of the Dominican Sugar Industry: From Competition to Monopoly, from National Semiproletariat to Foreign Proletariat." In *Between Slavery and Free Labor: The Spanish-Speaking Caribbean in the Nineteenth Century*, ed. Manuel Moreno Fraginals, Frank Moya Pons, and Stanley L. Engerman, pp. 215–34. Baltimore: Johns Hopkins University Press, 1985.

Clark, Victor S. "Labor Conditions in Cuba." *Bulletin of the Department of Labor* 41 (July 1902), 663–793.

Cok Márquez, Patria. "La introducción de los ferrocarriles portátiles en la industria azucarera, 1870–1880." *Santiago* 41 (March 1981), 137–47.

Corbitt, Duvon C. "Immigration in Cuba." *Hispanic American Historical Review* 22 (May 1942), 280–308.

———. " 'Mercedes' and 'Realengos:' A Survey of the Public Land System in Cuba." *Hispanic American Historical Review* 19 (May 1939), 262–85.

Cubillas, Vicente. " 'Yo fuí el primer guía de Fidel al llegar el Granma.' " *Revolución,* December 2, 1959, 2.

Deere, Carmen Diana, and Magdalena León de Leal. "Peasant Production, Proletarianization, and the Sexual Division of Labor in the Andes." In *Women and Development,* ed. Lourdes Beneria, New York: Praeger, 1982.

Dennison, Edgar W. "Cuban Development." *Pan American Union Bulletin,* XXIX (August, 1909), 365–371.

Duvant, J.M.W. "Real Estate Titles in Cuba." *Cuba Review and Bulletin* 4 (June 1906), 13–15.

Earle, F. S. "Agricultural Cuba." *World Today* 11 (November 1906), 1175–84.

Fernow, B. E. "The High Sierra Maestra." *Bulletin of the American Geographical Society* 39 (1907), 257–68.

Fortune, George. " 'What's Doing' in Cuba for the Younger American." *Cuba Magazine* 3 (February 1912), 336–40.

Franco, José Luciano. "Panamá: refugio de la rebeldía cubana en el siglo XX." *Casa de las Américas* 15 (July–August 1974), 16–26.

García, Tomás Simón. "Notes from Baracoa." *Cuba Review* 4 (November 1906), 13.

García Montes, Oscar. "Los derechos de los colindantes en el deslinde de fincas no comuneras." *Cuba Contemporánea* 3 (November 1913), 248–67.

González Guerrero, Roger. "Por la ruta de la columna num. 6." *Verde Olivo* 7 (September 18, 1966), 6–7, 66–69.

González Valdés, José. "La Guardia Rural." *Boletín del Ejército* 4 (February 1919), 783–85.

Griffith, P. Merrill. "Santiago." *Cuba Review* 14 (November 1916), 10–19.

Harrah, Grace E. "The Hacienda Comunera (I–II)." *Cuba Review and Bulletin* 4 (July–August 1906), 9–12, 9–10.

———. "The Present Status of Properties in Land in Eastern Cuba." *Cuba Review and Bulletin* 5 (June 1907), 12–14.

Henrickson, H. C. "A Journey Through Eastern Cuba." *The Cuba Magazine* 1 (April 1910), 8–12.

Hidalgo, Juan. "Guillermo García: el primer campesino que se unió a Fidel en la Sierra Maestra." *Hoy* 2 (June 21, 1963), 6.

Hinton, Richard J. "Cuban Reconstruction." *North American Review* 164 (January 1899), 92–102.

Hitchman, James H. "U.S. Control Over Cuban Sugar Production, 1898–1902." *Journal of Inter-American Studies and World Affairs* 12 (January 1970), 90–106.

Hobsbawm, Eric J. "Social Banditry." In *Rural Protest: Peasant Movements and Social Change,* pp. 142–57, ed. Henry A. Landsberger. New York: Harper and Row, 1973.

Hoernel, Robert B. "Sugar and Social Change in Oriente, Cuba, 1898–

1946." *Journal of Latin American Studies* 8 (November 1976), 215–49.

Hone, Basil. "Buena Vista." *Cuba Magazine* (July 1913), 490–91.

Iglesias, Fe. "Algunos aspectos de la distribución de la tierra en 1899." *Santiago* 40 (December 1980).

———. "Azúcar y crédito durante la segunda mitad del siglo XX en Cuba." *Santiago* 52 (December 1983), 119–44.

———. "The Development of Capitalism in Cuban Sugar Production, 1860–1900." In *Between Slavery and Free Labor: The Spanish Speaking Caribbean in the Nineteenth Century,* ed. Manuel Moreno Fraginals, Frank Moya Pons, and Stanley L. Engerman, pp. 54–75. Baltimore: Johns Hopkins University Press, 1985.

Janvry, Alain de, and Carlos Garramon. "The Dynamics of Rural Poverty in Latin America." *Journal of Peasant Studies* 4 (April 1977), 206–16.

Knight, Franklin W., "Jamaican Migrants and the Cuban Sugar Industry, 1900–1934." In *Between Slavery and Free Labor: The Spanish-Speaking Caribbean in the Nineteenth Century,* ed. Manuel Moreno Fraginals, Frank Moya Pons, and Stanley L. Engerman, pp. 94–114. Baltimore: Johns Hopkins University Press, 1985.

Lacosta, Perfecto. "Opportunities in Cuba." In *Opportunities in the Colonies and Cuba,* pp. 131–272. New York: Scribner's and Co., 1902.

Lavedán, Enrique. "Los ladrones de tierras en Oriente." *Gráfico* 3 (February 7, 1914), 10.

León, Waldemar. "Caicaje: batalla final de una revuelta." *Bohemia* 52 (May 22, 1960), 100–02, 113.

LeRiverend Brusone, Julio E. "Sobre la industria azucarera cubana durante el siglo XIX." *El Trimestre Económico* 11 (April–June 1944), 52–70.

Livi-Bacci, Massimo. "Fertility and Population Growth in Spain in the Eighteenth and Nineteenth Centuries," *Daedalus* 97 (Spring 1968), 523–35.

Lockmiller, David A. "Agriculture in Cuba During the Second United States Intervention, 1906–1909." *Agricultural History* 11 (July 1937), 181–88.

López Segrera, Francisco. Cuba: "Dependence, Plantation Economy, and Social Classes, 1762–1902." In *Between Slavery and Free Labor: The Spanish-Speaking Caribbean in the Nineteenth Century,* ed. Manuel Moreno Fraginals, Frank Moya Pons, and Stanley L. Engerman, pp. 77–93. Baltimore: Johns Hopkins University Press, 1985.

Loret de Mola, Luis. "Sobre la guerra civil de 1917: Memorandum." *Boletín del Archivo Nacional* 10 (January–December 1961), 179–86.

Luaces, Roberto L. "Cooperation at Bayate." *Cuba Magazine* 4 (October 1912), 465–66.

Lundahl, Mats. "A Note on Haitian Migration to Cuba, 1890–1934." *Cuban Studies/Estudios Cubanos* 12 (July 1982), 23–36.

Lussón, Enrique. "El paso de la columna 9 al Segundo Frente Oriental." *Verde Olivo* 5 (March 3, 1964), 9–14.

Macaulay, Neill. "The Rebel Army: A Numerical Survey." *Hispanic American Historical Review* 58 (May 1978), 284–95.

Marino Pérez, Luis. "La actual situación económica de Cuba." *La Reforma Social* 6 (March 1916), 521–31.

———. "La inmigración jamaiquina desde el punto de vista social, económico y sanitario." *La Reforma Social* 8 (October 1916), 391–97.

Marshall, Edward. "A Talk with General Wood." *Outlook* 68 (July 20, 1901), 669–73.

Martí, Carlos. "Holguín." *Cuba y America* 13 (November 1, 1903), 161–66.

Martín, Regino. "Charla con el comandante Crescencio Pérez: un heroe de leyenda." *Carteles* 40 (February 8, 1959), 38–40, 82.

Masferrer, Marianne, and Carmelo Mesa-Lago. "The Gradual Integration of the Black in Cuba: Under the Colony, the Republic and the Revolution." In *Slavery and Race Relations in Latin America*, ed. Robert Brent Toplin, pp. 348–84. Westport, Conn.: Greenwood Press, 1974.

Matthew, Franklin. "The Reconstruction of Cuba." *Harper's Weekly* 43 (July 15, 1899), 700–01.

Mayo, J. "Dos décadas de luchas contra el latifundismo." *Bohemia* 70 (May 26, 1978), 84–89.

Moreno Fraginals, Manuel. "Plantations in the Caribbean: Cuba, Puerto Rico, and the Dominican Republic in the Nineteenth Century." In *Between Slavery and Free Labor: The Spanish-Speaking Caribbean in the Nineteenth Century*, ed. Manuel Moreno Fraginals, Frank Moya Pons, and Stanley L. Engerman, pp. 3–21. Baltimore: Johns Hopkins University Press, 1985.

O'Malley, Pat. "Social Bandits, Modern Capitalism and the Traditional Peasantry. A critique of Hobsbawm." *Journal of Peasant Studies* 6 (July 1979), 489–501.

Oquendo, Leyda. "Despojo y rebeldía del campesino cubano." *Bohemia* 69 (February 25, 1977), 84–89.

Padrón, Pedro Luis. "Desalojos campesinos." *Verde Olivo* 15 (February 25, 1973), 26–28.

Pazos, Felipe. "La economía cubana en el siglo XIX." *Revista Bimestre Cubana* 47 (January–February, 1941), 83–106.

Pepper, Charles. "Bandits in Cuba." *Washington Evening Star*, December 29, 1900, p. 8.

Pérez, Lisandro. "Iron Mining and Socio-Demographic Change in Eastern Cuba, 1884–1940." *Journal of Latin American Studies* 14 (November 1982), 381–405.

Pérez, Tubal. "Why the Attack on Moncada? Nieves Cordero Tells His Story." *Granma*, February 11, 1973, p. 9.

Pérez de la Riva, Francisco. "La inmigración antillana en Cuba durante el primer tercio del siglo XX." *Revista de la Biblioteca Nacional "José Martí"* 18 (May–August 1975), 74–88.

Pérez de la Riva, Juan. "Estudio demográfico del Alto Naguas." In *El barracón y otros ensayos*, pp. 317–37. Havana: Editorial de Ciencias Sociales, 1975.

Pérez de la Riva, Juan, and Blanca Morejón Siejas. "La población de Cuba, la guerra de independencia y la inmigración del siglo XIX." *Revista de la Biblioteca Nacional "José Martí"* 13 (May–August 1971), 17–27.

Pérez Vega, Oscar. "El frente interior y la Guardia Rural." *Boletín del Ejército* (May–June 1955), 83–91.

Petinaud, Jorge, and Raúl Rodríguez. "Manuel García no fué un bandido." *Granma,* December 1, 1985), p. 8.

Pierson, Carrie E. "In Eastern Cuba." *Cuba Magazine* (April 1912), 465–66.

———. "Omaja." *Cuba Magazine* 4 (July 1913), 485–89.

Pino-Santos, Oscar. "Los mecanismos imperialistas de apropiación de la tierra en Cuba (Caso de la United Fruit Co.)." *Santiago* 23 (September 1976), 181–89.

———. "Raíces económicas del 24 de febrero." *Carteles* 37 (February 26, 1956), 48–50, 73, 77.

Portell Vilá, Herminio. "La Chambelona en Camagüey." *Bohemia* 52 (May 8, 1960), 12–13, 119.

———. "La Chambelona en Occidente." *Bohemia* 52 (May 22, 1960), 36–37, 82.

———. "La Chambelona en Oriente." *Bohemia* 52 (April 24, 1960), 36–37, 82.

———. "La Chambelona en Las Villas." *Bohemia* 52 (May 15, 1960), 36–37, 98.

Poumier, María. "La vida cotidiana en la ciudades cubanas en 1898." *Universidad de La Habana,* nos. 196–97 (February–March 1972), 170–209.

"Property in Cuba." *Scientific American* 119 (July 27, 1918), 66.

Quijano Obregón, Aníbal. "Contemporary Peasant Movements." In *Elites in Latin America,* ed. Seymour Martin Lipset and Aldo Solari, pp. 301–40. New York: Oxford University Press, 1967.

Quintana, Jorge. "Lo que costó a Cuba la guerra de 1895," *Bohemia* 52 (September 11, 1960), 4–6, 107–08.

Rea, George Bronson. "The Destruction of Sugar Estates in Cuba." *Harper's Weekly* 41 (October 16, 1897), 10–34.

Reno, George. "Oriente, the California of Cuba." *Cuba Review* (August 1927), 14–20.

Rivero Muñiz, José. "Los cubanos en Tampa," *Revista Bimestre Cubana* 74 (Primer Semestre, 1958), 5–140.

Rosell, Eduardo. "Diario de operaciones del comandante Eduardo Rosell, jefe de Estado Mayor del Brigadier Pedro Betancourt." In Carlos M. Trelles y Govín, *Matanzas en la independencia de Cuba* pp. 142–74. Havana: Imprenta "Avisador Comercial," 1928.

Schwartz, Rosalie. "Bandits and Rebels in Cuban Independence: Predators, Patriots, and Pariahs." *Bibliotheca Americana* 1 (November 1982), 91–130.

Scott, Rebecca J. "Class Relations in Sugar and Political Mobilization in Cuba, 1868–1899." *Cuban Studies/Estudios Cubanos* 15 (Winter 1985), 15–28.

Serrano, Violeta. "La hacienda comunera." *Economía y Desarrollo* 39 (January–February 1977), 108–31.

Tellería Toca, Evelio. "Más de un cuarto de millón de braceros importados." *Granma*, April 14, 1970, p. 2.

Trelles y Govín, Carlos M. "El censo de Cuba de 1899." *Cuba y América* 5 (February 1901), 285–97.

———. "El censo de Cuba de 1899." *Cuba y América* 5 (March 1901), 413–23.

Van Hermann, H. A. "Immigration and Monopoly." *Modern Cuba* 2 (March 1914), 3–7.

Vázquez Candela, Euclides. "El Segundo Frente Oriental Frank País: pequeña república insurgente." *Revolución*, March 11, 1963, p. 8.

Venegas Delgado, Hernán. "Acerca del proceso de concentración y centralización de la industria azucarera en la región remediana a fines del siglo XIX" *Islas* 60 (September–December 1982), 63–119.

———. "Apuntes sobre la decadencia trinitaria en el siglo XIX." *Islas* 46 (September–December 1973), 159–251.

Welsh, Osgood. "Cuba As Seen From the Inside." *Century Magazine* 54 (August 1898), 586–93.

Whitbeck, R. H. "Geographical Relations in the Development of Cuban Agriculture." *Geographical Review* 12 (April 1922), 223–40.

Willetts, Gilson. "Business Opportunities in Our New Colonies." *Leslie's Weekly* 88 (January 5, 1899), 9–12.

Wolcott, Henry M. "Cuba." *Cuba Review* 14 (August 1916), 22–27.

Wolf, Donna M. "The Cuban 'Gente de Color' and the Independence Movement, 1879–1895." *Revista/Review Interamericana* 5 (Fall 1975), 403–21.

Wood, Edmond. "Can Cubans Govern Cuba?" *Forum* 32 (September 1901), 66–73.

Wood, Leonard. "The Need for Reciprocity with Cuba." *Independent* 52 (December 12, 1901), 2927–29.

Wright, Irene A. "The Guantánamo Valley." *Cuba Magazine* 2 (March 1911), 15–22.

———. "The Nipe Bay District." *Cuba Magazine* 2 (October 1910), 6–17.

———. "Oriente." *Cuba Magazine* 3 (February 1912), 330–35.

Yanes, Lorenzo, and René Batista Moreno. "Retratos de una vida hazañera." *Bohemia* 63 (January 22, 1971), 98–99.

Index

PITT LATIN AMERICAN SERIES

Cole Blasier, Editor

Argentina

Argentina in the Twentieth Century
David Rock, Editor

Discreet Partners: Argentina and the USSR Since 1917
Aldo César Vacs

Juan Perón and the Reshaping of Argentina
Frederick C. Turner and José Enrique Miguens, Editors

The Life, Music, and Times of Carlos Gardel
Simon Collier

The Political Economy of Argentina, 1946–1983
Guido DiTella and Rudiger Dornbusch, Editors

Brazil

External Constraints on Economic Policy in Brazil, 1899–1930
Winston Fritsch

The Film Industry in Brazil: Culture and the State
Randal Johnson

The Politics of Social Security in Brazil
James M. Malloy

Urban Politics in Brazil: The Rise of Populism, 1925–1945
Michael L. Conniff

Colombia

Gaitán of Colombia: A Political Biography
Richard E. Sharpless

Roads to Reason: Transportation, Administration, and Rationality in Colombia
Richard E. Hartwig

Cuba

Cuba Between Empires, 1878–1902
Louis A. Pérez, Jr.

Cuba, Castro, and the United States
Philip W. Bonsal

Cuba in the World
Cole Blasier and Carmelo Mesa-Lago, Editors

Cuba Under the Platt Amendment
Louis A. Pérez, Jr.

Cuban Studies, Vols. 16–18
Carmelo Mesa-Lago, Editor

Intervention, Revolution, and Politics in Cuba, 1913–1921
Louis A. Pérez, Jr.

Lords of the Mountain: Social Banditry and Peasant Protest in Cuba, 1878–1918
Louis A. Pérez, Jr.

The Origins of the Peruvian Labor Movement, 1883–1919
Peter Blanchard

The Overthrow of Allende and the Politics of Chile, 1964–1976
Paul E. Sigmund

Panajachel: A Guatemalan Town in Thirty-Year Perspective
Robert E. Hinshaw

Peru and the International Monetary Fund
Thomas Scheetz

Primary Medical Care in Chile: Accessibility Under Military Rule
Joseph L. Scarpaci

Rebirth of the Paraguayan Republic: The First Colorado Era, 1878–1904
Harris G. Warren

Restructuring Domination: Industrialists and the State in Ecuador
Catherine M. Conaghan

Social Security

The Politics of Social Security in Brazil
James M. Malloy

Social Security in Latin America: Pressure Groups, Stratification, and Inequality
Carmelo Mesa-Lago

Other Studies

Adventurers and Proletarians: The Story of Migrants in Latin America
Magnus Mörner, with the collaboration of Harold Sims

Authoritarianism and Corporatism in Latin America
James M. Malloy, Editor

Authoritarianism and Democrats: Regime Transition in Latin America
James M. Malloy and Mitchell. A Seligson, Editors

Female and Male in Latin America: Essays
Ann Pescatello, Editor

Latin American Debt and the Adjustment Crisis
Rosemary Thorp and Laurence Whitehead, Editors

Public Policy in Latin America: A Comparative Survey
John W. Sloan

Selected Latin American One-Act Plays
Francesca Collecchia and Julio Matas, Editors and Translators

The State and Capital Accumulation in Latin America: Brazil, Chile, Mexico
Christian Anglade and Carlos Fortin, Editors

Transnational Corporations and the Latin American Automobile Industry
Rhys Jenkins